THE HANDBOOK FOR

POOR STUDENTS, RICH TEACHING

ERIC JENSEN

A joint publication

ASCD · Solution Tree

Visit **go.SolutionTree.com/instruction** to download the free reproducibles in this book.

555 North Morton Street
Bloomington, IN 47404
800.733.6786 (toll free) / 812.336.7700
FAX: 812.336.7790
email: info@SolutionTree.com
SolutionTree.com

Printed in the United States of America

Library of Congress Cataloging-in-Publication Data

Names: Jensen, Eric, 1950- author.
Title: The handbook for Poor students, rich teaching / Eric Jensen.
Description: Bloomington, IN : Solution Tree Press, [2019] | Includes
   bibliographical references and index.
Identifiers: LCCN 2018045173 | ISBN 9781947604650 (perfect bound)
Subjects: LCSH: Children with social disabilities--Education--United
   States--Handbooks, manuals, etc. | Poor children--Education--United States
   v Handbooks, manuals, etc. | Educational equalization--United States v
   Handbooks, manuals, etc.
Classification: LCC LC4091 .J465 2019 | DDC 371.826/94--dc23 LC record available at https://lccn.loc.gov/2018045173

Solution Tree

Jeffrey C. Jones, CEO
Edmund M. Ackerman, President

Solution Tree Press

President and Publisher: Douglas M. Rife
Editorial Director: Sarah Payne-Mills
Art Director: Rian Anderson
Managing Production Editor: Kendra Slayton
Senior Production Editor: Todd Brakke
Senior Editor: Amy Rubenstein
Proofreader: Miranda Addonizio and Elisabeth Abrams
Text and Cover Designer: Laura Cox
Editorial Assistant: Sarah Ludwig

Visit **go.SolutionTree.com/instruction** to download
the free reproducibles in this book.

Table of Contents

PART ONE

IMPLEMENTING THE RELATIONAL MINDSET. 5

PART TWO

IMPLEMENTING THE ACHIEVEMENT MINDSET 37

PART SEVEN

About the Author

Eric Jensen, PhD, is a former teacher from San Diego, California. Since the early 1990s, he has synthesized brain research and developed practical applications for educators. Jensen is a member of the invitation-only Society for Neuroscience and the President's Club at Salk Institute of Biological Studies. He cofounded SuperCamp, the first and largest brain-compatible academic enrichment program, previously held in fourteen countries with over sixty-five thousand graduates. He is listed as a Top 30 Global Guru in Education and does professional development internationally.

Jensen has authored over thirty books, including *Teaching With Poverty in Mind, Tools for Engagement, Engaging Students With Poverty in Mind, Turnaround Tools for the Teenage Brain, Bringing the Common Core to Life in K–8 Classrooms, Teaching with the Brain in Mind, Different Brains, Different Learners,* and *Poor Students, Rich Teaching, Revised Edition.*

To learn more about Eric Jensen's teacher workshops and leadership events, visit Jensen Learning (www .jensenlearning.com).

Introduction

The core title for this book and its companion, *Poor Students, Rich Teaching, Revised Edition*, suggests they are about succeeding with students from poverty. But really, it's about something much more than that: rich teaching. Here, the word *rich* means full, bountiful, and better than ever. Teachers can make a difference in students' lives with richer teaching. They just need the knowledge and tools to do it. It's also about developing the high-impact mindsets necessary to accomplish this.

In *Poor Students, Rich Teaching, Revised Edition*, I establish the knowledge component of this equation—the research and strategies that high-performing teachers can use to defeat toxic narratives and help students succeed through richer and more abundant teaching. This handbook takes a tool-focused approach to these strategies. With a lesser focus on the supporting research, this book instead provides a plethora of tools you can use to help bring these strategies to life. There are graphic organizers for your students, brainstorming and worksheets for you to plan lessons, checklists to ensure you're hitting all of a strategy's key points, surveys to self-assess your current thinking and practices, and reflection questions to help you consider how you can change your practices (your teaching mindsets) to enrich your teaching.

To kick things off, we'll take a quick tour of how I've organized this book, how it works as a critical part of your teaching toolkit and how you can get the most of it. Then we'll take a quick look at why these mindsets have such a high impact on bringing out the best in your students from poverty.

About This Book

This book's major theme is developing the most powerful tool for change: mindset. A mindset is a way of thinking about something. As Stanford University psychologist Carol Dweck (2008) explains, people (broadly) think about intelligence in two ways: (1) either you have it or you don't (the fixed mindset), or (2) you can grow and change (the growth mindset). Those with a fixed mindset believe intelligence and competency are a rigid unchangeable quality. Those with a growth mindset believe that intelligence and competency can develop over time as the brain changes and grows.

This book broadens and deepens the mindset theme to many new areas of student and teacher behaviors that you'll find highly relevant. It continues in seven parts, each highlighting a specific mindset with chapters that offer easy-to-implement and highly effective strategies and tools you can use immediately. Every part begins with a series

1

of self-assessment questions to get you in touch with your current approach and thinking related to the mindset. Similarly, every chapter begins with a simple survey related to that topic. These are about understanding where you are starting from so that you're ready to embrace the new thinking that comes from changing your mindset. As you dive in, you'll find the strategies and tools you need to make these changes. Here are the seven parts.

- **Part one: The relational mindset**—Chapters 1 through 3 explore the relational mindset and begin to discover why the types of relationships teachers have (or don't have) with students are one of the biggest reasons why students graduate or drop out. Everything you do starts with building relationships with your students.

- **Part two: The achievement mindset**—Chapters 4 through 6 teach you about powerful success builders with the achievement mindset. Students from poverty can and do love to learn, when you give them the right tools.

- **Part three: The positivity mindset**—Chapters 7 through 9 home in on your students' emotions and attitudes. Each chapter focuses on building an attitude of academic hope and optimism in both your students and yourself. If you've ever put a mental limitation on any student (don't worry, we all have), these chapters are must-reads. Your new, rock-solid positivity mindset will help your students soar.

- **Part four: The rich classroom climate mindset**—Chapters 10 through 12 offer strategies to take all that positivity you've generated and use it to create an energetic, high-performing class culture, using the rich classroom climate mindset. You'll learn the secrets that high-performing teachers use to build an amazing classroom climate.

- **Part five: The enrichment mindset**—Chapters 13 through 15 focus on building breakthrough cognitive capacity in students. A big problem for students from poverty is their mental bandwidth, often known as cognitive load. Here, you'll see the clear, scientific evidence that shows, without a molecule of doubt, that you can ensure your students build cognitive capacity in the form of memory, thinking skills, vocabulary, and study skills.

- **Part six: The engagement mindset**—Chapters 16 through 18 dig into student involvement in a new way with the engagement mindset. You'll gain quick, easy, and practical strategies for maintenance and stress, for buy-in, and to build community.

- **Part seven: The graduation mindset**—Chapters 19 and 20 help you focus on the gold medal in teaching: students who graduate job or college ready. Each chapter centers on school factors absolutely proven to support graduation. You'll learn the science of *why* these factors can be such powerful achievement boosters, and you'll discover a wide range of positive alternatives to what your students are doing at school.

Each chapter and part ends with a series of reflection questions about the topic or mindset you just read and how your thinking on it has evolved. There's much more for you to learn, but these seven high-impact mindsets and the accompanying strategies and tools will make a world of difference if you implement them well. That's my promise.

Why These Mindsets

Before we get into part 1 and all seven mindsets for change, it's important that I establish for you that these mindsets and strategies are not simply feel-good measures. They have the backing of years of research into how the brain reacts to poverty and how intervention counteracts poverty's detrimental effects. You will find additional information in *Poor Students, Rich Teaching, Revised Edition* that plumbs the depths of how pervasive poverty affects students and why, in America, it is all a part of a new normal that teachers must be prepared to confront. But for the purposes of this handbook, the key takeaway is that the brain is not set and even your most troubled students are not locked in to self-destructive cycles.

The fact is, humans can and do change (Mackey, Singley, Wendelken, & Bunge, 2015). When people don't change, it is often because others have given up on them, their daily environment is toxic, or others are using an ineffective strategy that doesn't help. Often, teachers feel powerless to help students if there is a lack of support at home, but the truth is the classroom teacher is still the single most significant contributor to student achievement; the effect is greater than that of parents, peers, entire schools, or poverty (Hanushek, 2005; Haycock, 1998; Rivkin, Hanushek, & Kain, 2005; Rockoff, 2004).

Given this, it's important that we have a way to measure a strategy's effect. In most sports, the team that scores the most points (or goals, runs, and so on) wins. This scoring system is simple and easily understood. In our profession, the scoring system that decides a winning classroom strategy is called the *effect size*. This number is simply the size of the impact on student learning. In short, it tells you how much something matters. The mathematics on it are simple: it is a standardized measure of the relative size of the gain (or loss) in student achievement caused by an intervention (versus a control; Olejnik & Algina, 2000). See figure I.1.

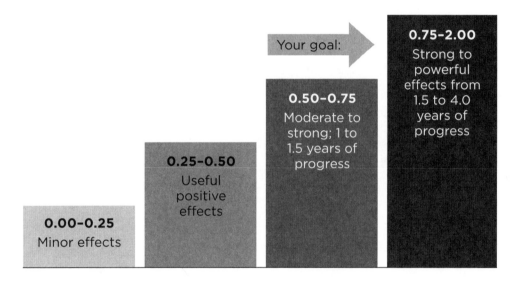

Source: Vacha-Haase & Thompson, 2004.

Figure I.1: Effect sizes made practical.

Researchers simply measure the difference between doing something and doing nothing. Ideally, one uses an experimental group (using a new strategy) and a control group (using an existing norm). The strongest analysis includes large sample sizes and multiple studies with varied population demographics. Then, you know your data are very, very solid.

Classroom interventions typically have effect sizes between 0.25 and 0.75 with a mean of about 0.40 (Hattie, 2009). One full year's worth of academic gains has a 0.50 effect size, and two years' worth of gains have a 1.00 effect size. This means that effect sizes above 0.50 are just the baseline for students in poverty. Teachers have to help students catch up from starting school one to three years behind their classmates, and it takes good instructional practices for effect sizes to be well above 0.50.

To ensure students from poverty graduate, you'll want to teach in ways that give them one and a half years' worth of gains (or more) in each school year. What if, by just replacing one strategy you already use (for example, saying "Good job!" to a student) with another (a far more effective one, like "Your steady, daily studying really paid off. That's going to help you graduate on time!"), you could get five to ten times the positive effect on student achievement? Not only do I show you how to do that in this book, I give you more than one hundred tools to help implement each strategy.

An amazing journey is about to begin. Are you game?

PART ONE

IMPLEMENTING THE RELATIONAL MINDSET

In this part, we begin with building the narrative of relationships as the core underpinning of high-performance teaching with students from poverty. Sometimes we find it easy to connect with students who share our own background, but it becomes much more challenging with students who don't; yet it's essential to build relationships with those students before any real learning can happen. If you're not connecting by giving respect, listening, and showing empathy, you risk losing your students. When students lose interest in school, they will most likely find somewhere else to invest their energy and may make poorer choices. Some will get their respect and connections through peers and sports, others through drugs or even gangs.

To begin this part, use figure P1.1 (page 6) to self-assess how you already approach building (or not building) relationships with your students.

As you think about your answers to these questions, it's paramount for you to build your awareness that all of us are in this together—you, me, colleagues, students, and parents. Relationships between everyone that touches students' lives affect their success. When your students succeed, you succeed. There is no *us* (teachers) and *them* (students). Maintaining an erroneous narrative of separation will ruin your chances of success in teaching. The relational mindset says, "We are all connected in this life together. Always connect first as a person (and an ally) and second as a teacher."

> The relational mindset says, "We are all connected in this life together. Always connect first as a person (and an ally) and second as a teacher."

1. Consider the relationships you had with teachers when you were going through elementary and secondary school. What teachers did you feel connected to? Which did you have difficult experiences with? How did each affect your learning?

_____

_____

_____

_____

2. When you stand at the front of your classroom and look out over your students, how do you feel about what you see? Do you feel connected or bonded with your students? Do you feel distance and separation? Why?

_____

_____

_____

_____

3. Describe how you feel about your role in teaching. What is its scope? Do you see yourself purely as a subject-matter resource to impart knowledge? Do you consider yourself a source of emotional support?

_____

_____

_____

_____

4. Consider all the students in your classroom. Do you know which students come from poverty and which do not? What are some of the challenges students from poverty face? What are some ways you've witnessed poverty affecting their behavior or academic outcomes?

_____

_____

_____

_____

5. Do you feel empathy for the students in your class who come from poverty? What tools do you use to show students that you have an understanding of and empathy for their challenges? How do you ensure you make connections with students that foster empathy?

_____

_____

_____

_____

Figure P1.1: Assess your understanding of how poverty affects students.

*Visit **go.SolutionTree.com/instruction** for a free reproducible version of this figure.*

Do not confuse this mindset with me telling you that it is impossible to succeed with *every student* unless each likes or respects you. Some students (those from strong, intact families) come from such stability at home that they need *less* relationship time at school. When a student has an emotionally stable family, good friends, and positive relatives, the need for relational stability at school is less. Ask yourself, "How can I show my students I care about their home life as well as their classroom life?"

Your students will care about academics as soon as you care about them. As neuroscience tells us, we are hardwired to connect (Commission on Children at Risk, 2003; Moriceau & Sullivan, 2005), and effective teacher-student relationships contribute to student achievement. Also, this contribution varies depending on students' socioeconomic status and grade level. The research tells us that relationships mean more to students who have instability at home than to students who have a stable, two-parent foundation (Allen, McElhaney, Kuperminc, & Jodl, 2004). Among all students, good relationships have a 0.72 effect size, which makes them an exceptionally significant and strong effect size catalyst (Hattie, 2009). Among secondary students, the effect size is an even larger 0.87 (Marzano, 2003).

The scope of the relational effect goes much further, and I explore it in depth in *Poor Students, Rich Teaching, Revised Edition* (Jensen, 2019). The bottom line is that relationships influence engagement in multiple ways. First, quality interactions within a relationship provide instruction, correction, modeling, and support for students, forming the basis of a teacher-student relationship (Hughes & Kwok, 2006). Second, a positive teacher-student relationship enhances students' sense of classroom security and increases their willingness to engage in the classroom (Baumeister & Leary, 1995). Third, evidence shows that quality relationships can help students achieve more through greater connected engagement (Roorda, Koomen, Spilt, & Oort, 2011). Another study reveals that students' positive or negative classroom relationships *are equal to* IQ or school achievement test scores in predicting if a student will drop out (Jimerson, Egeland, Sroufe, & Carlson, 2000).

The next three chapters offer the following strategies to help you build relationships with your students that will get them on board emotionally and socially.

1. Personalize the learning.
2. Connect everyone for success.
3. Show empathy.

In these chapters, you'll see how relationships offer the emotional environment through which all course content flows. There is no classroom content without some sort of context, even if the context is a digital device. Let's dig in.

Questions for Daily Reflection

Each day, consider your own mindset for fostering connection and relationships with your students, and answer the following questions.

1. Have I recently seen other teachers successfully build quality relationships with their students? How did they do it? Could I do something similar?

2. Which students in my classroom have I not taken the time to get to know? In what ways can I connect with those students that will make a difference for them?

3. Are there students in my classroom who appear to feel unsafe, not respected, or disconnected from their peers? How can I change those things?

CHAPTER 1

PERSONALIZE THE LEARNING

Think about the faces you see in your classroom every day. How many of these students are more than faces? How many can you look at and say that you know something personal about them, about their lives and the challenges they face? Take a moment to think about how you make learning in your classroom personal. As you consider your current practices, fill out the survey in figure 1.1.

How many students' names do you know within the first thirty days of the year or semester? (Circle one.)	Less than half	More than half	All
Do you engage students in classroom activities that allow them to get to know you as a person and allow them to get to know each other? (Circle one.)			Yes No
How often do you share a personal story or challenge with your students? (Circle one.)	Never	At least once a month	At least once a week
Do you have personal or professional goals that you share with your students? (Circle one.)			Yes No
Before reading about the personalization strategies in this chapter, list some things you could do to get to know your students better and let them get to know you.			

Figure 1.1: Assess how well you personalize learning in your classroom.

Visit go.SolutionTree.com/instruction for a free reproducible version of this figure.

As you reflect on your answers, remember that to get personal in this context means connecting in a personal way so that your teaching gets students to perk up and pay attention to that which is relevant: themselves. Even if you can say that you make an effort to make the learning in your classroom personal, there is always room to re-examine your practices and look for ways to improve. That's why this chapter is all about fostering teacher-student relationships by creating a culture of personalization. In this chapter, you will engage with the following four strategies.

1. Learn students' names.

2. Create a Me Bag.

3. Share an everyday problem.

4. Share progress on goals.

The strategies in this chapter lay the groundwork that makes the other mindsets in this book effective; as you engage with them, reflect on what you already do and how you can evolve your existing practices. Maybe it will also inspire you to add something new.

Learn Students' Names

To create a culture of personalization starting on day one, learn every student's name, and make sure students all know each other. Neither you nor your students need to be a memory champ to do this. You just need to care and take the time to set up the learning process, then practice, just like the students in your class. When you use a student's name, be sure to smile and make eye contact. Many times, a simple handshake or other appropriate connection will show a lot to your students (you care). You may already be great at learning student names; but even if you are, many of your students have a hard time remembering the names of their peers, which is also important for the relational mindset. In this section, you'll find strategies to help both you and your students learn each other's names.

Name-Learning Strategies for Students

There are many smart ways to remember names and faces. One of the simplest is to first put your brain in a curious state. Say to yourself, "OK, what is this student's name? Is it _____?" That primes the brain to care and to listen better. Then, when you hear the name, use it! Use it under different circumstances such as standing, sitting, when giving a compliment, or standing at the door. You can also put together notecards on each student that you update as you learn about them and use those as often as necessary for you to remember details about him or her. See figure 1.2. Note you don't necessarily have to take your own photos for these profile cards. Most schools keep student profile photos you can access.

Having tools like this to help you keep track of your students can significantly speed up the process of getting to know them, but you have many other options at your disposal. Here are some strategies for learning names.

- **Introductions:** At the start of the school year, have students say their first names every time they speak. Do this for the first thirty class days (if you have thirty students, or twenty days if you have twenty students).

- **Desk nametags:** Have students create desk nametags from single index cards or cardstock (fold the paper in half horizontally). Have a box for each class of nametags and ask students to pick them up and return them to the box each period. The hard (but good) part is after two weeks, you pick out each name and try to place it on the right student's desk.

- **Checks:** When students are writing, ask yourself quietly, "What's his or her name?" Try to answer it first, then walk over, and check out your answer by looking at the student's name on a paper or asking.

	Student: _____
Student photo	Period or class: _____
	Favorite subject: _____
	Favorite hobby: _____

Things I know about this student:

Figure 1.2: Student profile card.

*Visit **go.SolutionTree.com/instruction** for a free reproducible version of this figure.*

- **Alliteration:** Link a word that begins with the same consonant as the student's first name. Use connections like, "Laura longhair," "Benny in a bowtie," "Michael has a motorcycle," and "Jasmine likes jam." Then, visualize the connection in your mind's eye.

- **Self quizzes:** As students enter the class, greet them by name, or ask them to give you a prompt or cue to trigger their name. Tell students they can't enter your classroom until you say their names correctly. Then, use their names as you make eye contact and give a compliment. ("Eric, good to see you today.")

- **Likes:** Do a quick energizer by asking students to stand in areas of the room by likes or dislikes. ("If you like green vegetables, stand over there. Stand over here if you are a St. Louis Cardinals fan.") The point of this activity is to help you remember students by associating them with their preferences. If you print out profile cards for your students (refer to figure 1.2), you can jot down notes about each student's answer on their profile card.

- **Nametags:** For the first two weeks or so have students wear nametags. Make a contest to see who can learn the most names in class. For younger students, tags will last longer on their backs.

- **Rhyming:** Link a word that sounds like the student's first name to each student. ("Jamal at the mall," "Tim is slim," or "Jake swims in a lake.")

- **"I'm going shopping" game:** Students stand up, one by one. The game begins like this: "My name is Eric, and I am buying medicine for my earache." The next student stands and says, "His name is Eric, and he is buying medicine for his earache. My name is Kim, and I am buying a coke." Each student stands, repeats prior students' statements, and adds his or her own shopping item. You can be the last person to add to the shopping list.

- **Returns:** When you return papers or assignments in the first three to four weeks, use names as you give the paper back to the student ("Loved your perfect spelling, Kenisha").

- **Interviews:** Give students two to three minutes in pairs to interview each other and discover something that no one can forget. Each pair stands, then asks students to introduce each other, allowing about one minute per pair.

- **Classroom roles:** Students apply for (or are given) jobs so you can tie the student to his or her class job ("Ryan the reporter" or "Kayla the class leader"). You can read more about assigning classroom jobs in chapter 12 (page 128).

Name-Learning Strategies for Students

Ensuring students also know each other's names is also a useful way to build relationships between peers, because strong social glue builds valuable respect, familiarity, and trust. That can break down barriers and reduce cliques in class.

A fun activity for students to learn each other's names is the name game. On a blank, 3" x 5" notecard, ask everyone to write one word that begins with the same letter as his or her first name. The word should connect with something about him or her ("Eric is energetic"). Then, put your students in small groups of four to six. In a circle, ask everyone to say his or her name, the word, and the connection to the word. Then, the group can put the cards in the center of the circle in a box or basket. Using a timer, ask a pair of volunteers to see how long it will take them to return the correct card to the other students in the group. Next week, switch up students so all of them are in a new group. Continue this for the first four weeks until everyone is pretty good at others' names. Use the tracking sheet in figure 1.3 to help you keep track of the names and attributes for each student in a class.

Student	Attribute or characteristic	Student	Attribute or characteristic	Student	Attribute or characteristic

Figure 1.3: Name-learning tracking sheet.

*Visit **go.SolutionTree.com/instruction** for a free reproducible version of this figure.*

These memory tools will build the confidence and social glue to foster cognitive capacity (for attention and for short- and long-term memory). Additionally, during group work, invite students to always address each other by name. When students pair up with a new partner, ask them to introduce themselves to others with eye contact, a greeting, and a handshake.

Create a Me Bag

Another way to build a culture of personalization is to use variations of the Me Bag activity during the first week of school. This is a great activity for all K–12 students because most students, no matter their age, want to know some personal things about their teacher. First, you'll model the process for your own students. Start with a paper bag that has small objects, items you collect about yourself: photos, receipts, ticket stubs, a favorite snack, keys, or mementos that help tell a story about yourself. Share those objects and stories in about seven to ten minutes. Use figure 1.4 to brainstorm some items you could put into a Me Bag and what you might want to say about them.

Item	The story behind this item

Figure 1.4: Ideas for a Me Bag.

*Visit **go.SolutionTree.com/instruction** for a free reproducible version of this figure.*

Share an Everyday Problem

Whether you want to be a role model or not, you *are* a role model. Give students what they need so badly—a real-world model of how to live as an adult. You can think of this as a way to extend the work you began with the Me Bag activity. That means about once a week, share a piece of your world, something that presents a challenge or problem that you had, maybe something you experienced over the weekend. A short, three-minute slice of a teacher's life can do wonders for fostering the relational mindset.

Consider the following teacher's story.

> Last weekend something weird happened. I had promised to help my friend move on Saturday. But when I went out to my car that morning, I turned the key to start it and click . . . nothing! My car wouldn't start, and I was freaking out because I made a promise to her. "Friends keep promises to friends," I said to myself. Now, what could I possibly do?

> Well, students, it's time for your challenge of the day. Work with a partner, and come up with two possible solutions to my problem. You see, even though I was freaking out, I found a way to solve the problem. How would you solve this problem?

Your story gives students a tiny window into your adult world, especially when you can turn it into a learning opportunity for them to learn to solve real-world problems, which is often something you can connect directly to the learning topic you intend to cover in your lesson. After you present your story, give students a minute to brainstorm how they would approach it. Then, call on students to give their thoughts, and don't judge their answers. Keep a modest, positive spirit, and say, "I hadn't thought of that. Thank you, Marcus" or "I appreciate the brainstorming you did. Thank you! Now, let's grab a few more ideas." I always thank students for their participation but never criticize, judge, or evaluate their efforts. I realize they're a fraction of my age and are unlikely to have the same coping skills.

After you call on many volunteers (thanking them for their effort), you should share the rest of the story. How did you decide what to do about the problem, and what did you learn from the results? If you need help organizing an activity for this lesson, use figure 1.5 to plan it out in advance.

Describe the problem or obstacle:	
Does this connect to the lesson topic? Yes ☐ No ☐	How will you make this connection clear to students?
How did you resolve the problem:	

Figure 1.5: Map an everyday problem.

*Visit **go.SolutionTree.com/instruction** for a free reproducible version of this figure.*

Even if you can't connect this exercise directly to an ongoing lesson, it is not a waste of time; it is an investment in your students that will pay off later since you're role modeling three things for your class. Yes, adults *do* have problems and *how* they deal with them can be useful. Just because a problem is tough, big, or stressful doesn't mean it is unsolvable. Finally, it is a chance for you to share the process of problem solving. You share your values, your attitude, and the procedures it takes to be a success.

Share Progress on Goals

The last tool for creating a culture of personalization is sharing your personal goals. Many teachers struggle to find a separation between their personal and teacher lives. However, all students, especially those from poverty, love the idea of goals. Setting personal goals and sharing them with your students is an effective way to foster the relational mindset. Post your personal goal in the classroom (since you are asking students to do the same) and share your progress all year (or semester) long. In addition, you'll also post your class goal. (You'll learn more about setting gutsy class goals in chapter 4, page 41.) Figure 1.6 provides a worksheet you can post in your room for achieving a personal goal.

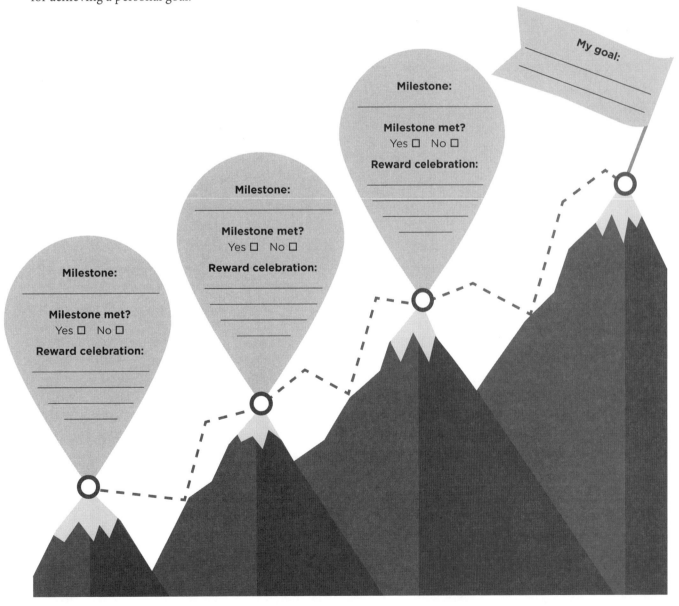

Figure 1.6: Goal and progress poster.

*Visit **go.SolutionTree.com/instruction** for a free reproducible version of this figure.*

Table 1.1 lists some sample goals you might consider, along with some milestones to associate with these goals.

Table 1.1: Examples of Personal Goals

Goal: Participating in community projects	**Goal:** Starting healthier eating and exercise habits	**Goal:** Completing a teaching improvement list
Milestones: • Identify a project. • Sign up to help. • Complete the project.	**Milestones:** • Identify a healthy eating and exercise routine. • Maintain the routine for four weeks. • Maintain the routine for three months.	**Milestones:** • Identify three habits for improvement. • Maintain these habits for three weeks. • Maintain these habits for three months.
Goal: Running a 10k	**Goal:** Mentoring someone	**Goal:** Growing a garden
Milestones: • Identify and download apps to improve from 0 to 5k and from 5k to 10k. • Complete the 0 to 5k app. • Complete the 5k to 10k app.	**Milestones:** • Identify a person who wants and will benefit from mentoring. • Maintain mentorship for four weeks. • Maintain mentorship for three months.	**Milestones:** • Plan a garden space and the plants that will go in it. • Create the garden space and plant the plants. • Nurture the plants to full growth.
Goal: Learning a skill or sport	**Goal:** Helping change the culture at your school	**Goal:** Helping your parents with a goal
Milestones: • Identify a skill to learn and a pathway to attaining it. • Complete the learning pathway that attains the skill. • Demonstrate mastery of the new skill by completing a related project.	**Milestones:** • Identify an aspect of school culture that could improve and three ways to improve it. • Achieve buy-in from relevant stakeholders for three months for improvement. • Cite evidence of the improvement's success or a new action plan to try again.	**Milestones:** • Talk to your parents and identify a goal they want to achieve and micro goals to achieve it. • Complete half the micro goals. • Complete all goals or reset and try again.

After selecting, displaying, and making progress toward applicable goals, begin routinely sharing and celebrating all your key milestones and how you overcame them. When you share all the micro steps forward and the nearly predictable setbacks you experience, students will see that mistakes are OK and make way for improvement.

Quick Consolidation: Personalize the Learning

This chapter was about a powerful path in your classroom—personalizing learning. The tools I present in this chapter are no secret. I'm just inviting you to choose one or two of them and make it a habit, but all of them are important assets in your relational toolbox. As you share part of your life with students, you allow them to understand your journey. Plus, they learn about the process you used, your values, and your choices. Answer the following reflection questions as you consider your next steps on the journey to making learning more personal in your classroom.

1. What did you learn about the importance of making the learning in your classroom personal that you didn't know when you started this chapter? How is your outlook changing?

2. What strategy from this chapter will you use to ensure you learn every student's name? How will you deploy this strategy in your classroom?

3. To better connect with your students, what are some items you could put in your Me Bag? How will you explain them?

4. What are some everyday problems you've experienced that you could share with your students? How might these change how your students perceive you?

5. What are some goals you have in your personal life that might humanize you in the eyes of your students and help them connect with you?

CHAPTER 2

CONNECT EVERYONE FOR SUCCESS

In this second of three powerful chapters on the relational mindset, we'll strengthen our skills in connecting everyone. Before we get started, use the survey in figure 2.1 to think about the connections you foster in your life and work and what they mean to you.

Who is someone from your youth that influenced the adult you became?				
What did that person do to have such an important impact on you?				
Who is one student or peer you have that you believe you have had a positive influence on?				
How did that connection first form? What did you do to help make it into something so beneficial?				
What percentage of time do you devote to in-classroom, collaborative activities? (Circle one.)	< 25%	25–50%	50–75%	> 75%

Figure 2.1: Assess the connections in your life and teaching.

*Visit **go.SolutionTree.com/instruction** for a free reproducible version of this figure.*

Every connection you have in your life influences you in some way, so it's important to bring awareness of that into your classroom where you have a connection that affects every single one of your students, whether you are aware of its effects or not. To help foster these connections into something that builds up your students from poverty, this chapter establishes the fifty-fifty rule for in-class interaction and supports that with five collaborative strategies that are sure to make your classroom a richer learning environment.

The Fifty-Fifty Rule

During a typical school week, how much time do you have students devote to individual studies (including lecture time), and how much do you devote to collaborative learning between students?

Two key social elements have a strong effect on academic success: (1) belonging and (2) cooperative learning (Adelabu, 2007). In fact, a strong feeling of acceptance in class and school helps protect minority students from damaging, environmental, and social threats (Cook, Purdie-Vaughns, Garcia, & Cohen, 2012). The effect size of cooperative versus individual learning is 0.59 (Hattie, 2009). This gain is solid; over a year's worth of difference.

To effectively impact academic achievement, teachers should split class time equally between social time and individual time—that's the fifty-fifty rule. Most high-performing teachers use one or more of the strategies in table 2.1 to create social time for students and balance it with individual learning time.

Table 2.1: The Fifty-Fifty Rule

Social Time	Individual Time
Cooperative groups and teams	Solo time for journaling and mind mapping
Study buddies or partners to quiz each other	Students practice self-testing
Temporary partners for summarizing time	Goal setting and self-assessment
Learning stations for social data gathering	Reading, reflection, and writing
Group projects for brainstorming and discussion	Seatwork for problem solving

To help you implement this, use the lesson-planning worksheet in figure 2.2 to choose a daily lesson and some activities you plan to use with it. Note whether this activity constitutes individual or collaborative time, and then gauge how much classroom time you need to provide students to complete the activity.

Day: _____ Lesson topic: _____		
Classroom activity	**Is this activity social or individual?**	**Time to complete**
Time spent on collaborative activities:		
Time spent on individual activities:		

Figure 2.2: Track time between individual and collaborative activities.

Visit go.SolutionTree.com/instruction for a free reproducible version of this figure.

Note that on any given day, you might split social and individual time seventy–thirty or even ten–ninety. The goal is to plan out your instructional activities so that, over a week, it all evens out. In the next section, we'll take a look at the collaborative activities that enhance social time to connect for success.

Collaborative Strategies

Much of what makes social activity work (to the degree it does) is our own biology. We are not just driven to be social; we are genetically primed for it. Because of this, students' emotional side gets a big boost when you add interdependency to lessons, which makes for more robust effect sizes. *Interdependency* means that student success depends on another student's success, which raises everyone's effort level. Four students in a cooperative group or team has a 0.69 effect size on student achievement (Hattie, 2009).

In the next section, I begin with strategies for building effective cooperative groups and teams that foster interdependency. In the sections that follow, we'll look at some other ways to build interdependency in the form of study buddies, mentors, and temporary partners. As you implement these in your classroom, remember it takes time to build and maintain relationships. Be patient, and your students will benefit from the good that comes from them.

Cooperative Groups and Teams

Ultimately, teams are just structures, and by themselves, they will accomplish nothing. Your students need social cues, prompts, and systems to establish and guide productive group behaviors. Let's break down how teams can work. In my middle school classes, teams of five seemed to work best. For elementary school, temporary cooperative groups of four or established teams of four work well. I have drawn the following ideas from many sources (for example, see Kagan, Kagan, & Kagan, 1997).

- **Allow teams to be unique:** Let each pick its own unique name, slogan, cheer, celebration, and logo. This builds social status and camaraderie. Give students time for each of these when building teams.

- **Give everyone a unique and valued role:** Roles engage more of the class and build positive interdependence (examples include summarizer, leader, personal trainer, stretch leader, energizer, joke teller, and courier).

- **Set class norms for all group behaviors:** This reduces students acting out and builds individual accountability. For example, share three things you expect every team to do, such as (1) contribute to the class, (2) be on time, and (3) support each other.

- **Give the group occasional downtime:** This allows for random acts of relationship building and fun. (Limit downtime to two to four minutes.)

- **Ensure the team works together daily:** Use procedures and rituals that involve everyone, every day. (You can learn more about designing effective rituals and find a worksheet to create some in chapter 18, page 191.) Foster equal participation using turn-taking that leadership and group norms regulate.

- **Encourage friendly competition:** This builds teamwork and effort and fosters identity. Consider the following ways to use friendly competition.

  - Student groups or teams can compete against each other when the topic is less academic and more behavioral. For example, what group is the fastest to get cleaned up at the end of class, who has the most team spirit, who will be the first to learn everyone's name in class, who has the best team cheer, or who has the coolest name?

- Students can compete against either the teacher or an outside force (another school, class, or virtual team)—an "us against the world" mentality.
- Student teams can compete against themselves. They record and display their prior scores or marks, and each week they try to best their last score.

For cooperative groups and teams to be most effective, coach the team leader, and ask him or her to coach and teach the team how to improve. Make it clear to the groups that this is the leader's role. Reciprocal teaching (students teaching peers) has a strong effect size of 0.74 (Hattie, 2009). To help you form cooperative teams among your students, use the planning sheet in figure 2.3.

Activity: _____	Team Name: _____	
Group members	**Role**	**Participation notes**
Group accomplishments and feedback:		

Figure 2.3: Sheet for forming cooperative teams.

Visit go.SolutionTree.com/instruction for a free reproducible version of this figure.

Study Buddies

At the beginning of the year or semester, many teachers set students up with a semipermanent study buddy who takes responsibility for the success of his or her partner in that class. The students share phone numbers and email addresses so they can call, text, and email. When done well, study buddies tend to form a sibling-like relationship. As a teacher, create stakes in the relationship. Say, "If you want an A or B, you must help your partner get an A or B." If one passes a test and the other does not, it's a shared failure. A teacher who uses this strategy finds it helps students at the secondary level build relationships and learn to help one another.

Study buddies should sit next to each other in class and share key content as well as be a cheerleader for the other. They will each know the other's progress and be mindful of changes in progress. Both can sign off on this process with their parents and the teacher. Give students time to make plans for what to do next after getting feedback on a quiz or any other formative assessment.

One way to assign study buddies is to have students write out a passion related to the subject area on an index card. That year or semester, students will work with another kindred soul who shares the same passion for change or a specific topic (Henderson, 2012). Using language arts as an example, you could have students complete the statement, "What I think needs changing in this world . . ." Figure 2.4 provides a template for a student contact card.

You can have students fill out cards like figure 2.4, collect them, and use them to sort students into similar interests and passions. You can pass out each student's card to his or her partner and have them spend a few minutes getting to know each other, so that every buddy already knows the best way to contact each other.

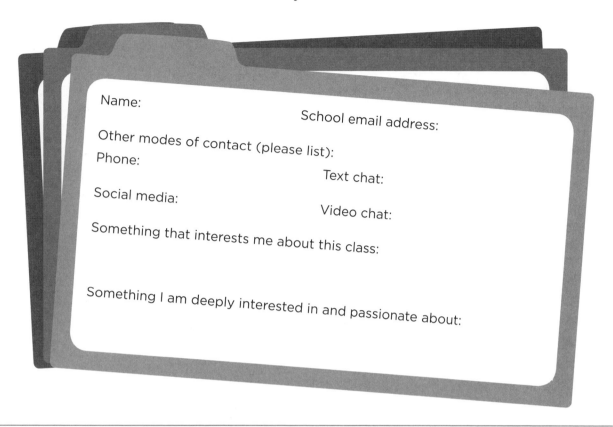

Figure 2.4: Study buddy contact card.

*Visit **go.SolutionTree.com/instruction** for a free reproducible version of this figure.*

If students don't want to work with the partner you assigned, give them some more time to work through the issue at hand using some collaboration-building tools like the one in figure 2.5 (page 24). Allocate relational time in your class to help students get to know their partner. Use simple one- to two-minute activities, and rotate them. For example, you could provide students with figure 2.5 and have them work together to answer just one question about each other's academic strengths, areas where they need help, or something that was important to them while growing up. Then provide them with it again the next day or week and have them tackle the next question.

These question activities help students build trust with others and give them a moment to exchange likes and dislikes. Additionally, pairing this activity helps with communication and conflict-resolution skills. Changing partners won't solve the problem if a student doesn't have the social skills to work with a partner. I provide further conflict-resolution strategies in *Poor Students, Rich Teaching, Revised Edition* (Jensen, 2019).

Student Mentors

Student mentors are also powerful. Every student can benefit from receiving guidance, encouragement, and leadership from someone who has more experience. Fourth graders can mentor second graders, eighth graders can mentor sixth graders, and eleventh graders can mentor ninth or tenth graders. Have students use the worksheet in figure 2.6 (page 24) to have them reflect on how a mentor guided, encouraged, and helped them.

For secondary students, set up a partnership with local colleges or universities for undergraduates to mentor (or tutor) juniors and seniors. For example, undergraduates can tutor students for forty-five minutes after school. High-poverty schools in Los Angeles used collegiate mentors for fourth and fifth graders with solid success (Coller & Kuo, 2014), noting that mentoring programs appear to be useful in promoting social relationships (with parents,

Directions: Fill out each other's name over a column, and then take turns having your partner tell you his or her answer to each question. Write down your partner's answer in the column under his or her name.

Name:	Name:
What does your partner feel are his or her strengths in school?	
What is something your partner finds challenging about school that he or she would like help with?	
What is something important to your partner outside of school?	

Figure 2.5: Relationship-building tool.

*Visit **go.SolutionTree.com/instruction** for a free reproducible version of this figure.*

Student: _____ Mentor: _____

What sorts of guidance has your mentor instilled in you to help you achieve academic success or meet personal goals?

_____

_____

_____

How has your mentor encouraged your successes or helped you overcome challenges?

_____

_____

_____

How has your mentor's influence helped you gain perspective about learning or aided your ability to achieve?

_____

_____

_____

Figure 2.6: Mentoring reflection sheet.

*Visit **go.SolutionTree.com/instruction** for a free reproducible version of this figure.*

mentors, or peers) and reducing conflict. Other mentoring programs have shown significant positive changes in youths' relationships with parents and teachers and were significantly associated with better youth outcomes, including self-esteem, academic attitudes, prosocial behaviors, and less misconduct (Chan et al., 2013).

Temporary Partners

Even well-managed teams and partners can get stale, so to freshen up the learning and social experience, teachers can use temporary partners. One way to effect this is to engage elementary or secondary students in a simple walk-and-talk activity.

> Oh! I've got a great idea that should only take a minute. Please stand up. Great! Now, when the music begins, and I say, "Go," please touch three walls and four chairs that are not your own. Once you get to the spot, wait for further directions. Ready, set, go!
>
> Now that you're in a new spot, look around, point to the person nearest you, and say, "You're it!" If you still need a partner, raise your hand. That new person will be your temporary neighbor for the next sixty seconds. Now that you have a partner, here's your challenge. Earlier we were discussing _____, and it's time to finish that.

You can then introduce the activity, such as students acting out a pro-and-con role, summarizing key points of the lesson, creating deeper and more interesting questions, or sharing what they know and need to learn. Once students finish the activity, they raise their hands. When all students have finished, ask them to thank their partners, using their first names, and head back to their seats. To further engage students, you can use music as a cue to end the activity and move forward. Use figure 2.7 to brainstorm and plan your temporary-partnership activities.

Lesson topic: _____

Goals for this lesson:

_____

_____

Describe the activity you want partners to engage in to accomplish your goals for this lesson. (Ideas include pro-and-con role-play, summarizing the lesson's key points, and crafting deep, interesting questions.)

_____

_____

With this activity in mind, describe your ideas for how you can create excitement for students to work with a new, temporary partner.

_____

_____

_____

_____

_____

Figure 2.7: Activity planning for temporary partners.

Visit go.SolutionTree.com/instruction for a free reproducible version of this figure.

Quick Consolidation: Connect Everyone for Success

As we've seen, many forms of interdependency can work to allow students to connect everyone for success. I have found interdependency to be one of the best tools for classroom success. Whatever strategies you adopt, no one method is perfect, because ultimately, students will crave a bit of novelty when they get tired of a social structure. The idea is to develop multiple sources that allow students to work with others in which the stakes are high for the common goals. Answer the following reflection questions as you consider your next steps on the journey to making learning more collaborative in your classroom.

1. What did you learn about the importance of collaborative-learning activities that you didn't know when you started this chapter? How is your outlook on group work changing?

2. Given the importance of splitting classroom time (over the course of a week) between individual and collaborative study time, what changes do you need to make to get closer to an even split between the two?

3. How will you approach using collaborative time with your class that ensures it creates effective (and not wasted) time?

4. If conflict arises between group members, study buddies, or temporary partners, what strategies will you use to achieve a productive outcome that allows the group or partnership to function better in the future?

5. What is your plan for observing the benefits of student collaboration? What will you look for to know these collaborative activities are benefitting students?

CHAPTER 3

SHOW EMPATHY

Many teachers struggle with providing students with what they need the most—someone who cares about their personal life as much as their school progress. As we know, bad things happen to everyone. However, students from poverty may not have the cognitive skills, emotional support, or coping skills necessary to deal with adversity. Use the survey in figure 3.1 to think about what you understand empathy to be and its importance to your teaching practices.

How do you define empathy? What differentiates empathy from sympathy?				
It is important for teachers to show students empathy in the classroom. (Circle one.)			True False	
Why or why not?				
How often do you go out of your way to show students that you care about them and their lives outside your classroom? (Circle one.)	Every day	A few times a week	A few times a month	Hardly ever
What examples can you think of where you showed students you care about their lives and what happens to them after they leave your classroom?				

Figure 3.1: Consider how you value empathy.

*Visit **go.SolutionTree.com/instruction** for a free reproducible version of this figure.*

In figure 3.1, the reason I asked you to define empathy and what it means to you is that I've found that people define empathy differently. So, it's important to understand what we mean here when we talk about empathy, because empathy and sympathy are not the same thing. Sympathy is the ability to understand another with feelings of sorrow for their misfortune. Empathy is a bit different; it is the ability to understand and share the same feelings. The key to this aspect of the relational mindset isn't to be sympathetic but to show empathy and provide tools. The good news is, empathy is something you can learn (Schumann, Zaki, & Dweck, 2014). Knowing this, does it change how you answered any of the questions in figure 3.1?

This chapter offers strategies to help you understand the need for empathy, tools for offering students empathic responses, and three quick-connect tools for making empathic connections with students.

Understand the Need for Empathy

In *Poor Students, Rich Teaching, Revised Edition* (Jensen, 2019), I write in detail on the research that supports why your students *need* empathy. Students in poverty don't need to be told their lives are tough; they often need a caring adult or a shoulder to lean on and an empathic teacher who listens. When students do not get support and empathy, they have more than just hurt feelings; they have stress, and students from poor families typically experience more stressors and have fewer skills to cope with that stress (Evans & Kim, 2007). Students of color are also more likely to experience chronic stress (Brody, Lei, Chen, & Miller, 2014). (Note that in addition to the empathy tools in this chapter, I offer some stress-management strategies to maintain student engagement in chapter 16, page 175.)

Now for some good news: positive relational experiences can mitigate the damaging effects chronic stress has on the brain. Our brain structures respond to empathic support by reducing stress hormones (like cortisol) and increasing the serotonin for well-being (Williams, Perrett, Waiter, & Pechey, 2007). When empathy is strong, emotional support fosters greater growth of the hippocampus, which enhances learning and memory. Plus, emotional support builds new mass in this structure, which is healthy (Luby et al., 2012, 2013).

If you are struggling to help students learn and behave, this is critical: foster quality, empathic relationships. Next, here are tools to accomplish this.

Use Empathy Tools

To keep coming to school, students need a caring adult, not a judge and an executioner. When a student shares something adverse that happened, avoid any impulsive or judgmental reaction, and instead start with empathy. There are many ways to show you care. Make your caring explicit. Not every student will read your face or body language, which might be your primary way of showing empathy. Take a moment to think about how you typically respond to students from poverty who come to you with a challenging personal matter, and answer the questions in figure 3.2.

When a student confronts you with issues like these, does your reaction demonstrate to him or her that you understand what they're dealing with? Or, do you focus only on their responsibilities to you and your class without any consideration of what his or her life is like outside of school? If you need help forming more empathic responses, consider starting with one of the following five empathy-response tools instead.

1. "I am so sorry to hear that." (Saying this with a sad face shows you care.)
2. "This makes me sick." (Be sad, upset, or very concerned for the student.)
3. "We were worried about you." (Say many others cared about the student; be worried.)
4. "Are you OK?" (Physically check on a student's safety and well-being.)
5. "That's awful. I don't know if I could handle that as well as you are." (This tells the student that the problem was a tough one and that you are showing empathy and admiration.)

Student challenge	Your response
"I had to miss school last week because one of my family members was injured in a violent incident."	
"I can't keep up with all this material because I work at night to support my younger brother."	
"I couldn't do my homework because it wasn't safe for me to go home last night."	
"It's very hard to pay attention to your teaching when I haven't eaten for two days."	
"Nobody in my family thinks school is important, so why should I even try?"	

Figure 3.2: Respond to student problems.

Visit **go.SolutionTree.com/instruction** *for a free reproducible version of this figure.*

Judging a student's situation gets in the way. Stop telling him or her how to fix it. That comes later, much later. Even if you're in a lousy mood (it happens), you're likely to find that saying one of these triggers your own empathy, so start there. Likewise, regularly engaging counselors by telling them about students who need extra support is also a tremendous way to help students feel cared about. Counselors can build stronger relationships and help students navigate life and the system. When your school adds just one counselor, it increases college attendance by 10 percent (Bouffard, 2014).

This applies to less extreme situations as well. Remember the first of Stephen R. Covey's (2013) seven habits: seek first to understand. Listen more, and talk less. The next time a student doesn't complete an assignment, say, "I'm sorry it didn't get done. Tell me what happened?" The next time a student is late for class, say, "Hey Eric, good to see you. Go ahead and join your teammates. They'll get you caught up." You can talk to him or her privately a bit later. When you do, and before anything else (like a reprimand for tardiness), check for safety. Ask the student, "Usually you're good about being on time. What happened today? Are you OK?"

Knowing this, would you change your approach to any of the questions in figure 3.2? If so, visit **go.SolutionTree .com/instruction** to access and print out a clean version of the figure. Keep refining your approach until you feel like you've got a toolbox of responses that show genuine empathy.

Use Quick-Connect Tools

On day one, students want to know who you are you and whether you care for and respect them, so don't wait until you have friction in your classroom to begin showing empathy. As I detailed in chapter 1 (page 9), using student names is a great start to building the class. Many teachers fall short at this. Use the following quick, easy tools to fast-track your relationships with students in your classroom. These are as simple as 1–2–3.

- **One and Done:** In the first thirty days of school, do one favor, make one connection, or show empathy that is so powerful that an individual or whole class remembers it. For example, a student shares a hobby he or she has with you. Let's say it is video games. You go home and search the internet for the nearest gaming convention dates and discuss with them what you found. Use figure 3.3 (page 30) to track your progress.

- **Two for Ten:** Identify one to two students who most need a connection early on. For ten consecutive days, invest two minutes a day in connecting time to talk about anything. This could be right before class, during seatwork time, or when the student comes up to you for something else. This gives you the relational foundation for the whole semester or year. Use figure 3.4 to track your progress.

- **Three in Thirty:** Ask just enough questions, through any conversation, to discover three things (other than a name) about every student you have in the first thirty days. For example, do you know who else is at home in the family? Do you know what interests the student has outside school? Do you know what the student wants to do when he or she gets older? Use figure 3.5 to track your progress.

	Who needed empathy?	Why?	What did you do?
Do one favor:			
Make one connection:			
Show powerful empathy:			

Figure 3.3: One and Done tracking sheet.

Visit go.SolutionTree.com/instruction for a free reproducible version of this figure.

	Student 1: _____	Student 2: _____
	What we talked about	**What we talked about**
Day 1:		
Day 2:		
Day 3:		
Day 4:		
Day 5:		
Day 6:		
Day 7:		
Day 8:		
Day 9:		
Day 10:		

Figure 3.4: Two for Ten tracking sheet.

Visit go.SolutionTree.com/instruction for a free reproducible version of this figure.

Student's name	Thing one	Thing two	Thing three

Figure 3.5: Three in Thirty tracking sheet.

Visit go.SolutionTree.com/instruction for a free reproducible version of this figure.

Consider the three preceding strategies as a quick start. Additionally, use the following three quick strategies as add-ons to show you care: (1) connect early, (2) connect late, and (3) connect with students' home lives.

Connect Early

During the first few minutes of class (or before it starts), make the rounds with students. Assess how students are doing on the opening activity, and take a moment to check in with them emotionally. You can build rapport, connect, and show empathy even with brief conversations. This is also a great way to complete your Three in Thirty worksheet (refer to figure 3.4). Use figure 3.6 as a list of common conversation starters; use the empty spaces in the reproducible version to add some of your own ideas based on what you know about your students individually and as a class.

Conversation starters	
"How are things going with your _____?"	"How are you feeling about _____?"
"Do you like to play any sports?"	"Do you have any fun skills (such as fixing things, performing, cooking, or building)?"
"What shows do you like to watch?"	"Where in the world would you like to visit?"
"Do you have any pets?"	"What dreams do you have for your future?"
"Who are your friends? What do you do together for fun?"	"How are you feeling today?"

Figure 3.6: Conversation starters.

*Visit **go.SolutionTree.com/instruction** for a free reproducible version of this figure.*

Some teachers will engage in friendly small talk with students (for example, about their favorite sports team and if that team lost or won). You may politely compliment a student on his or her new hair style or new shoes or ask about an upcoming community event or a family activity. Use the first three to seven minutes to see if anyone is struggling academically and needs extra help.

Connect Late

When students are leaving class, check their body language. Often their nonverbal signals will indicate their emotional state without you even needing to ask. See figure 3.7 (page 32) for a feelings poster for students. You can laminate the poster and have students circle the face that represents how they feel. Students can use this poster upon entering and exiting the class and during instruction.

How Am I Feeling?

Figure 3.7: Feelings poster.

For example, if a student is dragging himself out of class, maybe he or she does not want to go to his next class, maybe the student does not understand how to do homework, or maybe he or she is sorting out a big emotional issue. On his feelings poster, the teacher notices he circled frustrated all class period. This is the time to check in. Ask, as a student leaves, "Have you got a second?" Then say, "You know I'm always here for you, right? If something's going on, maybe I can help things move along a little easier." Your student will either talk or he or she won't. At least you reached out, and you planted that seed. Maybe next time you say that, he or she will open up.

Many high-performing schools, especially secondary, use the last school period for an all-student homework hour. Although research on the value of homework is mixed, at the secondary level, the effect size is strong—0.64 (Hattie, 2009). You can use this time to show students empathy. Each day, select a different student to invest a few minutes with—to not just help with homework but to listen and let him or her know you care. See figure 3.8. If your school does not have this valuable option in place, use classroom seatwork time to connect.

Connect With Students' Home Lives

There are many ways to widen your relationships with students outside the classroom. Because the time you invest to build relationships with your students is critical, do things early in the year or semester to show you care. On a deeper level, learn about your students' lives (without any judgments) in ways that help foster insights and different ways of thinking, acting, and feeling, as well as an appreciation of where they're coming from. This comes from quality time. Use the tool in figure 3.9 to keep track of the things you learn from your conversations with each of your students.

Student's name	Notes on his or her body language	Last date I invested one-on-one time with this student	What did I learn during this time?

Figure 3.8: Invest in your students.

*Visit **go.SolutionTree.com/instruction** for a free reproducible version of this figure.*

Student's name	Notes about this student's life outside of school

Figure 3.9: Track your interactions with students.

*Visit **go.SolutionTree.com/instruction** for a free reproducible version of this figure.*

You might attend something that students do after school, such as go to a sporting event, the mall, a movie, a concert, a pick-up basketball game, a funeral, or an activity in the park. Understanding their home lives allows you to show that you really do care. This may seem like asking a lot, but remember, investing one to two hours early in the year (or semester) can have a bigtime payback the rest of the year and throughout students' lives.

Quick Consolidation: Show Empathy

Something shifts when another *gets* you. We feel special, more important, and more connected when another gives us a moment of empathy. Remember, empathy does not mean letting a student off the hook for a bad behavior. It means you care about the student. It means you want to help him or her get better so that he or she knows better options for next time. It is about you being an ally for how your students feel as much as how they behave. When you can consistently demonstrate empathy toward your students, you've just added another good reason for them to come to school, especially to your class. Answer the following reflection questions as you consider your next steps on the journey to connecting with your students using empathy.

1. What did you learn about the importance of empathy that you didn't know when you started this chapter? What differentiates empathy from sympathy?

2. What will you do or say the next time a student comes to you with a difficult problem to show that your first concern is for his or her safety?

3. Which of this chapter's quick-connect tools will you use to build empathy with your students? How could you adapt the tool to work even better for your teaching style and classroom culture?

4. How could you change your beginning-of-class and end-of-class routines to make time to get to know your students better?

5. What can you do to get to know your students better outside the classroom?

Reflect on the Relational Mindset

All meaningful and lasting change starts with a mirror. Now that you understand the concept of the relational mindset and have strategies to foster its growth in your classroom, it's time to self-assess and reflect on what comes next. Use the following questions to accomplish this.

1. What can you do to bring a stronger relational mindset into your class every day?

2. What evidence do you expect to see to let you know that you're improving your students' chances of succeeding academically?

3. What strategy could you use or adapt from part one in your very next class to start building a relational mindset with your students or with specific students in need?

4. What challenges do you expect to encounter as you adopt this strategy? How will you react to and overcome these challenges?

5. What benefits can you envision when you find success building stronger relationships with your students? How will you benefit? How will your students benefit?

Your decision to help students grow means that you generate a new narrative that includes the relational mindset. Begin with a fierce urgency, and choose one of the chapters' strategies to get started with better relationships. Encourage colleagues to help, and set goals for progress. Once the message is in your heart, and you've built the activities into your lessons, the mindset will become automatic.

PART TWO

IMPLEMENTING THE ACHIEVEMENT MINDSET

The achievement mindset asks you a simple question: "Are your students' brains stuck for the rest of their life at their current cognitive level or can they be lifted?" If their brains are not stuck, then you are invited (and maybe even compelled) to help each student develop his or her drive, effort, and intention. Start with the mindset that every single student can and will learn and then help them learn it. This is a way to frame equity from the conversation to action steps. In this part of the book, you'll gain strategies and tools to develop steady motivation to help foster student efforts to produce greater achievement by choice. However, before we dig in, let's start with a quick self-assessment regarding how you approach student achievement in your classroom. See figure P2.1 (page 38).

Many teachers complain that their students lack effort. At the same time, it is a simple fact: a student who appears lazy or unmotivated for one teacher will often work hard for another teacher. This simple fact shows us that the student is different with a different teacher. This is extremely important to keep in mind as you reflect on your answers to these questions. It is the teaching that makes the difference, and the achievement mindset changes everything. The achievement mindset says, "I can build student effort, motivation, and attitudes to succeed. They are all teachable skills."

> The achievement mindset says, "I can build student effort, motivation, and attitudes to succeed. They are all teachable skills."

I sometimes hear teachers say things like, "By this grade, they should be able to motivate themselves. If they can't do it, they're not going to make it anyway." If you blame the students, parents, or your circumstances and make

1. Have you ever concluded that a student just "isn't good" at a particular subject or lesson? Why did you believe this? What efforts did you make to help the student overcome the challenge?

_____

_____

_____

_____

2. What goals do you usually set for yourself and your students? Are they ambitious, or are they goals you already know you or your students can achieve?

_____

_____

_____

_____

3. What are your strategies for giving students feedback on their work? What do you do to ensure students know what they need to do to improve their learning outcomes?

_____

_____

_____

_____

4. How do you approach students who struggle to keep up with a class or topic? How do you help them overcome doubt or frustration when they struggle with their work?

_____

_____

_____

_____

5. In what ways do you think poverty affects your students' belief in their own ability to achieve? What strategies do you already use to raise expectations for these students?

_____

_____

_____

_____

Figure P2.1: Assess your understanding of how poverty affects student achievement.

*Visit **go.SolutionTree.com/instruction** for a free reproducible version of this figure.*

every teaching problem someone else's fault, you're stuck as a professional and won't get better. But if you choose to help your students succeed, you'll bravely hold up a mirror. The mirror reminds all of us, "If it's to be, it's up to me." The achievement mindset shows that when the conditions are right every one of us can and will achieve.

Think about your current approach to students' successes and failures. When students succeed, you'll want to consistently attribute it to their preparation, effort, planning, strategies, focus, positive attitude, and persistence—elements under a student's control. Therefore, when students fail, avoid using comfort words for failure, like "You tried so hard" or "At least you have other strengths." These are detrimental, and when you use phrases like these, it lowers the student's expectations of himself or herself, motivation drops, and the student actually does worse (Rattan, Good, & Dweck, 2012).

You can learn even more about the full scope of research backing the achievement mindset in *Poor Students, Rich Teaching, Revised Edition* (Jensen, 2019); for our purposes, your three main takeaways are the following.

1. **Learn the invisible motivators:** Our brain is designed to pick up countless social, physical, and linguistic cues, which I narrow down to the following five: (1) approach, frame, and define a task appropriately; (2) manage the self-talk from you and the student; (3) provide core background subskills needed for the task; (4) identify stereotype threats and remove them; and (5) frame failures so students grow from them.

2. **Foster a growth mindset in your students:** Put simply, an achievement mindset *is* teachable. Lisa Blackwell, Kali Trzesniewski, and Carol Dweck (2007) found that students taught with a growth mindset outperformed a control group on test scores and had more effort and interest over three times as often.

3. **Drop the labels:** Avoid labels like *minority students* (Latino, African American, and Asian students make up 50.3 percent of U.S. public K–12 classrooms; Maxwell, 2014), *low achievers* or *low students* (these terms imply some sort of deficit when the truth is that the student may have had underperforming teachers for several years), and *disadvantaged* or *disabled students* (students from poverty are more likely to be school dependent for their enrichment, and many are inappropriately labeled as disabled).

The upcoming chapters dig into three of the most effective achievement boosters of all time. There is no ascending or descending order of importance. In fact, these ideas play off each other with a synergistic effect.

1. Set gutsy goals.
2. Give fabulous feedback.
3. Persist with grit.

Be patient in building the class campfire of energy. Every spark you bring to the classroom campfire will build the student fires of desire. The content you teach might remain the same; however, the circumstances for learning, your context, and your strategies can create highly motivated students, if you know how to do it. Get psyched!

Questions for Daily Reflection

Each day, consider your own mindset for helping students approach their learning with the conviction that they can achieve academic success, regardless of any challenges they have outside of school. Then, answer the following questions.

1. What can I do today to ensure I help a student who is struggling to overcome an academic obstacle and have success?

2. What big-picture goals have I set for my students, and how are they progressing toward that goal? What micro goal will I help them achieve on this day?

3. Have I given my students the feedback they need to improve and overcome mistakes? What can I do better?

CHAPTER 4

SET GUTSY GOALS

What would you predict is the greatest single contributing factor to student achievement? Would you say parental support, genes, or school quality? Would you guess effort, past achievement, or socioeconomic status? Any of those would be a pretty good guess. But there's a factor that contributes almost three years' worth of gains. The problem is most teachers don't know what it is.

The research is solid. Students' self-reported grades and expectations of their success (or failure) in class have a whopping effect size of 1.44, ranking it near the top of all contributors to student achievement (Hattie, 2009), contributing to nearly three years of growth. Students having some control over more short-term goals also has an effect size of 1.21 (Willett, Yamashita, & Anderson, 1983).

Before we begin, use figure 4.1 (page 42) to list three goals you have set for students in the past or that you would consider strong goals to use in the future.

As you look over the goals you listed, how do they strike you? Do they reflect highly ambitious results, results that are "good enough," or did you feel yourself compelled to set goals for students low because doing so feels more realistic?

Low-performing students expect (based on their own past performance) to struggle or fail at school each year. That's why high-performing teachers never allow students' low expectations to become the norm. For example, if you ask a student who has failed in mathematics for three years in a row his or her goal, it would likely be to just pass. But that student goal will not cut it in a high-performing teacher's class where goals are advanced or expert level, not just basic proficiency. Starting the first day of school, strong teachers encourage students to set the long-term bar sky-high. For the moment, don't worry about buy-in. Later in this chapter, I'll show you how you get students to believe (with even more strategies in chapter 16, page 173).

In this chapter, we begin our implementation of the achievement mindset with the baseline tools you need for creating gutsy goals that lead to mastery, look at the practice of setting those goals, establish ways you can get buy-in from students (give them a reason to believe), and then use micro goals to help close any gaps.

Creating Gutsy Goals for Mastery

Gutsy goals are jaw-dropping, nearly impossible, shoot-for-the-stars milestones. Why would you set goals you might not reach? James Cameron, director of two of the highest-grossing films of all time (*Titanic* and *Avatar*), said we should set impossibly high goals so that when we fail, we will fail above others' successes (as cited in Goodyear, 2009). For teachers, this means setting

Goal 1: _____

Why is this a strong goal? How did students react to it? (Or, how do you think they would react?) What challenges do you foresee in meeting it?

_____

_____

_____

Goal 2: _____

Why is this a strong goal? How did students react to it? (Or, how do you think they would react?) What challenges do you foresee in meeting it?

_____

_____

_____

Goal 3: _____

Why is this a strong goal? How did students react to it? (Or, how do you think they would react?) What challenges do you foresee in meeting it?

_____

_____

_____

_____

Figure 4.1: List and support three ideas for classroom goals.

Visit go.SolutionTree.com/instruction for a free reproducible version of this figure.

goals of mastery, not merely basic understanding or proficiency. Setting goals for mastery is what leads all students to graduate (see part seven, page 199).

The mastery process is one where a teacher says, "I don't just want them to get it right. I want them to become so proficient that they can't get it wrong. Only then will we move on." In mastery, there is no personal best or just good enough. Remember, even modest, achievable goals have a positive 0.52 effect size (one year's gain), but mastery as a goal has a huge 0.96 effect size (two years of growth) for disadvantaged and lower-ability students (Kulik & Kulik, 1987). High-performing, high-poverty schools have this core achievement driver (mastery, not basic or proficiency levels) in common, and it's a must for your classroom (Johnson, Uline, & Perez, 2014).

Understand, the big-picture goal is the process as well as the destination. This means gutsy goals are those you cannot meet until you grow into one who can reach them. To that end, the best gutsy goals are revised SMART goals (Conzemius & O'Neill, 2014): specific and strategic, measurable, amazing (rather than *attainable*), relevant, and time bound.

Consider the goals you outlined in figure 4.1. Now, use figure 4.2 and the SMART system to clarify your vision for making these goals masterful. Don't worry about creating final gutsy goals at this point. Use this instead to think about the qualities that will make your goals gutsy. We'll take that final step in the next section.

Goal 1: _____	Goal 2: _____	Goal 3: _____
Make it specific:	Make it specific:	Make it specific:
Make it measurable:	Make it measurable:	Make it measurable:
Make it amazing:	Make it amazing:	Make it amazing:
Make it relevant:	Make it relevant:	Make it relevant:
Make it time bound:	Make it time bound:	Make it time bound:

Figure 4.2: Make your goals SMART.

*Visit **go.SolutionTree.com/instruction** for a free reproducible version of this figure.*

In the next section, you'll use your explorations in figure 4.2 to set some truly gutsy goals.

Setting Gutsy Goals

Growing up in the digital generation, most students feel like anything they need to know is just a quick google search away. The gratification is split-second fast. However, becoming a good learner requires the capacity to dig deeply into a topic, which requires having persistence, thinking about it, clarifying it, analyzing it, and developing a complex, yet clear, understanding. This is hard work, and most students don't know how to do it. Yet, in higher-performing urban schools, the deeper, mastery learning is a key part of the solution (Johnson et al., 2014). To truly have a consistent achievement mindset, you must have something special worth doing.

In your classroom, student goals should produce something of value—something that is personally or culturally relevant—and be part of something bigger than themselves. Second, the goal must have specificity for a big impact (0.94 effect size; Marzano, 1998). Third, you must tell students why they can believe in you and the goals you have set for them. Finally, you'll need to set micro goals (see page 48) so they can get concrete evidence that the gutsy goals are happening.

Let's learn how to create high class expectations with high goals to get students to the promised land of consistent high effort. Following are elementary and secondary examples of gutsy goals as well as an opportunity to rethink your own goals and write them down. After that. I offer some examples of gutsy goals students can set for themselves.

Elementary Teacher Examples

Let's say that last year a teacher had 50 percent of her students reach proficiency in mathematics. I have heard those teachers set what seems like lofty new goals for class like, "At least 80 percent of my students will be proficient in mathematics, and 20 percent or more will get to mastery level." These might be higher goals than you've ever had before, but sorry, they are not gutsy goals. Here's a gutsy goal: "My first-grade students will read, write, do mathematics, and behave so that by the end of the year, they are ready for third grade, not second." This goal makes two years of gains with your students.

I have also heard teacher goals like, "This year, all my students will reach their potential." Unless you have a specific way to measure your students' potential, how would you know what their potential is? Remember, if you work in a school with high-poverty students, getting one and a half to three years of academic progress per year is just basic progress. Without very aggressive goals, you increase the likelihood for students to drop out or fail. Make your own goals jaw-dropping, amazing, and unlikely (but possible) to reach. Here are examples of teacher gutsy goals.

- **A process goal:** "This year, I will engage my students every nine minutes or less for the entire year."
- **A relational goal:** "This year, I will learn at least three things (outside of a name) about every student, and I'll do a One and Done (from chapter 6) with my two class leaders in the first thirty days."
- **A result goal:** "My second-grade students will read, write, do mathematics, and behave so that by the end of the year, they are ready for fourth grade, not third."

Secondary Teacher Examples

If you teach at the secondary level, let your students know about your own gutsy goals. You'll want to set goals so high that you're unlikely to (but maybe you might) reach them. That sends a message to your students to shoot for the stars.

- **A process goal:** A science teacher's goal might be to teach students how to rebuild a city from scratch when disaster strikes. A middle school English teacher might ask her students to write a paper to change the world. Their final papers could be read to community leaders, and the feedback would be life changing. A mathematics teacher's goal might be, "My students will write a handbook of tips for 'How to succeed in math,' during the last month of the semester."
- **A relational goal:** "I will complete a One and Done with one or two students in every class and do name-learning activities until every student knows every other student by first name."
- **A result goal:** "I will get two years of academic progress for every year I teach" or "I will become a top 50 finalist for the Fishman Prize for Superlative Classroom Practice."

Your Own Examples

Now that you've looked at some examples of some genuinely gutsy goals, use what you've learned so far in this chapter to lay out one of each type of gutsy goal—a process goal, a relational goal, and a result goal. Make sure each

Process goal:	
Is this goal specific and strategic?	Yes ☐ No ☐
Is this goal measurable?	Yes ☐ No ☐
Is this goal amazing?	Yes ☐ No ☐
Is this goal relevant?	Yes ☐ No ☐
Is this goal time bound?	Yes ☐ No ☐
Describe whether your process goal is SMART. If it isn't, how can you make it SMART?	

Relational goal:	
Is this goal specific and strategic?	Yes ☐ No ☐
Is this goal measurable?	Yes ☐ No ☐
Is this goal amazing?	Yes ☐ No ☐
Is this goal relevant?	Yes ☐ No ☐
Is this goal time bound?	Yes ☐ No ☐
Describe whether your relational goal is SMART. If it isn't, how can you make it SMART?	

Result goal:	
Is this goal specific and strategic?	Yes ☐ No ☐
Is this goal measurable?	Yes ☐ No ☐
Is this goal amazing?	Yes ☐ No ☐
Is this goal relevant?	Yes ☐ No ☐
Is this goal time bound?	Yes ☐ No ☐
Describe whether your result goal is SMART. If it isn't, how can you make it SMART?	

Figure 4.3: Your gutsy goals.

*Visit **go.SolutionTree.com/instruction** for a free reproducible version of this figure.*

of them meets the criteria for a SMART goal. See figure 4.3. Note that, if they apply, you are free to evolve your goals from figure 4.2 (page 43), or you can set some entirely new goals. If you find yourself answering "no" to any of the SMART questions, return to figure 4.2 and keep refining until it does meet these criteria.

Student Examples

Beyond the goals you set, it's important for your students to set goals that give them ownership over their own ambitions and growth. So, after you have established classwide gutsy goals and presented them to your students (along with information about what gutsy goals are and why they're important), it's a great idea to have them set some of their own. Here are student examples for gutsy goals.

- **A process goal:** "I will read at least five pages a day and take at least two pages of notes every school day of the year."

- **A relational goal:** "I will know every other student in class by first name." Or, "I will initiate three new friendships from this class before we end."

- **A result goal:** "I will get an A or B in every class."

Note that it's important for students to share their goals with you and each other as well. To that end, pass out notecards like those illustrated in figure 4.4, and have students fill them out. Then, have them form teams of four to six peers. Each team member stands to read his or her goals. When each student has finished, the team gives a standing ovation.

> **Name:** _____
> **Process goal:** _____
> What makes this goal gutsy? (Make sure it is specific and strategic, measurable, amazing, relevant, and time bound.)
>
>
>
> **Relational goal:** _____
> What makes this goal gutsy? (Make sure it is specific and strategic, measurable, amazing, relevant, and time bound.)
>
>
> **Result goal:** _____
> What makes this goal gutsy? (Make sure it is specific and strategic, measurable, amazing, relevant, and time bound.)

Figure 4.4: Gutsy goals for students.

*Visit **go.SolutionTree.com/instruction** for a free reproducible version of this figure.*

Giving a Reason to Believe

When you share gutsy goals, those around may be tempted to roll their eyes. It is as if they are saying, "Yeah, sure, right; like that's going to happen." Students may have trouble buying into the gutsy goals you set and those you ask them for, which is why it's essential for you to give them a reason to believe in you. Big goals *sound good*, but unless you can back them up, you will lose your followers. How you do this is critical.

Believe it or not, it takes just twenty seconds to give students a reason to believe in you. All you have to say is some variation of, "I care about you, I'm good at what I do, and I'll work hard, persist, and learn from my mistakes. You do your part, and I guarantee I'll do my part. I won't let any of you fail. Now, let's get to work!" Did you ever have a teacher say this to you in school? I didn't. That kind of confidence, when backed up by subsequent action, can move mountains.

Use figure 4.5 to write down your gutsy goals from figure 4.3 (page 45), and this time add in your plans for making your goals relevant to your students and how you're going to approach achieving their buy-in.

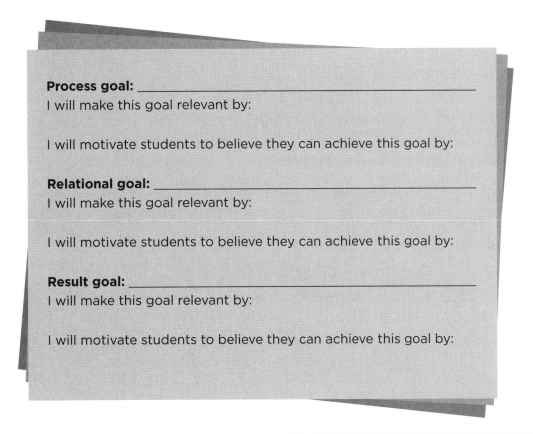

Process goal: _____

I will make this goal relevant by:

I will motivate students to believe they can achieve this goal by:

Relational goal: _____

I will make this goal relevant by:

I will motivate students to believe they can achieve this goal by:

Result goal: _____

I will make this goal relevant by:

I will motivate students to believe they can achieve this goal by:

Figure 4.5: Making your gutsy goals relevant.

*Visit **go.SolutionTree.com/instruction** for a free reproducible version of this figure.*

Reinforce your gutsy goals weekly, so that students can visualize them, hear them echo in their minds, and feel them viscerally. Post reminders and encourage students to talk to others about them. Many teachers (at both elementary and secondary levels) post college banners around the classroom. These are inspiring, especially if you write the names of past students who have gone on to that college below the banners. Unless you help students understand that it is the pursuit of the goals that makes life worthwhile—and that we all will encounter temporary failures—they may quit on you and on themselves.

Finally, and maybe most important, help teach students how to deal with failure. Tell them that failure is part of life and part of progress. Remind them often that failure is simply feedback on what did not work. Failures are lessons. Failures teach us. They can be positive when we positively accept and learn from them. When you have a student who experienced a failure and needs encouragement to build back up, use the worksheet in figure 4.6 to plan how you will approach him or her.

Student: _____
Describe the setback: _____
List three ideas you can use to approach this student to help him or her overcome this challenge in the future.

1. _____
   _____
2. _____
   _____
3. _____
   _____

Figure 4.6: Learning from and overcoming failure.

*Visit **go.SolutionTree.com/instruction** for a free reproducible version of this figure.*

How we respond to failure defines us, not the encounter itself. Getting knocked down is nothing; getting back up is everything. Students will show their true grit (see chapter 6, page 67) and get back up if their vision of worthwhile goals is strong enough and they have reinforcement along the way. That's where micro goals come in.

Using Micro Goals to Close the Gaps

For most students, having gutsy goals is exciting. However, it's difficult to reactivate the long-term sky-high goals over and over on cue. Any of us would find it hard to stay psyched about a goal that seems so far away. Training for the Olympics or trying to get an advanced degree are big motivators, but still, we all need those hourly, daily, and weekly nudges to keep us going. It is the trail of emotional highs that keep us moving forward, not the once-a-year goal.

That's why you'll need to constantly set micro goals that your students can reach within a week or less. These specific, concrete goals can:

- Reaffirm a specific competency
- Give measurable progress toward the gutsy goals
- Provide a quick emotional affirmation and moment for a celebration

Because micro goals allow students to get immediate feedback for themselves, the effect size is a sizzling 0.97 (Marzano, Pickering, & Pollock, 2001). That's almost two years' worth of gains! Set daily and weekly goals that students can reach with a solid effort. This step is critical. They need to see that they can reach the big gutsy goals, one bite at a time. When students set their own micro goals, the effect size is a strong 1.21—well over two years' worth of academic progress (Marzano et al., 2001).

Although adults understand the power of greater expectations, students will use their past experiences to set goals and often set them too low. However, they don't know how far they can go with an amazing teacher (like you). You can help them set and link the micro goal completion to the bigger gutsy goal. Every week, check in on your goal progress. See figure 4.7. For example, a student's gutsy goal might be to finish fifth grade ready for seventh grade. On week one, he might set a micro goal to get 100 percent proficiency on assessments; for week two, he wants to be on time every single day; and so on.

Gutsy goal: *Finish fifth grade ready for seventh grade.*	
Week One	Micro Goal
✓	*Get 100 percent proficiency this week.*
Week Two	Micro Goal
	Be 100 percent on time every day.

Figure 4.7: Micro goal checklist.

*Visit **go.SolutionTree.com/instruction** for a reproducible version of this figure.*

Remember that some weeks are dedicated to holidays, tests, or professional development, so you'll have to include these additions in your achievement calendar. When students get questions right or reach their micro goal, make time to celebrate. For example, every time your class reaches a micro goal, pause for quick celebrations, saying, "Hey class, we did it! We are one step closer to our big goal this year." Celebrations are important because they promote the values and standards that are fundamental to your class. Ultimately, these micro goals are about maintaining engagement, a mindset we cover in detail in part six. In particular, you'll find even more ways to celebrate small victories and student accomplishments in chapter 18 (page 191).

As a final summation of your work in this chapter, use figure 4.8 as a combined checklist to affirm that a goal you've set is gutsy, relevant to your students, and has suitable micro goals.

Gutsy goal:		
This goal is:	**Yes**	**No**
Specific and strategic		
Measurable		
Amazing (rather than attainable)		
Relevant		
Time bound		
What micro goals have I or my students thought of to achieve this goal?		

Figure 4.8: Gutsy goal with micro goal checklist.

continued ⇨

How will I celebrate achievement of micro goals or major milestones?

_____   _____

_____   _____

_____   _____

_____   _____

_____   _____

_____   _____

*Visit **go.SolutionTree.com/instruction** for a reproducible version of this figure.*

Quick Consolidation: Set Gutsy Goals

Many students get discouraged when you try to put them on the path to gutsy goals. Some will interpret the roadblocks they encounter as a lack of ability. This is why you must continually build the growth mindset. If they struggle, help them uncover the false assumptions or strategies that undercut their belief in their own ability to improve. Help them grow. Higher learning requires not only the achievement mindset but also the emotional safety for a relentless intellectual curiosity. Assume the best of your students, and pursue the gutsy goals with a high expectation for mastery. With this firmly in mind, answer the following reflection questions as you consider your next steps.

1. What did you learn about the importance of setting gutsy goals that you didn't know when you started this chapter? Why are they so important?

2. What distinguishes an ordinary goal from one that demands mastery?

3. How will you help students believe in their own ability to master the content you teach?

4. What is the role of micro goals in the mastery process? How can you set and celebrate micro goals to keep students on the path to mastery?

5. When students struggle and grow frustrated with the standards you've set, what will be your strategies for helping them break through these blocks?

CHAPTER 5

GIVE FABULOUS FEEDBACK

The topic of this chapter may be the holy grail of generating real student motivation and stronger effort. Here, you get tools to generate better quality feedback. As soon as you and I see progress, we get inspired. With feedback, the goal moves closer, and hope rises. That's how it works for your students too. Think about the nature of the feedback you give your students, and take a moment to answer the survey questions in figure 5.1.

Do you make it a priority to give all students constructive feedback as often as possible? (Circle one.)	No Yes
Describe the strategies or approach you use when giving feedback. What makes your feedback effective? How does it reach students and help them improve their work?	
What percentage of your assignments are formative or summative?	Formative: ____% Summative: ____%
Describe your approach to formative assessment. Is it a core component of how you assess learning?	
Do you provide opportunities for students to self- or peer assess? (Circle one.)	No Yes
Describe your approach to self- and peer assessment. If you don't use it, why not?	
Do you provide opportunities for students to assess your teaching? (Circle one.)	No Yes
Describe how you feel about having students critique your work with them. Do you feel defensive? Do you embrace the opportunity to fine-tune your approach?	

Figure 5.1: Consider how you approach assessment and feedback.

*Visit **go.SolutionTree.com/instruction** for a free reproducible version of this figure.*

Your students need and want quality, ongoing feedback to help them learn. Engage the mindset that great feedback is the breakfast of champions. Making sure that all your students get the feedback they need to grow from their mistakes can feel overwhelming, but it's an essential part of your teaching toolkit. When you intervene with students by giving them constructive feedback on their learning, you can expect a strong 0.65 effect size (Hattie, 2009), meaning more than one year's worth of academic gains. Give more positives than negatives (3:1 ratio) and be specific enough to focus on key things students can change.

We start this chapter with a look at the value of providing students with ongoing formative assessment and then details four specific forms of feedback: (1) qualitative feedback, (2) quantitative feedback, (3) micro–index card (MIC) feedback, and (4) student feedback. Unfortunately, these types are often those teachers least use. But you can change that path.

Ongoing Formative Assessment

The term *formative assessment* means you are using the evidence of learning (or lack of it) to adjust instruction toward a goal during the process, not just at the end. (See figure 5.2 for the feedback loop.) Formative feedback measures progress over the long haul. Formative evaluation for both students and teachers has a very high effect size of 0.90 (Hattie, 2009). This factor is effective across many variables, including student ages, duration, frequency, and special needs. Researchers conclude in one meta-study that regular use of classroom formative assessment raises student achievement by a substantial level—from at least 0.40 to 0.70 standard deviations (Black & Wiliam, 1998; Wiliam, 2018).

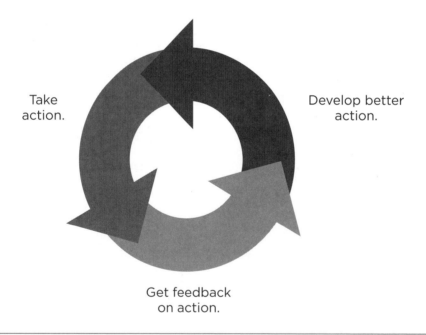

Take action.

Develop better action.

Get feedback on action.

Figure 5.2: Feedback loop.

One of the dangers of teaching without ongoing formative assessment is that you might go a week or two and still be unsure if your students are really getting it. But if you set up your class for daily multiple checks for understanding, you'll learn fast and adjust fast too. Higher-performing teachers notice quickly what is not working and adjust rapidly, revise, and redo a lesson.

No matter what kind of feedback you use in your class, quality formative assessment needs the following five benchmarks to work well: (1) clear, shared goals; (2) progress; (3) actionable feedback that moves learning forward; (4) students as owners of their own learning; and (5) tracking. Use the checklist in figure 5.3 to gauge the effectiveness of the formative assessments you use with your students.

Assessment name or topic:		
Does this assessment:	**Yes**	**No**
Have specific goals for learning and criteria for success? (share these with learners)		
Make clear to students where they are successful and where they need help?		
Provide a way for students to find out how to get better at what they're doing?		
Empower students to engage with the learning alone or collaboratively to grow?		
Allow students to see the big-picture trends and the details available?		
If you answered no to any of the preceding questions, what adjustments do you need to make to this assessment to make it more effective? How can you adjust rapidly, revise, or redo a lesson to ensure students get it?		

Figure 5.3: Assess your formative assessments.

*Visit **go.SolutionTree.com/instruction** for a free reproducible version of this figure.*

When your assessments reflect all of these feedback benchmarks, it leads to far more effective strategies than saying "Nice work" or "Good job." Using this checklist to evaluate and improve all of your formative assessments might be the single best way to boost achievement. Also, easy-to-use classroom activities can serve as powerful formative assessments. Here are my three favorites from Robert J. Marzano's (1998) *A Theory-Based Meta-Analysis of Research on Instruction*.

1. **Relevant recall questions (average effect size of 0.93):** Before you begin a unit, find out what students know and don't know. Use a brief quiz packed with questions designed to bring out useful and essential prior learning into the foundation time. Consider just ten questions, and have students correct their neighbor's paper and turn it in. See figure 5.4 (page 56). This gives you a better idea of where to start a unit.

2. **"I Decide, You Decide" (average effect size of 0.89):** Students in pairs alternate deciding and sorting information. Students have the content information on cards, papers, or digital media. You call out the decision to make, and the two students work out the answer. For example in science, you might say, "Compare and contrast oxygen and helium." The students can create a Venn diagram showing the overlap between the two elements, do a mind map, or just make two columns. Then, they share it with the class and get feedback.

3. **Graphic organizers and mind maps (average effect size of 1.24):** Show students an example first and then a blank framework. Figure 5.5 (page 56) highlights one such example, and you can find many others online (visit http://imindmap.com). Sell them on why this is a great way to learn ("It is just like your brain works—it goes from idea to idea to details, then it connects them"). Your students create their own personalized representation of what they are learning and then add illustrations, pictures, or emoticons. Once they are done, they trade organizers with a partner for peer-editing feedback. Then, ask them to turn in their organizers and recreate it from memory. The version they turned in to you can be for their final feedback.

Question	Answer	Peer feedback
1.		
2.		
3.		
4.		
5.		
6.		
7.		
8.		
9.		
10.		

Figure 5.4: Plan a quiz with feedback options.

*Visit **go.SolutionTree.com/instruction** for a free reproducible version of this figure.*

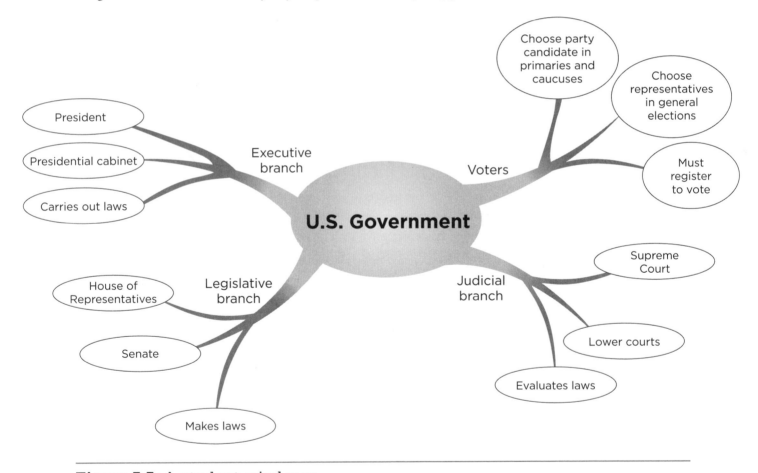

Figure 5.5: A student mind map.

*Visit **go.SolutionTree.com/instruction** for a free reproducible version of this figure.*

This chapter has four more high-performing feedback strategies that draw on the five benchmarks.

SEA for Qualitative Feedback

Students have no control over their DNA, their parents, or their neighborhood. However, students do have a huge amount of influence over the choices they make (strategy), how hard they work (effort), and the mindset (attitude) they bring to learning. The SEA strategy is a way to reinforce these in the classroom and ask, "How am I doing?"

You will find that although SEA is specific, the real reason it is effective is that you don't want to have to think in the moment, "*How* can I give specific feedback?" It has to become automatic and fast. SEA does this by giving you three quick ideas you can use without having to rack your brain. Each of the SEA qualities is a clear and potent replacement for using delayed tests (effect size of 0.31; Hattie, 2009) or saying "Well done" or "Good job" (effect size of 0.09; Kluger & DeNisi, 1996). Instead, using SEA, teachers give specific feedback in regard to strategy, effort, and attitude. Figure 5.6 offers a format to give students effective SEA assessment by simply attaching a quick note to the work you return to students. You could also give these blank forms to students for them to self-assess.

Student name:	
Subject:	
Strategy	
Effort	
Attitude	

Brainstorm some ways to give effective feedback in regard to strategy.

Brainstorm some ways to give effective feedback in regard to effort.

Brainstorm some ways to give effective feedback in regard to attitude.

Figure 5.6: Use SEA feedback.

*Visit **go.SolutionTree.com/instruction** for a free reproducible version of this figure.*

For example, you could offer the following feedback for strategy, effort, and attitude.

- **Strategy:** "I loved how you kept trying so many strategies on the third problem until you got it."
- **Effort:** "I like that you refused to give up. That extra effort will help you succeed again and reach your goal of mastering this content."
- **Attitude:** "Before you began, you thought you could succeed. Your positive attitude showed that you had a growth mindset and helped you come through."

Use the SEA feedback to build drive and long-term effort by changing who, when, and how often you give feedback. The *who* means you should never be the only source of student feedback. The majority should come from the student him- or herself, peers, computers, the physical results of actions, a rubric, or a standard set as a model or a checklist. The *when* means that sooner is better than later. The *how often* might be the most important question of all. Because feedback's contribution to motivation, learning, and achievement is so high, ensure that your students get some kind of feedback (by their peers, the activity itself, reflection, or you) at least once every thirty minutes, every school day of the year. By using specific high-scoring, self-awareness feedback strategies with an effect size of a huge 0.74, you give students the gift of affirmation and light a fire (Marzano, 1998).

3M for Quantitative Feedback

The 3M (milestone, mission, and method) feedback process focuses on orienting students to learning in an empirical way. The beauty of it is its simplicity. This feedback answers the three most essential questions students have about how they are doing: (1) "Where am I?" (milestone), (2) "Where am I going?" (mission), and (3) "How do I get there?" (method). The effect size is a whopping 1.13, which tells you it is highly effective (Wiliam & Thompson, 2007).

The 3M process involves using feedback with students and training them to use the process, which includes three steps: (1) teach students the 3M process, (2) ask students to track their progress, and (3) guide students to improvement. Let's look deeper at each of these.

Teach Students the 3M Process

Before students can use the 3M process on their own, you need to first teach them its critical pieces. Give them a filled-out 3M notecard like the one in figure 5.7. Later, I will show you a version you can give students to set and track their progress over time.

Student name: Kimani Hudson	
Subject: Vocabulary, section 6.1	
Milestone (Where am I?)	Here's where you're at right now. You got eight out of fifteen vocabulary words correct.
Mission (What's my goal?)	Your mission is always to get a 100 percent on the end-of-the-month quiz.
Method (How do I get there?)	You'll need a new strategy and plan to get where you're going. I've posted some ideas you can choose from. Now, let's set some fresh micro goals.

Figure 5.7: Introduce students to 3M feedback.

Visit go.SolutionTree.com/instruction for a free reproducible version of this figure.

Once you begin to use the 3M process with students, they will see its value. Over time, students will learn to self-assess.

Ask Students to Track Their Progress

For students to self-assess, they need data to track how they are doing. The data are simply their scores, which can come from self-assessments, a returned assignment, a student-graded quiz, or any other form of written, numerical score. So, quality data could be as simple as sixteen out of twenty points on a quiz. Provide them with a tracking sheet to track all scores for a unit and for any score less than 100 percent, instruct them to write notes about what they must do to improve. See figure 5.8.

Unit: _____

Date	Item (assignments, quizzes, tests)	Score	What can you do to improve this score?
__/__/__		__/__	
__/__/__		__/__	
__/__/__		__/__	
__/__/__		__/__	
__/__/__		__/__	
__/__/__		__/__	
__/__/__		__/__	
__/__/__		__/__	

Figure 5.8: Track progress.

*Visit **go.SolutionTree.com/instruction** for a free reproducible version of this figure.*

When tracking their data, students should be aware of their mission during this step. The mission is always simple; it is 100 percent. You may have students with special needs who start at a much lower score than the rest of the class. In their case, the mission focus is on 100 percent improvement (from three correct to six correct is a 100 percent improvement). These high expectations are a critical part of the achievement mindset. Keep them high, and focus on the micro goals (the method) necessary to make them happen. (If you need a refresher on goal setting and micro goals, refer to chapter 4, page 48.)

Guide Students to Improvement

A key benefit of the 3M strategy is developing student autonomy. They will quickly figure out their milestone and mission but often need help with their method—how to improve their learning. Post a list of "How I Can Get Better at Learning" tips on the classroom wall to encourage students to try various ways of learning and to figure out, on their own, how they learn best. See figure 5.9 (page 60). You can make your own developmentally appropriate list of student-learning tools.

You can also have students draw the list and post it. Imagine the powerful effects when students can take their milestone data (like "Eight of fifteen words correct"), reaffirm their mission ("100 percent on my next vocabulary test"), and decide for themselves how to improve their learning ("Maybe I should ask more questions in class"). See figure 5.10 (pages 60–61) for a goal tracker students can use to set their milestone, mission, and method.

Students can keep their goal tracker in a folder or digital file, or teachers can post them on the wall as ongoing student work. I love empowering students to know and be able to act on the results of their own learning. They'll know their milestones and their goal (mission), and they'll choose their next step to get better (method). Finally, it's most effective when classrooms use the 3M process at least once or twice a week. Use the four-week planning sheet in figure 5.11 (page 61) to help you do this. To empower your students to become better learners, help them learn the tools to do the work, then connect the dots for them. Students learning to regulate their own growth is the heart of the 3M feedback system.

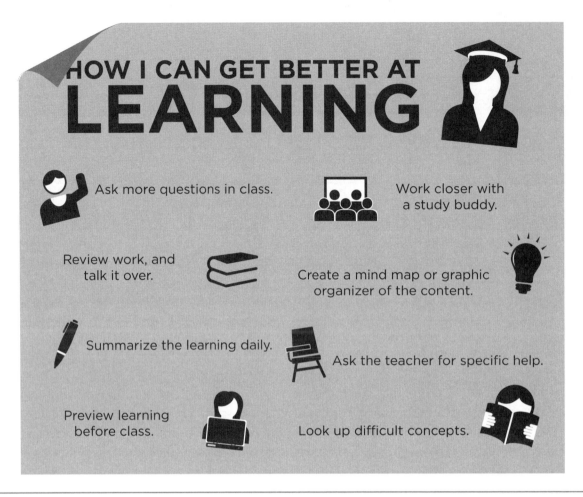

Figure 5.9: Poster of student-learning tools.

*Visit **go.SolutionTree.com/instruction** for a free reproducible version of this figure.*

My Goal Tracker	
Week One	
Milestone	9/15 vocabulary words correct
Mission	15/15 vocabulary words correct
Method	Practice with a partner.
Week Two	
Milestone	12/15 vocabulary words correct
Mission	15/15 vocabulary words correct
Method	Do homework.
Week Three	
Milestone	14/15 vocabulary words correct
Mission	15/15 vocabulary words correct
Method	Draw pictures to symbolize words, and self-test.

Week Four	
Milestone	15/15 vocabulary words correct
Mission	15/15 vocabulary words correct
Method	Stay the course and continue.

Figure 5.10: 3M feedback tracker.

Visit go.SolutionTree.com/instruction for a free reproducible version of this figure.

Track how often you used the 3M process this month.

	Number of times students used the 3M process	**What activities did they use it with?**	**Notes**
Week One			
Week Two			
Week Three			
Week Four			

Figure 5.11: 3M planning sheet.

Visit go.SolutionTree.com/instruction for a free reproducible version of this figure.

MIC Feedback

MIC is an acronym for *micro–index card* feedback. It is a fast way to help students get unstuck and move ahead. In many classes, students with less confidence dread taking on challenges, creating, producing, completing, writing papers, or doing projects. One issue they have is starting off on the wrong foot and never quite catching up. MIC feedback deals with that issue. It is a way to get inside a student's head to discover his or her thinking paths (and stuck areas) that might hurt his or her chances for success.

As you start the year (or semester), gathering MIC feedback is simple. Ask students to write their name on the back of an index card. On the other side, ask students to write on *one* specific topic. This portion of the card will look something like figure 5.12 (page 62).

The prompts that could appear here are infinite, but consider using one of the following.

- Two things about themselves that you (the teacher) should know but most don't know
- Past experience in the subject area (in five sentences or less)
- How the week has been (what they liked and what they'd change)
- Goals for the class
- About parts of a paper (introduction, theme, thesis, evidence and support, argument rebuttals, summary, and conclusions)
- Three friends in the classroom (to learn how much social glue each student has)
- A five- to ten-word outline of what they are currently working on
- Advice for another younger student about how to approach most mathematics problems

Topic: *Write two things about yourself that I should know but most don't know.*

1. _____

_____

_____

2. _____

_____

_____

Figure 5.12: Notecard for MIC feedback.

*Visit **go.SolutionTree.com/instruction** for a free reproducible version of this figure.*

For the first two weeks, ask for students to do one of these activities every other day. Read and sort these cards. You will quickly identify which students need which types of differentiation.

With this method, you can learn about specific topics that you would never have time to ask for individually. Over time, students realize they can get help from you (privately, if needed). Initially, this seems like more work. But quickly, students (and you) get the early information correct, and they can move forward in larger chunks faster.

On the social side, you can use the class time to have students work with just the right partner or in a small group to talk about what they put on their card and what they will do next. (Review chapter 2, page 21, for some group-work strategies.) With peer support, students' assignments and projects will fit basic proficiency requirements and then you can focus on moving to mastery levels. Each time you use this process, the students will get just a bit better at using the MIC strategy. See figure 5.13.

MIC feedback topic:		
Student	**Response**	**How can I best use this information?**

Figure 5.13: Track MIC feedback responses.

*Visit **go.SolutionTree.com/instruction** for a free reproducible version of this figure.*

Student Feedback

Perhaps surprisingly, the all-time best feedback is student feedback to you, the teacher (Hattie & Timperley, 2007). Getting feedback from students is simple. Consider the following four student feedback strategies and use figure 5.14 to record which forms you use, record key points on the feedback you receive, and reflect on how you will use that information.

Select one or more strategies for gathering student feedback. Reflect on what you observed from this feedback and how you can use it.

	Which feedback strategies did you use or observe?	What stood out in the feedback you received?	How will you adjust your teaching to reflect this feedback?
Week One:	☐ Nonverbal ☐ Retrieval practice ☐ One-minute summaries ☐ Suggestions box		
Week Two:	☐ Nonverbal ☐ Retrieval practice ☐ One-minute summaries ☐ Suggestions box		
Week Three:	☐ Nonverbal ☐ Retrieval practice ☐ One-minute summaries ☐ Suggestions box		
Week Four:	☐ Nonverbal ☐ Retrieval practice ☐ One-minute summaries ☐ Suggestions box		

Figure 5.14: Student feedback tracking sheet.

*Visit **go.SolutionTree.com/instruction** for a free reproducible version of this figure.*

1. **Nonverbal information:** Observe students during seatwork time. Look for signs of physical or emotional distress during the task so you can stop and ask what your students are experiencing ("Can I check in with you for a moment?"). When you introduce something to your class, watch the body language. If any students roll their eyes and slump back in their seats, that's feedback to you. Your hook or buy-in did not work (or it was missing from your lesson). If everyone except a couple of students is hooked, let each student get started, then go check on the isolated, concerned, or checked-out students. Marzano describes this use of real-time information as *withitness*, which has a massive effect size of 1.42 (Marzano et al., 2001; Marzano, 2017).

2. **Yesterday's learning:** Retrieval practice has a positive impact on learning (Ritchie, Della Sala, & McIntosh, 2013). To find students who are lost, use an activity to get feedback from the previous day's class. Give students a blank sheet of paper and twelve minutes to write down everything they can recall from yesterday's lesson. Collect their work, and quickly sort it to identify the struggling students. Then,

reteach confusing concepts and correct your own teaching mistakes. This way, the students get better and so do you.

3. **One-minute summary:** At the end of class (as an exit pass), ask students to write an anonymous one-to-two-minute note on two topics. First, they answer, "What is the most important thing from class today?" Then, your students answer, "What is still a bit confusing to you about today's class?" Even though they're anonymous, which helps students be honest, they'll give you immediate, useful feedback on your teaching. Figure 5.15 shows an example notecard with this kind of feedback.

4. **Suggestions box:** Instead of having students use your classroom suggestions box in a passive way, use the suggestions box as a feedback tool. Ask students before class if they got a bit lost in the previous day's class (and where). Then, during class give everyone a one-minute suggestion moment for feedback, and encourage them to keep it specific. These tools help you collect valuable feedback, especially if you have already taught students how to tell you what they need. At the end of class, use it as an exit pass. After you sort through the suggestions box once a week, tell students what you read, how much you appreciate their responses, and how you'll use their ideas to get better as a teacher.

Please provide me with the following feedback on today's class.	
What is the most important thing you learned from class today?	It was really interesting to learn how feudal Japan divided people up into only two classes (nobility and peasants) and how almost 90 percent of the population were peasants.
What is still a bit confusing to you about today's class?	I have a hard time understanding the difference between the emperor's role and the shogun's role. Why did they need to have both?

Figure 5.15: Notecard for student feedback.

*Visit **go.SolutionTree.com/instruction** for a free reproducible version of this figure.*

Students are remarkably candid and accurate in their perceptions of classroom climate. Without quality, continuous feedback, you may as well be teaching in a vacuum.

Quick Consolidation: Give Fabulous Feedback

When you use the tools in this chapter, you are likely to get pretty good feedback, which informs better teaching. Students cannot control everything that happens to them in class, but through student feedback, they can respond to your teaching. Seek it out, use it, and enjoy the difference. With this firmly in mind, answer the following reflection questions as you consider how you can improve your feedback practices to better support your students.

1. What do you understand about the value of formative assessment and feedback that you didn't know before you started this chapter?

2. What are some ways you can provide more consistent, ongoing formative assessment to your students?

3. What feedback strategy from this chapter will you try first? What makes this strategy a better fit for your students and teaching than the others?

4. How will you specifically integrate it into your teaching, and what are your expectations for results?

5. How will you plan for transitioning between giving students direct feedback from you into having students conduct self- or peer feedback?

CHAPTER 6

PERSIST WITH GRIT

School is not a sprint; it's a marathon. There is a lot of deferred gratification before actually graduating. As the study "The High Cost of High School Dropouts" highlights (Alliance for Excellent Education, n.d.), a significant portion of students who don't graduate simply give up (versus pursue something perceived as "better"). If you want students to achieve their gutsy goals, while overcoming the inevitable discouragement and failures that are a part of succeeding in school, they need grit, and it's a core component of the achievement mindset. Use figure 6.1 to think about your current mindset toward the level of grit your students show (or don't show) in their work.

When you see students who are quick to give up, how do you feel about them? (Circle one.)	I can't help them if they don't want to try.	I will never let them give up on themselves.
Think openly and honestly with yourself about the answer you chose. Why do you feel this way?		
Do you see grit as something students either have ingrained in them or don't have? (Circle one.)	Grit is ingrained.	Grit is teachable.
Think about and describe what it means to you for students to show grit in their work and studies. What does grit look like?		
How do you define the difference between grit and self-control?		
What strategies do you use to help develop grit in your students or give them a boost when grit levels drop?		

Figure 6.1: Assess your approach to building grit in students.

*Visit **go.SolutionTree.com/instruction** for a free reproducible version of this figure.*

Whatever your personal experience, it's critical to understand many of your students already have plenty of grit. In fact, they probably have traits that you never expected. Start with the mindset that every single student either already can persist through adversity or learn to do so. This is a way to frame equity from the conversation to action steps.

When a student's effort drops, it is easy to say, "She's not motivated" or "He doesn't want it very badly." However, you may be confusing self-control with grit. Self-control is the short-term ability to manage attention and effort while avoiding distractions to reach a goal, such as concentrating for a big test. Grit is the tenacity and strength to pursue your long-term goals (think gutsy goals like getting an advanced degree), even in the face of obstacles, for something worthwhile (Duckworth, Peterson, Matthews, & Kelly, 2007).

With low grit (and low self-control), student by student, the collective energy and effort in your classroom drop. This can prompt some teachers to lower their goals and settle for more typical goals of passing or proficiency. However, setting goals for passing or proficiency doesn't challenge students or allow them to grow. This chapter details strategies to develop grit and offers tools you can use to build it up when grit drops.

Ten Ways to Develop Grit

Here are ten of the best-researched ways to develop grit, some from an interview with MacArthur Fellowship grantee Angela Duckworth, a pioneer of grit (Winerman, 2013).

1. **Help students continually value their gutsy goal:** Reference student long-term goals in a variety of ways (such as posters, celebrations, micro goals, and stories) so they see the journey as a worthwhile path to the goal. Many times, a student will become gritty in a project that is highly personal and meets his or her values.

2. **Show students what grit looks like:** There are many superb movies that feature grit. Consider scenes in movies such as *Forrest Gump, Bend It Like Beckham*, and *Remember the Titans*. But talk about self-control and grit before you show it. Ask students to share something they have already done that shows grit. Most have at least some *partial* grit examples.

3. **Model grit:** Set a gutsy goal for yourself, and share it with the class—for example, learn a new language, run a half-marathon, get a book published, or so on. Then, share the ups and downs with your class as you pursue your own gritty challenge using a poster like the one we showed you in chapter 1 (see figure 1.6, page 15). Students need to see, hear, and feel close up what grit is. Truly gritty people have a history of setting especially challenging long-term goals. If students don't see it, they won't know how to do it.

4. **Teach students the ability to stay in the moment:** Value right now. This focusing tool is more than a bit of Zen because it teaches students to let go of any thoughts about what else they could be doing. A simple deep-breathing activity or quiet reflection activity may start the process for your students and help them develop self-control. Remember, your life is simply a very long sequence of right-now moments. Make each one count.

5. **Create a common grit vocabulary:** Tell students what being gritty is, and what it is not. "Doing that shows me a lot of grit!" Your students need specific ways to identify and describe grit when it occurs. A good starting point is to create a grit baseline. Ask students to stand up and when you say "Go," they run (in place) as hard as they can for thirty seconds. You might have three-fourths of your class slow down before the thirty-second mark. So, your fitness baseline for grit is 25 percent of the class is gritty for running in place.

6. **Assess grit:** You can help your students (middle and high schoolers) assess grit at the start and end of your school year (or semester) using a grit index (see University of Pennsylvania School of Arts and Sciences, 2011; https://angeladuckworth.com/grit-scale). Visit **go.SolutionTree.com/instruction** to access a direct link to this grit index.

7. **Foster conditions for grit:** Build classroom positivity through celebrations, smiles, upbeat music, and affirmations. Positive emotions like optimism tell students that the future is good and it is worth working toward a big goal. You get maximum value in resilience and grit building when the ratio of positives to negatives is about 3:1 (Catalino & Fredrickson, 2011). Ensure that every student, before he or she goes home, has gotten much more positives (affirmations, quality feedback, nonverbal encouragement, and so on) than negatives (criticism, negative nonverbals, exclusion, and so on).

8. **Make grit real in many ways:** Use metaphors, quotes, and analogies to refer to grit so students understand it and know exactly what it is. Tell your students that they may not be responsible for getting knocked down, but they are responsible for getting back up. Jamie Irish, a high school mathematics teacher in New Orleans, uses two objects to highlight what grit is (Irish, 2012). One is a real egg, and the other is a special bouncy ball—a Super Ball. The question he asks is, "Are you an egg or a Super Ball?" For a demonstration, he drops both the egg and Super Ball on the floor. The egg breaks, but the Super Ball bounces back stronger than before. "Which one are you?" Jamie asks. If students casually say, "Super Ball," he will say, "I didn't hear you! One more time." Finally, the class roars, "*Super Ball!*"

9. **Reinforce grit in action:** Every time you see a student pushing through obstacles, say, "Love the way you're being so gritty with that task." When a student gets frustrated, do not make excuses ("I understand that not everyone succeeds" or "Maybe this is not your thing"). Affirm students' strengths and give them a pep talk on how you are all in this for the long haul and that this was just a glitch and a time to adapt.

10. **Give grit a chance:** If everything you do over the course of a semester can be done in a few seconds, minutes, or hours, students will never get a chance to develop grit. In arts, students learn to perfect a skill over a period of months or years. In sports, grit develops over the course of a season. You'll need to create opportunities for students to develop tenacity over the long term with at least one project. The team (or partner) project should take months to complete (students might work on it weekly). For example, students might write a twelve-page guide for success to give next year's students that illustrates what they've learned over the course of a semester or year.

As you consider these strategies, think about which of them you want to use in your classroom. Use figure 6.2 (page 70) to write down the three strategies that most interested you and then support those selections with your ideas for how you could use them with students in your class. These ideas can be to better support a specific student, a student group, or the entire class.

Keep your perspective developmental. For a first grader, grit might mean sticking with something for a week or even a day. Students can start the year with small, twenty-minute activities, but remember the power of asking. Ask for great things out of your students. Students won't do what you don't expect or ask them to do. After a short time, they're ready for something that takes some work every day over two weeks. Soon, and as students mature, you'll be ready to offer projects that take weeks or months.

	How I will present this strategy to my students	How I will help students get past negativity
Strategy 1:		
Strategy 2:		
Strategy 3:		

Figure 6.2: Build grit in your classroom.

*Visit **go.SolutionTree.com/instruction** for a free reproducible version of this figure.*

Tools for When Grit Drops

All of us have had lapses in our grittiness. Researchers have uncovered strategies that reignite the passion to get the grit back in action. When grit drops, connect their *values* and *identity* to the task to infuse new energy and effort for success (Cohen, Garcia, Purdie-Vaughns, Apfel, & Brzustoski, 2009). Here are several ways to do this.

- **Ask students to take a five-minute break:** For the first two minutes, give students a stretch, deep-breathing activities, or a faster energizer (see page 206). For the next three minutes, ask them to sit and write down a list of their qualities or personal characteristics. For example, their list might include honesty, humor, and loyalty. Once they think they are finished, ask them to think a bit and add some more. The beauty of this list is that it allows the student to see right there in front of him or her "Who am I?" It usually fosters more grittiness.

- **Adopt an expert-in-training identity in your students:** For example, a student who is poor in mathematics wouldn't hang in there for twenty minutes trying to solve a problem. However, an expert in training *would* hang in there for twenty minutes.

- **Refer to your students as scholars:** This label is critical when you want to build character traits such as grit. Say to students, "In the past, a few of you might not have stuck with this task. But you're scholars now. Mistakes are our friend, and as an expert in training, you realize it takes time to get good." Encouraging posters (like Working Harder Gets You Smarter) can help foster grit.

Finally, encourage students to use the following simple three-step strategy to deal with grit breakdowns.

- **Step 1: Listen**—When you're about to take on a task or a big challenge, listen to your self-talk. Listen for any sign of the fixed mindset. What does it say in your head? Is it a voice that limits you? If it is, switch to the growth mindset voice, which says, "I am not defined by my past or my mistakes. I can learn and solve this problem no matter what it takes."

- **Step 2: Reactivate**—What's the goal that you have, and why is it important for you to achieve it? Activate a clear, sensory-rich image and sound of the goal you want. See it, hear it, and feel the joy of accomplishing your goal right in the moment. Tell a partner why it is important to reach the goal. Next, share how you (or those you help) will feel when you reach the goal.

- **Step 3: Choose again**—Remember that it's your own brain and your own voice, and you're not a robot. What's the new achievement mindset that will best help you get your goal? If your voice says, "I don't think I can do this. It's a huge job, and I'm not sure how to do it. I'm afraid

I'll fail" choose an alternative. Change the predictive self-talk. Talk to yourself and say, "I have succeeded at many things before when I was unsure at the start. If I need help, I'll ask for it. When I make mistakes, I'll learn from them. My goal is important and nothing worthwhile is easy. I'm ready!"

Figure 6.3 includes a checklist and worksheet for effecting this three-step strategy with your students.

	Have I:	Yes	No
Step 1: Listen	Engaged myself in positive self-talk?		
	What will I do to adopt a growth mindset?		
Step 2: Reactivate	Focused on what my goal is and why it's important?		
	Why is my goal important? What will it look or sound like? What will it feel like to achieve it?		
Step 3: Choose again	Made a choice to believe in myself and what I can do?		
	What are some reasons for me to believe I can achieve this goal? What will I do to ensure it happens?		
	What adjustments does this assessment need to make it more effective?		

Figure 6.3: Checklist and worksheet for rebuilding grit.

*Visit **go.SolutionTree.com/instruction** for a free reproducible version of this figure.*

When it comes to maintaining goals, constantly reactivate students' grit so they remember why they wanted to reach their goals. Over the course of days, weeks, and months, your students' enthusiasm will go up and down. Your role is to find a variety of ways to make the same gutsy goal interesting.

Quick Consolidation: Set Gutsy goals

Every one of the strategies in this chapter can help boost your students' grit, but if you start by using three, four, or more of these, your class grit will rise like a hot-air balloon. Yes, grit is important, you can build it, and it's free and fairly easy to do it. With this firmly in mind, answer the following reflection questions on how you will approach building up grit in your class.

1. What do you know and understand about grit and its importance to learning that you didn't know when you started this chapter?

2. What new ideas did the strategies in this chapter instill in you to build your own strategies for fostering grit in your students?

3. When students show a lack of grit, how will you change your approach in the future from what you have done in the past?

4. When you feel your own grit level dropping, what will you do to restore it and better support your students?

5. When you see your students showing grit in their coursework or achievement outlook, how will you recognize and support it?

Reflect on the Achievement Mindset

All meaningful and lasting change starts with a mirror. Now that you understand the concept of the achievement mindset and have strategies to foster achievement in your classroom, it's time to self-assess and reflect on what comes next. Use the following questions to accomplish this.

1. Are effort and achievement issues in your class? Remember, you always have a choice: Do you want students to graduate job or college ready, or do you want to make excuses for why they failed?

2. What strategy could you use or adapt from part two in your very next class to start building an achievement mindset with your students?

3. What challenges do you expect to encounter as you adopt this strategy? How will you react to and overcome these challenges?

4. What makes mastery a critical aspect of the achievement mindset? When you have students struggle to achieve mastery, how will you approach them?

5. What benefits can you envision from helping students believe they can grow and achieve in their academic life? How will you benefit? How will your students benefit?

Your decision to grow students in a more self-confident, achievement-minded mindset includes a new narrative about yourself and your students, achievement boosters to develop the mindset with a fierce urgency, and a support process to ensure successful implementation.

PART THREE

IMPLEMENTING THE POSITIVITY MINDSET

A logical next step from establishing relational and achievement mindsets involves a crucial way to change how you think of your job: the positivity mindset. You may have heard teachers' comments about how students from low-income families are harder to teach or have behavior problems: "Of course I try to be positive, but look at what I'm up against. Have you seen our students? Do you know where they live, and their friends, and their parents? How are we supposed to succeed?" What similar statements might you have said out loud or even thought to yourself? Use figure P3.1 (page 76) to gauge your existing approach to positivity with your students.

As you consider your answers to these questions, think about how you perceive your work and how you help your students to be their best selves. As you start each day, do you approach it with a sense of hope and positivity or hopelessness that you cannot reach students who don't want to be in your classroom in the first place? Your students often grow up in environments that may have chronic stressors that contribute to illness or depression. Start with the mindset that every single student will love your positive ways. This is a way to frame equity from the conversation to action steps.

When working with students from poverty, it's important to understand that other factors (see the next section) influence their behavior and erode students' ability to feel hopeful about their futures. To combat this, and as I establish in chapter 3 (page 27), the most important trait you can sharpen is your empathy, not sympathy. A positivity mindset enhances the benefits of empathy. It says, "I am an optimistic and grateful ally who helps students build a successful narrative of their future."

1. How often do you feel helpless to positively impact learning and outcomes for your students from poverty? Why do you think you can't have a positive impact? What experiences have you had with students that made you feel more positive and successful about your work?

   _____

   _____

   _____

2. How do you think poverty affects students' ability to feel positive about their lives? How might poverty impact students' ability to believe in their own academic success?

   _____

   _____

   _____

3. What do you think about when you feel positive and hopeful about your work and your students? What steps do you take to encourage positivity and hope from your students and yourself?

   _____

   _____

   _____

4. What activities do you engage in with students to foster positive attitudes in yourself and your students? What do you do to encourage students to take responsibility for themselves and self-regulate their emotions?

   _____

   _____

   _____

5. If you or your students feel constantly negative, what do you think you could do to change this emotional set point so that it evolves into a more positive outlook?

   _____

   _____

   _____

   _____

Figure P3.1: Assess your understanding of how poverty affects students.

Visit go.SolutionTree.com/instruction for a free reproducible version of this figure.

> The positivity mindset says, "I am an optimistic and grateful ally who helps students build a successful narrative of their future."

To become both positive and empathic, and give some of that positivity back to your students, you've got to understand what's *really* going on, because it starts at home. You need to acknowledge this because persons in poor households have more than double the rate of violent victimization than those in high-income households (Harrell, Langton, Berzofsky, Couzens, & Smiley-McDonald, 2014). Students didn't choose their DNA, parents, neighborhood, or culture. You would be amazed at the power of your positivity to impact your students' brains and improve their success (Jensen, 2019).

Even if you consider yourself a negative person, know that we can learn a positive mindset as a type of *cognitive control* (versus feeling like a victim without choices). This trait (or lack thereof) makes a significant difference in the brains of students from poverty (Noble, Norman, & Farah, 2005; Noble, Tottenham, & Casey, 2005). If you truly want students to succeed in a middle- or upper-class world, help them develop the psyche to survive and thrive.

The content you're required to teach will always be in transition; changing standards are a given. The one reliable, unstoppable force in your class must be *you* using a positive attitude, tone, climate, and sky-high expectations each day. In the next three chapters, you'll read about the following strategies to promote a positivity mindset in your classroom.

1. Boost optimism and hope.
2. Build positive attitudes.
3. Change the emotional set point.

Positive affect in school contributes to more kindness, better health, increased participation, fewer absences, and greater achievement. Turn to the next chapter to learn how to boost optimism and hope every day.

Questions for Daily Reflection

Each day, consider your own mindset for bringing out positivity in yourself and your students. Then, answer the following questions.

1. How am I feeling about my work and my students today? If I have feelings of negativity or hopelessness, what can I do to change them *before* I set foot on school grounds?

2. If I see a student in my classroom who doesn't believe in him- or herself and shows no interest in learning, what will I do to help him or her feel a sense of hope and optimism in my class?

3. What strategy will I use today to build and foster positive attitudes in my classroom?

CHAPTER 7

BOOST OPTIMISM AND HOPE

The positivity mindset focuses on building both optimism and hope, which are two distinct feelings. Hope is an orientation of spirit. It is the certainty that something will ultimately take a turn for the better, regardless of the outcome. A hopeful person often has a low level of personal control and yet lives knowing that his or her life is in good hands (Bruininks & Malle, 2005). Because the poor often feel less in control, building hope is powerful. Optimism requires a belief that things will get better due to the efficacy of one's own progress (Bailey, Eng, Frisch, & Snyder, 2007). It is also about perspective; one can learn to see the good side of nearly any event or person. Use the survey in figure 7.1 to think about your own understanding of hope and optimism and the roles they play in your classroom.

At the start of a typical teaching day, how do you feel about teaching? (Circle one.)	I feel excited and can't wait to start.	I like what I do, but I don't make a difference.	I can't wait to go home at the end of the day.
Describe some of the reasons you feel this way.			
Do you get the sense that your students feel like they can succeed in school and life? (Circle one.)	My students are generally positive and energetic.	Many of my students seem despondent or disinterested.	My students don't want to be there.
How do you think a sense of hopelessness or negativity affects student performance?			
What are some things you currently do (or could try) to help build in students a sense of hope and optimism about their learning and lives?			

Figure 7.1: How you approach hope and optimism.

Visit go.SolutionTree.com/instruction for a free reproducible version of this figure.

Very often, people associate negativity and positivity as ingrained, fixed traits in people, but here's the truth: optimism and hope are both teachable traits (Seligman, 2006). Optimistic students with hope are more cheerful and work harder. They make teaching more fun and perform better. If you don't teach this, who will? See table 7.1 for what hope and optimism sound like. After reviewing the examples in table 7.1, consider how you've instilled hope and optimism in your classroom. Jot down a few of the ways and refer back to them as you dive into the strategies for the chapter.

Table 7.1: Teaching Hope and Optimism

Hope	Optimism
"I know good things will happen. It will all turn out for the better."	"Due to the efficacy of my own progress, things will get better."
"Bad things have happened before; I'm sure it will be all right in the end."	"I learned what I did wrong in the past. I know just what to change, so I think it will be better tomorrow."
"Some things we just don't have control over. We just have to trust everything's going to be OK."	"I have been working on this for a while. I think I got it right. Next week, it's going to be amazing."

Here are your four strategies for optimism and hope.

1. Model optimism daily.
2. Build hope daily.
3. Build students' self-concept and effort levels.
4. Encourage and support dreams.

These strategies may seem very familiar to you. They may trigger memories of strategies you have heard of or may have used before. But knowing about a strategy does not raise student achievement. I have a simple request for you. Read each as if it is the very first time. Then, ask yourself, "Am I actually doing this on a daily basis to the best of my ability?"

Model Optimism Daily

When you are optimistic, you believe that most negative events are temporary, limited, and manageable. Notice how this model also assumes you can take potential action to ensure you will survive. For many students, optimism is the only way they can begin to see the world differently. Model optimism for students every day in every way you can think of. When a student asks, "How ya doing?" answer with phrases like, "Never been better," "I'm living my dream," or "It's a great day to learn!" Then, add, "And, how about you?" Show them what it's like to love your job and help others and how to ignore the negativity of bad news. Be the model of the teacher who loves teaching. Modeled optimism can be contagious. Consider the following strategies.

Teaching Perspective

Perspective helps students gain the real power of optimism. Teach your students how, upon hearing or reading about a news story or an event, to look at different sides of it. Simple activities in which students take different sides of a topic help them build alternate points of view and see the positives in each situation. In this activity, pair up two students, and offer them a scenario. Have them record their reactions to challenging scenarios using the worksheet in figure 7.2. Students should fill out their thoughts and alternate sharing their pros and cons with

Scenario	
"You got a low score on a test. How could you use this to your advantage?"	
A negative approach:	An optimistic approach:
Scenario	
"You didn't get accepted to your first choice for college. How could that be a good thing?"	
A negative approach:	An optimistic approach:
Scenario	
"You didn't get the job you wanted. How could that be a positive thing?"	
A negative approach:	An optimistic approach:

Figure 7.2: Worksheet to practice optimism.

*Visit **go.SolutionTree.com/instruction** for a free reproducible version of this figure.*

each other. To help students get started, share a few examples from your own life to make the activity real to them. Invite questions so students start to process this internally.

Using Word Nutrients

Word nutrients are daily words and actions that feed positive attitudes. As a role model for students, choose words that are like supplements to students' brains by sharing the "seed of something greater" attitude with them. When students enter the room, instead of saying "Hi," say, "It's stupendous to see you today!"

Word nutrients are also part of a powerful writing activity. Have students use the worksheet in figure 7.3 (page 82) to get them engaged with using language to influence their states of mind. Do not grade these; the very act of writing about their lives is a positive experience (Lyubomirsky, Sousa, & Dickerhoof, 2006).

Overcoming Setbacks

All of us fail. What counts is what we do after we fail. When you fall down, get up. That's the secret; never give up. Give classroom examples of how you have done this in the past. Then, have students share examples with the whole class, and ask, "How will you deal with it?"

Using quickwrites like the one in figure 7.4 (page 83) are a powerful way to help students understand themselves and see the world differently. Have students write for three to ten minutes on overcoming setbacks, such as "How might I solve a problem I'm having?" or "How can I improve my grade on an upcoming test?" It's important for students to reflect on times when they've failed but refused to quit. Most important, allow students to share what they wrote in small groups or in front of the class.

There are countless resources available for building a positive, behavior-changing daily attitude with your students. One of my favorites is Jack Canfield's (2015) *The Success Principles*. Most of the chapters are just five to ten pages. Read just one chapter per week. Take what you read and adapt it for your students. You can foster the positivity to overcome setbacks.

Record the ten positive words from the class brainstorming activity.

_____   _____
_____   _____
_____   _____
_____   _____
_____   _____

Write for three to five minutes about something good that happened last week.

Write for three to five minutes about something that troubled you last week.

Choose a positive word for the day (use this word at least five times today): _____

Figure 7.3: Worksheet for word nutrients.

*Visit **go.SolutionTree.com/instruction** for a free reproducible version of this figure.*

Describe a setback you recently experienced.
Write for three to ten minutes on how you overcame this setback or with your ideas for how you will overcome this setback.

Figure 7.4: Worksheet to overcome setbacks.

*Visit **go.SolutionTree.com/instruction** for a free reproducible version of this figure.*

Build Hope Daily

Building hope daily is not a check-the-box activity. This is a constant process of instilling a lifelong sense of possibility for something good. Begin with building a relationship based on respect and empathy for your students. This alone can create hope. In the following sections, I offer three specific strategies to build hope over time, and with a careful eye, you will see opportunities to use many of the other strategies in this book to foster students' sense of hope. You'll want students to practice new skills in class weekly, so they see that they are growing and improving. Use the planning sheet in figure 7.5 (page 84) to brainstorm and plan your hope-delivering strategies for each week.

Teaching Goal Setting

Managing your destiny is a hope builder. To that end, teach your students to set daily, weekly, and yearly goals. Make progress visible; it may inspire students. Teach students how to assess progress, get feedback, and correct their courses in order to score higher. Give each student a handout like the one in figure 7.6 (page 84) with room for his or her weekly, monthly, and annual goals. (Or, you can use a tablet.) Underneath the long-term goals, students can write their weekly goals and strategies.

Track how often you used the 3M process this month.

	Lesson topic	Strategy or goal for building hope	How will you implement this strategy or goal with your students?
Monday			
Tuesday			
Wednesday			
Thursday			
Friday			

Figure 7.5: Planning sheet for building hope.

Visit go.SolutionTree.com/instruction for a free reproducible version of this figure.

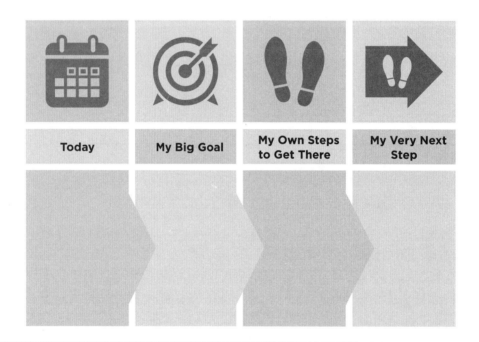

| Today | My Big Goal | My Own Steps to Get There | My Very Next Step |

Figure 7.6: Manage your destiny.

Visit go.SolutionTree.com/instruction for a free reproducible version of this figure.

Displaying Daily Progress

Continually point out and display progress. Students need to see that they are improving and getting closer to their goals, or they may give up on themselves. Post class progress reports (as a whole) and team progress reports using a template like the one in figure 7.7. Getting better is a hope builder.

Target goal:
Where we started:
How we're progressing as of _____:

Figure 7.7: Display our progress.

Visit go.SolutionTree.com/instruction for a free reproducible version of this figure.

Including Affirmations of Hope

Every day, affirm your students' goodness, positive energy, and success, and work to create a classroom climate where peers do the same to each other. Encourage your students to turn to their neighbors and say things like, "You're on fire today!" "You rock!" "Love your attitude, girl!" Getting peer and teacher affirmation are hope builders.

Class posters and placards should also contain affirmations of hope (for example, "The harder I work, the luckier I get"), and students should read books about hope and successful role models. For example, consider A Mighty Girl (www.amightygirl.com) books, which focus on girl-led titles for all ages.

Each day, a different student can be responsible for writing and sharing a positive affirmation for the class. Keep these fresh, and rotate them around the room. Over time, let students contribute their own affirmations. Affirming capacity is a hope builder. See figure 7.8 for a sample class poster including an affirmation of hope.

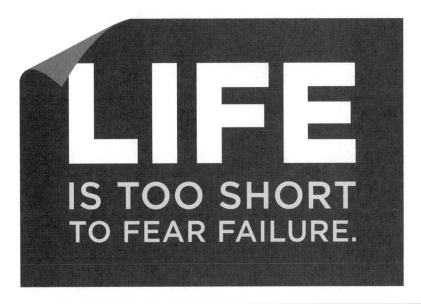

Figure 7.8: Sample class poster.

*Visit **go.SolutionTree.com/instruction** for a free reproducible version of this figure.*

Build Students' Self-Concept and Effort Levels

Strong teachers purposefully *choose* to affirm student strengths. They choose to build student self-concept and effort levels. To help your students grow, make it your mission to find and develop their strengths. This does not mean you are blind to their weaknesses. It means building them up enough that they can deal with error corrections and helpful feedback. Here's how you can do it.

Using a Power Minute

At least once a week (it's usually best on a Monday or Friday), have students share something about themselves in a *power minute*. Consider the following topics.

- One strength they have
- Someone they have helped recently
- Something they admire in others
- How they helped a friend lately
- A goal or milestone they have reached lately

Don't ask all students to share in a single day; stretch the activity out over a few months. To keep the activity fresh, rotate how you do it, and keep the sharing under four minutes. For example, students can share in four ways: (1) in a written journal, (2) to their study buddy, (3) within a cooperative learning group or team, or (4) with the whole class. Remember to respect their privacy, and give them time to become comfortable with these powerful self-affirmations. Also, remember to praise effort, choices, strategies, and attitudes, as a student can manage each of these. Never praise or showboat about a student's intelligence or how smart he or she is, as this is an ineffective form of feedback (Mueller & Dweck, 1998; Rattan, Savani, Chugh, & Dweck, 2015).

Affirming Student Strengths With a Connection

Use attribution in your affirmations. Attribution is connecting the cause and effect of an action to the outcome. Always affirm their strengths *with a detailed connection*. It's not enough to say, "Eric, you really write well" (Rattan et al., 2015). Say, "Eric, when you add practical strategies, I understand better what you are talking about. Plus, that strategy will help with your dream of publishing a book."

When students hear you (as an authority figure) affirm their effort and connect it to how that strength will do some good in the world, students take more pride in their strengths and work harder. Use the worksheet in figure 7.9 to practice your affirmations based on previous classroom interactions.

Student:
Positive thing this student did:
What I will say to affirm this action:

Figure 7.9: Practice attribution with affirmations.

Visit go.SolutionTree.com/instruction for a reproducible version of this figure.

One thing to keep in mind is how much a student's understanding of effort and ability is dependent on age. John G. Nicholls and Arden T. Miller (1984) describe four levels of attribution theory.

- **Level 1 (from five to six years old):** Students do not understand the difference between effort and ability or cause and effect.

- **Level 2 (from seven to nine years old):** Students attribute outcome purely to effort.

- **Level 3 (from ten to eleven years old):** Students can distinguish between ability and effort but will often still mix them up.

- **Level 4 (twelve years and older):** Students clearly understand the difference between effort and ability.

While attributing a success or failure to a trait that we have some control over (like effort, attitude, or strategy) remember to ensure your comments are developmentally appropriate.

Creating a Classroom Directory

Some teachers help students create a classroom version of Facebook, where students list two to three of their strengths and include details about their friends and family so the class gets a sense of who they are. This class directory can be a three-ring binder or posted online to the classroom webpage of the school's site. Using this information, some teachers create a classroom experts directory, so students know who to go to when they need help. Students can be the in-house experts on fixing technology, clothes purchases, trivia, sports, games, and yes, even classroom content. Have students fill out and submit a worksheet like the one in figure 7.10 and add it to the binder or transfer it to an online resource.

Name:
List two to three strengths you have: _____ _____ _____
Describe something important to you about your friends and family:

Figure 7.10: Classroom dictionary page.

*Visit **go.SolutionTree.com/instruction** for a free reproducible version of this figure.*

Encourage and Support Dreams

A great way to help students find their voices, paths, and strengths is to ask them about their dreams and visions of their own future. Consider asking the following introspective questions to get students to think about the future and current strengths.

- Where do I want to be in five, ten, or even fifteen years?
- What am I already good at?
- How could I help others?
- What kind of person do I want to be?

When you allow students to draw, sing, or share with others you help them affirm their dreams. Instill a class rule: "No dream killers." As students share their dreams with others, they may or may not get peer approval. But they will get support from their teacher—you!

Quick Consolidation: Boost Optimism and Hope

For many students, losing hope means the game is over—students may drop out. I have come to understand why daily optimism and positive energy work so well. It's more than engagement. It's more than a coping tool or happy face in the classroom. Use the positive strategies in this chapter every day, and you'll start seeing and hearing positive students over time. With this firmly in mind, answer the following reflection questions on how you can build more optimism and hope in your classroom.

1. How has your understanding of the importance of hope and optimism changed after reading this chapter?

2. What is a strategy for building optimism you learned about in this chapter that you will use or adopt in your classroom? What is your plan to implement it?

3. What strategy from this chapter will you use or adapt for use in your classroom to build a sense of hope in your students?

4. The next time a student of yours expresses a lack of self-confidence, what will you do to build him or her up?

5. What will you do to learn about and encourage your students' most treasured dreams and ambitions?

CHAPTER 8

BUILD POSITIVE ATTITUDES

Transforming your mindset to be positive, instead of negative, continues with a look at some research on building positive attitudes. In this chapter, we focus not on oneself but on others. To get started thinking about a mindset of building positive attitudes, consider the questions in figure 8.1.

Do you do any work outside of teaching that benefits others (such as volunteer work)? (Circle one.)	Frequently Sometimes Never
If you do this kind of work, how does it make you feel? If you don't do this kind of work, why not?	
List six things about your life inside and outside teaching that you are grateful for.	_____ _____ _____ _____ _____ _____
How do these things, and the gratefulness you feel for them, influence your state of mind when teaching?	
How might encouraging your students to engage in acts of kindness and take responsibility for their own self-talk help them improve their academic learning?	

Figure 8.1: How you approach hope and optimism.

Visit go.SolutionTree.com/instruction for a free reproducible version of this figure.

A simple (if challenging) shift in attitudes can have a profound impact on both your own teaching and your students' approach to their lives, including their education. That's way in this chapter, we cover the following life-changing social traits.

- Gratitude building
- Service work and acts of kindness
- Personal responsibility and self-regulation

Let's start with gratitude building.

Gratitude Building

Occasionally, teachers raise their eyebrows when I talk about gratitude, as if they think that gratitude is something only the elderly ask of their grandchildren: "Be grateful for what you have!" Nothing could be further from the truth (Algoe, Haidt, & Gable, 2008; Froh, Sefick, & Emmons, 2008). Gratitude affirms what we experience is good. It grants a gift to those receiving it and invites us to see how others have supported us. This makes gratitude both personal and social, and when we express gratitude in our relationships, we connect better (Algoe, 2012). Most of your students have not yet learned this skill, so you can begin by building an emotional bank account stacked with gratitude.

To start building an emotional bank account every day, share with your students something that you are grateful for (your health, family, job, friends, the weather, and so on). Students need to see an adult showing gratitude; if you're not grateful, they're less likely to buy into the attitude they need to learn. Your openness will, over time, help students to become more comfortable sharing their gratitude with others.

Figure 8.2 highlights some research-based tips for your gratitude process (Emmons, 2007; Sheldon & Lyubomirsky, 2006). You can use it as a handout for yourself and for your students. Consider how the tips can help your teaching be more effective.

To keep the gratitude process fresh, use the weekly planner in figure 8.3 (page 91) to choose a gratitude-builder to use on certain days of that week. To avoid having these activities evolve into simple time fillers, make the activity happen for five to seven minutes a day, three times a week, for two to six months. Constantly tweak the activity to keep it fresh with just enough novelty to prevent student boredom. Increase the challenge and complexity of the activity so the process becomes a worthwhile mental journey instead of a mindless routine.

Service Work and Acts of Kindness

Research shows that daily acts of kindness, including works of service, create changes in the lives of the giver and receiver (Otake, Shimai, Tanaka-Matsumi, Otsui, & Fredrickson, 2006). In fact, kind people who do work on behalf of others experience more happiness (Otake et al., 2006). Many programs that build student character include the simple strategy to help students become net *givers* instead of net *takers*. Pick just one day a week for extra kindnesses like those mentioned in this section. This experience seems to intensify positive emotions, creating a much greater emotional high. Use a worksheet like the one in figure 8.4 (page 92) to have students pick a day for their extra kindnesses and list them. Some examples are opening the door for someone, picking up something someone dropped, or helping a classmate with homework. You can use a similar worksheet to keep track of your own kindnesses.

Let's examine both service work and acts of kindness in turn.

Use the tips on this sheet to help you focus on the good things in your life for which you feel gratitude.

KEEP IT PERSONAL

When you think about what you're grateful for, focus on the people who have a positive impact rather than things you have. Think about others' support, sacrifices, and contributions.

What are you grateful for?

START WITH A GOAL

Set a positive, grateful goal in a personal or classroom journal. Using a journal to feel more satisfied and joyful helps add value to the journaling.

What's your positive, grateful goal?

FAVOR DEPTH OVER BREADTH

Elaborate deeply about one thing instead of focusing at the surface level of multiple things. Focus on what is surprising and unexpected. Think of facts about your life, such as advantages and opportunities.

What are you focusing on?

USE A TAKE-AWAY-THE-GOODNESS STRATEGY

Reflect on what your life would be like without a certain positive event (versus all the positives).

What would your life be like without this positive event?

REFLECT ON THE GOOD THINGS WEEKLY

When you expect a good thing every day, it can lose its impact, so write just once a week about something that is good and valuable in your life and for which you're thankful.

What are you grateful for this week?

Figure 8.2: Build gratitude.

*Visit **go.SolutionTree.com/instruction** for a free reproducible version of this figure.*

Strategy	Day of week
1. Share with a buddy: Have students share their feelings of gratitude with a partner.	Monday: _____ Tweak:
2. Use a journal: Have students write their feelings of gratitude in a gratitude journal.	Tuesday: _____ Tweak:
3. Start small: Have students share just one small thing (in detail) that they are grateful for with a peer.	Wednesday: _____ Tweak:
4. Share in a circle: Have students share in a small circle. After each speaks, others thank him or her.	Thursday: _____ Tweak:
5. Make a poster: Have students work with a partner or a small team to create a poster.	Friday: _____ Tweak:

Figure 8.3: Gratitude weekly activity planner.

*Visit **go.SolutionTree.com/instruction** for a free reproducible version of this figure.*

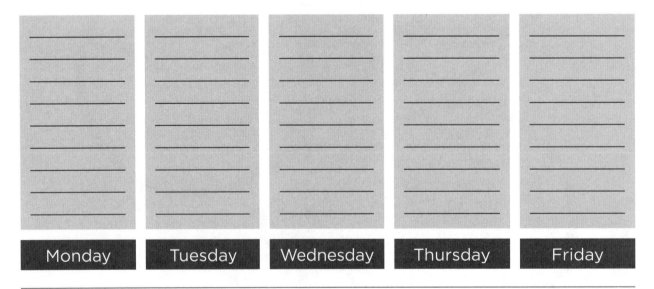

Figure 8.4: Stack up the kindness.

*Visit **go.SolutionTree.com/instruction** for a free reproducible version of this figure.*

Service Work

Service work means simply doing public work for the good of others. Why would students want to do this? First, it feels good. Second, students feel more capable and hopeful making changes. Third, students see that they make a difference in the lives of others.

To get started, use the following as sources for ideas.

- **Local and national news:** Look for the stories on existing projects that others are doing, like a book drive. Many of them could use help.

- **Local animal shelters:** Volunteers are used for animal support tasks, such as cleaning cages, answering phones, or making shelter waiting rooms a nicer area.

- **Parks, community orchards, and beaches:** Environments always have needs that students can fill. Students can plant trees, clean up unsightly areas, or do beach trash pickups.

- **Seniors and nursing homes:** Many senior citizens would relish the time and help as would a private nursing home where volunteers are also needed. Contact the recreation director who plans activities.

- **Agencies:** During the holidays, students can work with agencies that need temporary help. There are many agencies that need food or gifts for deserving families. Your students can ask for donations.

- **Military families:** Look up organizations that ship packages to troops, such as Operation Gratitude (www.operationgratitude.com) or Operation Troop Support (http://operationtroopsupport.org). Get donations and support our troops.

To go beyond this list, look for agencies that experience pervasive challenges, for example, shelters that feed the homeless daily need fresh vegetables. This problem is something that a school can eliminate by raising crops and donating the vegetables. (Visit http://katieskrops.com to learn how one student began growing and donating fresh cabbage to a local soup kitchen and how others have joined her.) If your students want to broaden their reach, visit www.dosomething.org/us/campaigns to read about what others are doing and find an already operating campaign. (Visit **go.SolutionTree.com/instruction** to access live links to the websites mentioned in this book.) As they do this, have them use the brainstorming sheet in figure 8.5 to record their ideas.

List five resources you've looked at to find service work.	What options for service work did you find here that resonate with you? Why?	What are your action steps for engaging with this work?
1.		
2.		
3.		
4.		
5.		

Figure 8.5: Service work brainstorming sheet.

*Visit **go.SolutionTree.com/instruction** for a free reproducible version of this figure.*

Acts of Kindness

In a study of nineteen elementary classrooms, researchers asked students to perform three acts of kindness per week over the course of four weeks. Students who did so experienced significant increases in peer acceptance, which translated to better behaviors (Layous, Nelson, Oberle, Schonert-Reichl, & Lyubomirsky, 2012). Acts of kindness are easy; simply invite students to try out these two strategies while at school.

The Magic Three

The Magic Three strategy uses the words *respect*, *agree*, and *appreciate* to defuse and de-escalate any situation. When a student experiences conflict, students start arguing, or a student starts shouting or gets upset, here's what to do. Remember, others need to feel that their voices are heard first.

1. If you want them to listen, you go first and say, "I *respect* (your right to say that, your feelings, the work you put in, your passion, or how you feel about that)."

2. You can also say, "I *agree* with (your position, strategy, understanding of the topic, or problems)." You may not agree with their strategy, but you can agree with their intention (the need to change a rule or system).

3. Finally, you can say, "I *appreciate* (the hard work you put in, the way you care about this, your commitment, or you wanting to talk this through)."

Notice how these three openings—*respect*, *agree*, and *appreciate*—slow things down, soften the tone, and let the student know that you do see good in him or her. Once students feel they've had a chance to be heard, you can have a much more productive (and less combative) conversation. To practice, use figure 8.6 to reflect on a conflict you've witnessed in your classroom and some ways you did or could have approached it to show your respect, agreement, and appreciation.

Which students were involved:
Describe the conflict. _____ _____
What do you respect?
What do you agree about?
What do you appreciate?

Figure 8.6: The magic three.

Visit go.SolutionTree.com/instruction for a free reproducible version of this figure.

Acts-of-Kindness Lists

Empower students to create their own acts-of-kindness lists so they can do the things they've chosen for themselves. Here are some suggestions to help students get started.

- Letting another student go ahead of you in line
  - Sharing food or a favorite movie or song
  - Helping a friend fix something
  - Helping another student with homework
  - Getting a tissue for someone who needs it (like after a sneeze)

Ensure students acknowledge each other publicly (if they give permission) as well as privately for their kind deeds. Over time, and especially when combined with service work, this will not just help students feel better about themselves but just may transform your school culture. Help students track both of these by providing them with a copy of figure 8.7.

List five acts of kindness you engaged in this week (or last week).

_____   _____

_____   _____

_____

What made you feel good about doing these things?

_____

How many hours did you devote to service work? _____

Describe the work you did.

_____

_____

_____

How did you feel about this work? What did you learn?

_____

_____

_____

Figure 8.7: Track acts of kindness and service work.

*Visit **go.SolutionTree.com/instruction** for a free reproducible version of this figure.*

Next, we look at the role of personal responsibility in building attitudes of gratitude and contributing to the positivity mindset.

Personal Responsibility and Self-Regulation

Many truisms become part of people for so long that it is easy to forget how powerful they are and the effect they have. For example, it's likely that years ago, someone said to you (or you figured out), "It's not what happens to you in life that shapes your future, it is how you deal with what happens."

In other words, you're not always responsible for what happens to you in life. But, as you get older, you sure are increasingly responsible for how you respond to what happens. When you learn to regulate your intentions, you become a player, not a bystander. You become a force to be reckoned with because you manage your emotions and have a better work ethic. Your students can deal with this process by mastering how to run their own brains, learn from real-world examples, reframe to stay positive, handle negatives constructively, and choose their battles.

In the following sections, I present four strategies for helping students take responsibility for and self-regulate themselves.

Learning From Real-World Examples

Share a real-world role model's quote or book with students. Choose someone who takes personal responsibility for his or her actions and writes about how to do that. Your students need to know they are not alone. Successful people have learned to be responsible because that is what works in life. See figure 8.8.

Role model	How this person took responsibility for his or her actions

Figure 8.8: Reflect on role models.

*Visit **go.SolutionTree.com/instruction** for a free reproducible version of this figure.*

Reframing to Stay Positive

Teach the skills of reframing to stay positive. Students can learn to say to themselves, "Maybe I am having a bad day" instead of "My life stinks" or "I didn't do well on this test" instead of "I'm an idiot." Find a way, mentally, to refrain from judgment or criticism and instead see another's point of view. Teach students that sometimes the source of the negativity is a constant, and it's best to spend less time around it. You can have students use a simple worksheet like in figure 8.9 to help them reframe their feelings in a more positive and constructive way.

Figure 8.9: Reframe negative thoughts.

*Visit **go.SolutionTree.com/instruction** for a free reproducible version of this figure.*

Handling the Negatives Constructively

Post the sign *What to Do When It's Not Working* in your class. The sign should have a simple five-step process that every student can follow: (1) take a deep breath, (2) say "I can do this," (3) list three things you might do differently, (4) try out your best of the three choices, and (5) evaluate progress and either continue or go back to step 1. Visit **go.SolutionTree.com/instruction** to download a free reproducible of this sign.

When you criticize a student, often he or she has no clue how to behave or respond. The student may not have been taught the right skills at home, or chronic stress could be dominating his or her behaviors. Neither of those are the student's fault. Stop telling students what to do. Teach them how to behave, or they will counterattack or go silent. Encourage upset students to say, "Listen, I am sorry I messed up. I just didn't know what else to do. Help me out, and please tell me what you want me to do instead of telling me what's wrong."

Without teaching them *the how*, students will get in trouble over and over and soon the suspensions will follow. Unless you help, they may drop out.

Choosing Your Battles Wisely

Teach your students never to argue with a constantly negative or angry person. Role model this with your students. See figure 8.10. In class, when things get out of hand with a student, simply say, "I respect your point of view and appreciate what you're saying. It does sound like you and I have to sort some things out. Let's do this privately a bit later so the rest of the class can move forward." Otherwise, both of you will end up feeling worse in the end. Listen to what the student said, but if nothing applies to you, let it go. If the shoe fits, pick it up and try it out. If it doesn't, leave it alone. Simply breathe in good thoughts, and breathe out the stress. You and your students have more important things to do.

> **Consider a disagreement you've had recently.**
>
> Did the argument get heated? If so, how can you defuse a similar situation in the future?
> _____
> _____
> _____
>
> If not, did you choose your battles wisely? (Circle one.)
>
> Yes   No
>
> What was the other person's reaction?
> _____
> _____
> _____
>
> How can you improve the situation in the future?
> _____
> _____
> _____

Figure 8.10: Reflect on a conflict.

*Visit **go.SolutionTree.com/instruction** for a free reproducible version of this figure.*

Quick Consolidation: Build Positive Attitudes

A surprising focus for high-performing teachers is on the power of emotions and how they impact others. Remember, no matter how good your students get, unless you help them internalize those strengths and feel good about themselves for a solid reason, they will always have paralyzing doubts that hold them back. With this firmly in mind, answer the following reflection questions on how you can build positive attitudes in your students.

1. How has your understanding of the importance of building positive attitudes shifted after reading this chapter?

2. What are three strategies you're going to use to help students build a sense of gratitude? Why did you choose these strategies?

3. What are some resources in your community you can connect your students with to help them find service work they can get involved in?

4. How will you help students understand the value in acts of kindness and encourage students to engage in them with frequency?

5. Who are some real-world examples of people who approached life with a positive attitude and achieved great results that you can share with your students to help motivate them?

CHAPTER 9

CHANGE THE EMOTIONAL SET POINT

Going back hundreds of years, two of the biggest mistaken beliefs include, "The Earth is flat" and "Brains can't change." Today, we know better. The Earth is round, and brains can change. In fact, the so-called *set point* for weight management (feeling full) can be changed, as well as your tolerance for pain (the *ouch* tolerance), your happiness (joy), and your stress level. The *emotional set point* signifies a person's most common emotional state. For some, it is frustration and anger. For others, it is calmness and joy. Use the survey in figure 9.1 to consider your own emotional set point and how you approach the set points of your students.

What do you consider your default emotional set point? (Circle one.)	I often feel calm, hopeful, or joyful.	I often feel anxiety, anger, or frustration.
Describe the reasons for the answer you chose.		
As a group, how many of your students appear to have an emotional set point rooted in frustration or anger? (Circle one.)	Less than one-third	About half / Two-thirds or more
What do you think are some of the reasons that students might appear to have a negative emotional set point? How do you think this affects their ability to learn?		
In what ways do you think you could help students operating from a negative emotional set point move toward a more positive one?		

Figure 9.1: How you approach emotional set points.

*Visit **go.SolutionTree.com/instruction** for a free reproducible version of this figure.*

The majority of school-age students living in poverty are exposed to multiple chronic stressors including violence, family turmoil, separation from family members, and substandard living environments (Evans & Kim, 2012). Students are also more sensitive to social stress (Sripada, Swain, Evans, Welsh, & Liberzon, 2014).

The human brain adapts to the chronic stress by creating a new normal set point. While it is a coping tool, this also sets up the brain for problems. Examples of new set points for stress are hypervigilance (aggressive, in-your-face behavior) and hyporesponsiveness (learned helplessness; Maier & Watkins, 2005). But you can help change this rewired brain if you know how to do it. It is all about the emotions, and in this chapter, I help you understand the functions of emotional set points and give you some strategies to help you shift the emotional set point of your students into a more positive mindset. To learn more about the research into emotions and the brain, make sure to read *Poor Students, Rich Teaching, Revised Edition* (Jensen, 2019).

How an Emotional Set Point Gets Set

Why are emotions so important in the classroom? The answer may surprise you. When people are grumpy or out of control, they occasionally make poor decisions. When depression, anger, or irritation is one's semipermanent life state, he or she may often make poor decisions.

The key to changing your students' happiness set point is consistency. When you consistently teach students to make better choices, foster a better emotional climate, and offer them some measure of control over their lives, their emotional set point changes. This is not simple to do, but it is well worth it. Improved emotions can foster better decisions, and better decisions can foster improved emotions. As you help make this happen, the next step is to ensure you're coaxing these improved emotions from the right place.

When students succeed and feel good at school, their daily happiness improves. But it turns out that the *type* of happiness they're feeling is what matters (Catalino & Fredrickson, 2011). You might think, "Happy is happy. It's just a matter of how mild or intense." There are three types of happiness, each of which has a very different effect on your students at both a practical level and even at a genetic level (Catalino & Fredrickson, 2011). Use figure 9.2 to build your understanding of these types of happiness and list some examples of them that you see in your teaching.

To understand how and why these tie into teaching, it's important to know how brains respond differently to each of the three happiness types.

The primary distinction of spontaneous happiness is that the joy is unplanned and unpursued. In the classroom, it could happen when a teacher surprises her students with a joke, a fun energizer, a funny story, or an early departure. The brain's response is the release of dopamine, the neurotransmitter of pleasure.

Hedonic happiness is distinguished by two qualities: (1) it is a planned pursuit, and (2) the person seeks pleasure as the outcome. In the classroom, you might reinforce hedonic happiness with the chronic use of material rewards such as bribes of sweets and treats or points redeemable for more rewards. This sort of hedonic pleasure has some problems (Disabato, Goodman, Kashdan, Short, & Jarden, 2015), because the brain quickly habituates to the reward. As a result, the pleasure response diminishes, and the rewarded behavior becomes a letdown. This type of happiness becomes harder and harder to achieve.

Eudaimonic happiness leads directly to meaningful goals—like graduating (see part seven, page 199). This happy state comes not from consuming but from producing something. It's the byproduct of a sustained effort in working toward something bigger than you: seeking purposeful and meaningful goals. It's the pursuit of big goals and mastery learning. This type of joy actually fuels the drive to achieve and helps the body thrive too. This is a dramatically healthier profile, and students who frequently experience eudaimonic happiness are more likely to stay healthy, avoid drugs, and exhibit greater resilience (Cohn, Fredrickson, Brown, Mikels, & Conway, 2009).

SPONTANEOUS HAPPINESS

This is the enjoyment to be found in the moment (ice cream, a surprise of a beautiful flower opening up, a smile, a gift, a kiss, or sunset).

List some examples of spontaneous happiness that occur in your classroom.

_____

_____

_____

_____

HEDONIC HAPPINESS

This is the pursuit of pleasure for its own sake (being addicted to video games, online shopping, unhealthy foods, gambling, excess TV, or hoarding).

List some examples of hedonic happiness that occur in your classroom.

_____

_____

_____

_____

EUDAIMONIC HAPPINESS

This is the joyful satisfaction of long-term pursuit of worthwhile goals (becoming part of an athletic team that has a good season, learning a tough new skill, building something relevant, or leading an interesting project).

List some examples of eudaimonic happiness that occur in your classroom.

_____

_____

_____

_____

Figure 9.2: Three types of happiness.

*Visit **go.SolutionTree.com/instruction** for a free reproducible version of this figure.*

How to Change Students' Emotional Set Points

There are two ways to change students' emotional set points: (1) intensity (like trauma, obviously not a good idea) or (2) relevant duration (language learning). In your classroom, this means you'll be doing relevant things over time. You can use meaningful projects, focus on the end product, tie feedback to quality, and reinforce what is working. For example, K–12 students who work hard for long-term goals (like high school graduation) may find meaning and joy in the process. Additionally, strong social ties, the capacity to derive meaning, and personal growth are common correlations for the eudaimonic state (Ryff, 2014).

Let's look at five strategies for achieving this state.

Use Meaningful Projects

Assign work projects that last longer than just a week or two. It turns out that adolescents (grades 6–12) who focus over a semester or a year on eudaimonic (long-term) pleasures have less risk of depression (Telzer, Fuligni, Lieberman, & Galván, 2014). Ideas for you include relevant project-based learning, service work, or team assignments with collaboration over weeks and months. When you help your students do meaningful, relevant projects (versus only short worksheets), they have a better chance of getting healthier and happier! High-performing teachers do these consistently. Use figure 9.3 to brainstorm some meaningful projects for your students.

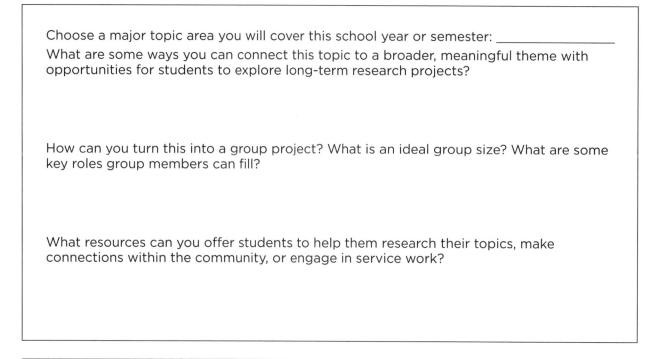

Choose a major topic area you will cover this school year or semester: _____

What are some ways you can connect this topic to a broader, meaningful theme with opportunities for students to explore long-term research projects?

How can you turn this into a group project? What is an ideal group size? What are some key roles group members can fill?

What resources can you offer students to help them research their topics, make connections within the community, or engage in service work?

Figure 9.3: Brainstorm meaningful projects.

*Visit **go.SolutionTree.com/instruction** for a free reproducible version of this figure.*

Focus on the End Product

Start an assignment by first focusing on the end product. That means you'll want to get buy-in to the end goal and then strengthen the intensity of the value. Tell students about the benefits, have them draw a picture of how they'll feel, ask them to share the benefits with a neighbor, and post up a colorful picture of students succeeding at the project. Next, move on to concentrate on the process. That is, the hook to involve students may be a relevant, gutsy goal (see chapter 4, page 41). But once students get into the process, then you can focus on the quality of the work. That's where the satisfaction is.

Tie Feedback to Quality

Students need to learn what great work looks like. They also need to see that their teachers care about the quality of their work, not how fast they can get it done. Show great quality sample student work to your students so they know what you want. Circulate the examples and post them in the class. This ties their emotional satisfaction to a more lasting event, product, or service.

Reinforce What Is Working

Ensure that you keep students in the game with simple reinforcers. These include smiles, affirmations, celebrations, written feedback, team bragging, shared individual success, partner comments, personal interactions, and acknowledgments of quality work. This approach echoes what researchers know: positive reinforcement works better than negative reinforcement (Nelson, Demers, & Christ, 2014).

The eudaimonic state of happiness is an everyday mood-generating state that works magic in your school. Students will attend class more when they are sick less often. They try harder and succeed more often in school. This cycles positive energy and hope back to the teachers, who in turn feel affirmed and rewarded. This process is invisible yet powerful (Algoe & Fredrickson, 2011). Use figure 9.4 to consider each of these strategies for setting an emotional set point and brainstorming ideas for putting them to use.

List some ideas for meaningful projects you can have students engage in.

What is the end point for an assignment you plan to give students? How can you improve its value and illustrate those benefits for your students? What will the process look like?

What are some examples of exemplary student work that you already have access to? How can you use your classroom environment to call attention to them?

What are some things that students are already doing well in your class? How can you reinforce these successes to them and highlight how those successes will benefit them going forward?

Figure 9.4: Ideas for changing students' emotional set point.

Visit go.SolutionTree.com/instruction for a free reproducible version of this figure.

Quick Consolidation: Change the Emotional Set Point

Although the serendipity of a simple, surprising happy moment is, of course, a wonderful thing, pursuit of pleasure for pleasure's sake is not very good for our well-being. The long-term pursuit of meaningful goals is more than invigorating; it's healthier and more positive than short-term pleasure seeking. This is why tough projects and goals can work miracles with your students. With this firmly in mind, answer the following reflection questions on how you can build positive attitudes in your students.

1. What do you know or understand about emotional set points that you didn't at the start of this chapter?

2. Think about what you've learned about the different kinds of happiness (spontaneous, hedonistic, and eudaimonic). What changes will you make to your teaching practices to focus on fostering eudaimonic happiness in your students and avoid hedonistic rewards?

3. What strategies from this chapter will you begin using in your own practices? What makes them the best fit for your students and teaching?

4. What changes could you make to the strategies in this chapter to adapt them to better serve your specific students and classroom environment?

5. When you encounter challenges helping students shift their emotional set points in a more positive direction, how will you use the entirety of the positivity mindset to help them break through?

Reflect on the Positivity Mindset

All meaningful and lasting change starts with a mirror. Now that you understand the concept of the positivity mindset and have strategies to foster hope and optimism in your classroom, it's time to self-assess and reflect on what comes next. Use the following questions to accomplish this.

1. How do you want to invest the rest of you career? Are you going to dismiss the hard scientific research on the power of positivity, claiming that it's not your thing, or are you going to make positivity your mindset, starting today?

2. What new narrative will you adopt about yourself and your students that fosters positivity in the classroom?

3. What strategy from part three can you use or adapt with fierce urgency to move the emotional set points in you students in a positive direction?

4. What support processes can you create to ensure you successfully implement this strategy?

5. How might you increase your ability to succeed by talking with and enlisting the support of colleagues, writing affirming notes to yourself, or adapting your lesson plans to use new strategies and narratives?

Keep this at the front of your brain: you always have a choice. If you aren't happy where you are, find a different job in education, move overseas and teach in an international school, or switch career paths and do something entirely different. Do what you ask your students to do: focus on optimism and hope, remember your strengths, be grateful, perform acts of kindness, and take responsibility for how you react to what happens to you. You can do this!

PART FOUR

IMPLEMENTING THE RICH CLASSROOM CLIMATE MINDSET

The title of this mindset plays off the word *rich* in the book's title. Again, the word *rich* refers to substantial, bountiful, ample, and plentiful. This metaphor is important because your classroom climate must be rich in affirmation, rich in relevancy, rich in engagement, and rich in relationships. In a rich classroom climate, students feel comfortable and safe enough to take academic and behavioral risks. It inspires them to dream big. Most of all, it gives students a voice, and it respects them. A climate composed of energy, participation, spirit, respect, learning, movement, listening, sharing, reflection, and big goals ultimately creates a high-performing classroom. The richness that you share with your students must feel like the good life. Take a moment to preassess how to approach your own classroom's climate in figure P4.1 (page 108).

Because your students often grow up without the rich climate mindset, this addition can literally change their brains for the better. This is a way to frame equity from just a conversation to genuine action steps. So as you consider your answers to these questions, let's take a moment to distinguish between a rich classroom climate mindset and a more traditional classroom climate mindset.

When your students come to you stressed or unprepared for the grade level or subject matter, it is easy to make students the cause of your problems. In this mindset, students should already know how to behave, how to form and maintain teams, how to ask appropriate questions, and how to learn tough concepts with no help. It says, "My job is teaching content. If students don't want to learn it, that's their loss, and they need to sit up and knock off the silly stuff." Conversely, the rich classroom climate mindset says, "I focus on what students need to succeed and build it into the learning and social environment every day." This mindset is critical to understanding your students.

1. How do you define the difference between your classroom climate and your classroom culture?

_____

_____

_____

_____

2. What are some aspects of climate and culture in your classroom? What do you do to cultivate a healthy classroom climate, or do you approach it as something that is reflective of your students (random)?

_____

_____

_____

_____

3. What strategies do you employ to make the content you teach relevant to your students and their lives? What do you do to ensure your students have a voice in your classroom? Do you engage students in establishing a vision of themselves and their future?

_____

_____

_____

_____

4. What steps do you take to ensure your students feel safe in your classroom, both physically and emotionally? What rules have you adopted in your classroom and how do they impact student behavior?

_____

_____

_____

_____

5. How do you foster a sense of academic optimism in your students, particularly those who come from poverty? Do you have strategies to get students to believe they can succeed and achieve mastery in your classroom?

_____

_____

_____

_____

Figure P4.1: Assess your understanding of classroom climate and culture.

Visit go.SolutionTree.com/instruction for a free reproducible version of this figure.

> The rich classroom climate mindset says, "I focus on what students need to succeed and build it into the learning and social environment every day."

Some believe that class climate is an aggregate of everything, including relationship formation, instruction, cooperative learning, discipline strategies, curriculum, expectations, and engagement. That's why it's so valuable. High-performing teachers say, "*How* do I affirm what's good and make up any differences?" They work hard at it every day. That's why the individual teacher's classroom climate has a powerful 0.80 effect size (Hattie, 2009). This is almost two years' worth of academic gains.

People often use the terms *climate* and *culture* interchangeably; however, there is a clear difference between the two, so let's start there. Culture is *what* we do (behaviors and character), but climate is *how* we feel. Culture establishes and predicts behaviors ("Who are we?"), but climate follows the crowd and the mood of the moment and is an aggregate of student states. To change culture, we must make decisions and actions that foster our collective culture. Culture takes purpose to change; climate can change in moments.

Your goal as a teacher is to create a classroom culture that encourages students to come to school on time, fully prepared, and willing to develop high self-regulatory skills, grit, and relationships in class. Make your culture welcoming for every student (not just your favorites or those on time every day). A culture should invite reflection on how our behaviors affect us, others, and our school and develop shared beliefs that we are a part of something special and great. Build your culture to foster language that facilitates personal pride, purpose, and energy.

In the next three chapters, we'll explore the following three factors that promote a rich classroom climate mindset.

1. Engage voice and vision.

2. Set safe classroom norms.

3. Foster academic optimism.

Each of these factors strengthens a different area of students' lives.

Questions for Daily Reflection

Each day, consider how your practices foster a rich classroom climate. Then, answer the following questions.

1. What will you do today to help students find their voice and vision?

2. Will you make time to look for students who seem to feel unsafe in your classroom, and make time to approach them about what you can do to change that?

3. How will you adapt your lesson plans to foster in students a sense of academic optimism that they can and will achieve success and mastery in their studies?

CHAPTER 10

ENGAGE VOICE AND VISION

The first step in creating a rich classroom climate mindset means creating a positive, responsive environment. From part three, you have the tools you need to build positivity, and this chapter expands on that by focusing on what students need to succeed and incorporating these into the learning and social environment every day. That means showing students who they are, what they care about, and how they feel about things. Otherwise, students will feel like it's "your class" and not "our class." Before we begin, use figure 10.1 to consider your existing assumptions and practice with regard to involving students in your classroom.

How often do you go out of your way to connect content to students' lives? (Circle one.)	Every day	Sometimes	Never
How would you answer a student who asks, "Why should I learn this?" How does your answer reflect aspects of a student's life he or she can connect with?			
How often do you let students speak and engage with content? (Circle one.)	Every day	Sometimes	Never
What are examples of things you do to get students vocally involved in their own learning? What could you do?			
How often do you take time to learn what students want out of their own lives? (Circle one.)	Every day	Sometimes	Never
Based on past interactions, what are some things your students aspire to? If you don't know, write your best guesses, and poll students to see how they align.			

Figure 10.1: Consider how you establish relevance, voice, and vision.

*Visit **go.SolutionTree.com/instruction** for a free reproducible version of this figure.*

This chapter touches on three elements that make all the difference to students: (1) relevance, (2) student voice, and (3) and student vision. Let's start with relevance.

Relevance

How often do you hear "Why do we need to learn this?"? Relevance is everything to your students. If their brains do not buy into classroom learning, they are not changing (Green & Bavelier, 2008). If the brain doesn't change, no learning will occur (Engineer et al., 2012). If no learning happens, why should students even come to school? (Chapter 17, page 184, will also address relevance regarding buy-in, but here, we'll touch on its importance for a rich classroom climate.) Students feel respected when teachers understand where they are coming from and apply that understanding by making connections in the classroom. Create a student's sense of meaning and belonging.

In a nutshell, ask yourself the following four questions to foster a great classroom environment. These four areas have to be rock solid or you'll risk losing students who fail to see you and the content as a relevant part of their learning experience. You will find a more in-depth exploration of these questions in *Poor Students, Rich Teaching, Revised Edition* (Jensen, 2019).

1. **"Are you affirming?"** Culturally relevant teaching is validating and affirming because it acknowledges the strengths of students' diverse heritages.

2. **"Is your teaching diverse?"** Culturally relevant teaching is comprehensive. It uses culturally familiar resources to teach knowledge, skills, values, and attitudes through the classroom environment, teaching methods, and even evaluation.

3. **"Are you empowering?"** Culturally relevant teaching empowers students, giving them opportunities to excel in the classroom and beyond: "Empowerment translates into academic competence, personal confidence, courage, and the will to act" (Gay, 2010, p. 34).

4. **"Are you life changing?"** Culturally relevant teaching is transformative because educators and their students must often defy education traditions and the status quo.

Use the worksheet in figure 10.2 to consider your own teaching practices and what specific changes you can make to address each of these questions.

Lesson or topic:			
Question	**Yes**	**No**	**How am I building relevance, or what can I change to build more relevance?**
Am I affirming?			
Is my teaching diverse?			
Am I empowering?			
Am I changing lives?			

Figure 10.2: Build relevance.

*Visit **go.SolutionTree.com/instruction** for a free reproducible version of this figure.*

Culturally responsive teachers get to know, respect, and care for every single learner by holding sky-high expectations, ensuring rigor in the curriculum, and providing every type of support needed for students to meet those high expectations (Banks et al., 2005). The teachers have purposefully reflected on their own biases and have discovered how their attitudes can and do shape students' behaviors. As a result, they make it a habit to avoid any racist and discriminatory words or actions (Gay, 2010). If this seems like taking a class in a foreign language, it might be one. All I can say is, "If the shoe fits, wear it."

Student Voice

Student voice is the right-now expression of feelings, opinions, and narratives. When students have a voice in class, they feel heard and validated (Novak & Slattery, 2017). This offers students a sense of control in their learning and strengthens self-confidence in learning because they can stoke the fire. This matters because students from poverty experience chronic stress and offering them a measure of control in their learning provides them with a potent coping mechanism that lowers stress (Yehuda, Flory, Southwick, & Charney, 2006). When control increases, a sense of personal efficacy also increases. The class becomes *our class* instead of only the teacher's class.

When you help students find their voices, it makes tasks personal, meaningful, and relevant. When students take advantage of this, affirm their dreams, opinions, stories, expressions, interests, and life experiences. Consider using the following responses with students, and modify them as necessary.

- "I'm glad we were able to talk. How you feel is important to me."
- "I love your dream; let's see what we can do to make it happen."
- "Thanks for telling your story; I really liked hearing from you."
- "I love the excitement in your answer. How did you come up with it?"
- "You also sound a bit hesitant and unsure. Tell us what your concerns are about the answer."
- "I love that you shared your opinion with us, and I hope to hear from you again tomorrow."

Figure 10.3 shows a sample worksheet with ideas for building opportunities into your instruction that inspire student voices. To brainstorm and work through your own ideas, download and print off a blank version of it from this book's webpage (visit **go.SolutionTree.com/instruction**).

	How can you foster student voice for each of these strategies?
Invite students to share needs	Ask questions, meet their learning style, seek help, advocate for academic success tools (like tutoring), use a suggestions box, and stand up for rights (gender, sexual orientation, ethnic, or religious).
Validate and use student currencies	Understand their knowledge, soft skills, social skills, and network affiliation.
Invite students to share personal issues	Encourage them to talk to a teacher, counselor, or anyone who respects privacy and listens well.
Encourage students to take risks	Have them challenge their school to change, run for office, create a social media presence, utilize clubs, and undertake school issues and community problems that need attention.
Invite students to make allies in life	Show students why and how adults can be helpful, help them communicate better with their parents, and learn from what doesn't work well.
Inspire students to write and speak publicly	Their voice can only be heard if they share it; help them get exposure to others who want to hear them.

Figure 10.3: Foster voice.

*Visit **go.SolutionTree.com/instruction** for a free reproducible version of this figure.*

When you give students the opportunity to share their voice and you affirm it, you have given them one of the great gifts that anyone can give another human being. You are saying, "You're important to me and worth listening to."

You have to be able to appreciate, respect, and understand your students' culture to hook them in. When you consider and implement cultural factors into daily classroom experiences, you reduce the separation between what students refer to as the real world and the artificial school experience.

Student Vision

Vision is the student's expectation about his or her own future. We learned in chapter 4 that a student's expectation of success has a powerful 1.44 effect size (Hattie, 2009). An empowering expectation affirms having a sense of creative decision making, control, and ownership over one's destiny. It means everything to students, especially students who come from adversity. This differs from the teacher-facilitated process of setting gutsy goals in chapter 4, which is about academic milestones. Helping a student find or uncover his or her vision is different. With a student's vision, we are all about discovering and allowing the student's big idea to emerge. A student's vision is about his or her personal life. Your goal here is to ensure that the two (gutsy goals and vision) match up. Sometimes that is easy, and other times it is a bit of work. Here are three ways to uncover or discover your students' visions.

1. **Start with asking students for their long-term dreams (their vision):** The vision often begins with a fuzzy ideal, but students can develop those fuzzy ideals into something big. Whatever they come up with, remember to be receptive, not judgmental. ("Tell me what you have so far, you can edit it later.")

2. **Help students refine their dreams by using the revised SMART (specific and strategic, measurable, amazing, relevant, and time bound) goals criteria:** Ask students to explain what the end result would look like, sound like, and feel like. Over time, you can help them crystallize this vision into a clear endpoint that they can describe and measure. For students with a vision, they now have an endpoint worth striving for. Now, you can work with students to set micro goals to move them toward their dreams.

3. **Set the goals:** Ask students to use a tablet, laptop, or flipchart paper to create a timeline. Put *Start* at one end and *Goal* at the other end. This process is ideally done with a partner. Allow students to start filling in the milestones they would need to reach to accomplish their life vision. Once the smaller milestones are filled in, ask them to work backward all the way to the start.

Figure 10.4 integrates this process into a worksheet you can use with your students to help them develop their vision.

Once students have a vision and a dream for themselves, help them get used to the end result. Ask students to show you the end product. Get students out of their seats, and ask them to stand. Here you should play songs like the theme from *Rocky* ("Gonna Fly Now") or "Unbelievable" by EMF. With the music playing, ask students (while standing) to physically rehearse success poses like graduating, getting an award, getting the job they want, winning a game, getting a medal in the Olympics, or winning a championship. Have students show three different success poses and then jump into a tough new task. These simple routines change the brain's chemistry, as demonstrating high-power poses influences elevations in testosterone, decreases in cortisol (stress), and increased feelings of power and tolerance for risk (Carney, Cuddy, & Yap, 2010). These changes can support better learning and are powerful for celebration. We get into even deeper benefits and strategies for integrating music and physicality into your classroom in chapter 19 (page 203).

Name: _____ My gutsy goal: _____

Describe your long-term vision for your future. Start big picture and support that vision with why it's important to you. (If you have trouble, google the phrase "teens or students who have changed the world" to get ideas.)

Share what you have with a partner (if you are comfortable with doing so) to help sort out what you need to do to reach your goals. Refine your vision using SMART criteria. How can you make your vision:

Specific and strategic	Measurable	Amazing	Relevant	Time bound

Create a timeline for achieving your vision. Start with the end and work your way back.

START   **MY GOAL**

Write three to five sentences on how your vision and process for getting there align and have things in common with our gutsy goal for this class.

Figure 10.4: Develop vision.

Visit go.SolutionTree.com/instruction for a free reproducible version of this figure.

Quick Consolidation: Engage Voice and Vision

The tools you can use to introduce the relevance of cultural responsiveness, student voice, and student vision into your class connect and draw students into the classroom experience. Students need to feel that their own culture is more than OK. They must feel it is valid and acceptable to talk about at school. They want to know if the school and staff care enough about them to give them a voice and help foster their vision. This empowerment is critical to the formation of a rich classroom climate. Students need teachers that will invest in them socially, emotionally, and cognitively. Without your investment, students feel like they can't invest in school. Don't wait for them. You have to go first. With this firmly in mind, answer the following reflection questions on how you can build positive attitudes in your students.

1. What do you know or understand about the importance of establishing relevancy and student voice and vision in your classroom?

2. What are some ways you can answer for students the question, "What's in this for me?" and then help them connect more fully with the content you teach?

3. What are some examples of affirming responses you can offer students when they talk to you about their opinions, interests, or life experiences?

4. How can you help students to better articulate their vision of what they want from their futures?

5. If students convey doubt about expressing or developing their voice or vision, how will you encourage them to think big and believe in themselves?

CHAPTER 11

SET SAFE CLASSROOM NORMS

A key part of the rich classroom climate mindset is the creation of a positive, responsive environment built into a great learning and social environment every day. When students first walk into a classroom, an overarching gestalt of sounds, lighting, people, and room setup tells them whether the environment is a safe, organized, and pleasant place to learn. Think about the norms that govern your classroom and answer the survey questions in figure 11.1.

Do you regularly make students aware of the physical safety systems and procedures for your classroom? (Circle one.)	Yes No
Describe what you do to ensure your students feel physically safe in your classroom. How often do you remind them of emergency procedures?	
Do you have systems or practices in place to ensure your classroom is an emotionally safe space for your students? (Circle one.)	Yes No
Describe how you identify when students might feel emotional distress and what steps you take when intervening.	
Do you have set rules that you post and enforce in your classroom? (Circle one.)	Yes No
Describe the rules you set. What were your goals when determining these rules, and what are your strategies for holding students accountable to them?	

Figure 11.1: Consider your classroom norms.

*Visit **go.SolutionTree.com/instruction** for a free reproducible version of this figure.*

Students spend over nine hundred hours a year in a classroom. That's nearly a second address for most students and a primary one for those who are homeless, evicted, or in the foster-care system. When a classroom feels safe and has rules that make sense, students know that only good things will happen to them while they are attending. If the classroom feels safe, students will drop their guard, become less oppositional, and take learning risks. When students do not feel safe or feel unsure about the environment, all bets are off. Your class won't work well because students feel on guard all the time.

In this chapter, we focus on how you can ensure the physical safety and emotional safety of your students and set up some *cool* rules for your class that foster a rich learning environment. Together, you can ensure a safe and positive climate.

Physical Safety

To ensure students feel safe, review all safety plans monthly, but focus on the high-probability concerns for that month. At the start of the year, ensure you share safety concerns and procedures for all months, including fire, snow, tornadoes, floods, or hurricanes. Teach about every chemical, cleaner, or glass product and the safety issues that go with it. Use a hall pass and bathroom pass policy with a simple logbook. Know which students exit and return to your classroom. Avoid sending two students to the restroom in sequence; ensure one has returned before another leaves. In a safe classroom, you have removed obstacles and unsafe objects and set up the groups so that there is easy in-and-out access in case of an emergency. Figure 11.2 shows a worksheet you can use to document any safety protocols for your classroom and what you want the procedures to be. Fill it in with any relevant issues and procedures you can think of and are relevant to your classroom, such as fire and tornado protocols, hall and bathroom passes, and classroom equipment use.

Safety issue	Procedure

Figure 11.2: Establish physical safety procedures.

*Visit **go.SolutionTree.com/instruction** for a free reproducible version of this figure.*

If you have trouble coming up with specific ideas for your classroom, just take a moment before the first day of school and visualize what you would do if there were any of the five most common emergencies (fire, shooting, flooding, storm, or bodily injury). Picture the actions that will go on in your classroom during the year or semester and if any of them involve the potential for physical safety concerns. If you can visualize those actions with a smooth transit, safe exit, and understood procedures for all your students, you may have a safe classroom.

Emotional Safety

Beyond developing their voices and visions, allowing students to express themselves in a safe environment creates emotional safety. Ensure that students' voices are respected. That means no laughing, smirking, giggling, or degrading opinions. Your standing rule in the classroom to be nice means valuing everyone's opinion. When you see others following this rule, acknowledge it: "Jared, I love the way you jumped in to help your neighbor. That helps our whole class see how being nice works." Consider the following classroom norms.

- When students express their opinions about the news, the neighborhood, or a personal event, always thank them.

- Keep eye contact while a student is speaking. Only break eye contact when you move to another student and have already thanked the contributor.

- Never argue, disregard, or move on to the next student until you thank the student who is speaking ("I appreciate your jumping in" or "Always good to hear from you; hope you jump back in again soon").

- When others interrupt, laugh at, deride, giggle at, or make fun of another student's response, stop the class. Remind students of the class rules and the need for respect and safety. Let students know there are two sets of rules: what is inappropriate for class, and what works at home. But still, focus on the good they do.

Everything you do communicates to your students something about you, them, and the class climate. For most teachers, when students make mistakes, they think it's bad, and the goal is to correct the mistake, push it under the rug, and move on. Bad idea! Think about this for a second; if you want students to be more willing to make mistakes to learn and grow, you'll need to *show* that as a class norm. For example:

- "I'm glad that you showed me your mistake. That will help me do a better job in teaching you this year."

- "The reason your wrong answers are helpful is because they tell us in what direction our thinking was off. Now we can correct it and get smarter."

- "I'm going to ask for some answers, but I predict there will be some very different answers, and that's OK. Let's find out if I'm right."

Expect students to make mistakes. Accepting mistakes as opportunities to grow is a new skill that takes time, coaching, and support. The joy in your work is when you can help students walk through the thinking steps, just one at a time, to help them get better answers next time. If you have trouble ensuring your responses generate emotional safety for your students, use the worksheet in figure 11.3 to think through your interactions with students.

Student's response, action, or mistake:	
How I responded:	
Did I seek out and understand the student's reasoning?	Yes ☐ No ☐
Did I acknowledge the student's contribution or effort?	Yes ☐ No ☐
How I should change or improve my response:	

Figure 11.3: Make your classroom emotionally safe.

Visit go.SolutionTree.com/instruction for a free reproducible version of this figure.

As your demeanor grows from neutral to mildly positive to fully positive, the positivity equips students with the adaptive bias to approach and explore new learning, people, or situations. As we cover in part three, you need lots of classroom positivity because the effects of negativity that some students get at home are stronger than equal effects of good (Baumeister, Bratslavsky, Finkenauer, & Vohs, 2001). To overcome any classroom toxicity of negatives, apathy, and skepticism, you'll need to not only be a neutral force but also a strong positive force in students' lives (Catalino & Fredrickson, 2011).

Cool Rules

Teachers understand the value of rules. However, one issue I find with rules is that when there are too many, it becomes harder for students to recall and implement them.

So do you really need a dozen (or more) classroom rules? To create a climate that works, it is critical that you have very few, but well-understood and well-followed, rules. We call those *cool rules*. Here are four examples.

1. Be nice (be good, fair, and supportive of others).
2. Work hard (come to class prepared to use every minute).
3. Make no excuses (don't blame others or play the victim; be responsible).
4. Choose well (life is full of choices—be thoughtful).

In the following sections, we examine each of these in more detail, but first take a moment to write down some of your existing classroom rules and your initial ideas for making them *cool*. See figure 11.4.

Current rule	Is this rule cool? (Circle one.)	What would make this rule cool?	Sum up the revised, cool rule in two to five words.
	Yes No		
	Yes No		
	Yes No		
	Yes No		
	Yes No		

Figure 11.4: Make your rules cool.

*Visit **go.SolutionTree.com/instruction** for a free reproducible version of this figure.*

Be Nice

Be nice is a simple but clear rule that everyone can learn to follow. It means no lying, cursing, arguing, tattling, cheating, or cutting in line and no name-calling, hitting, pushing, insulting, poking, teasing, swatting, or criticizing other students or the teacher. To be nice also means saying, "Please," "Thank you," "I'm sorry," and "I was wrong." It also means no stealing anything (pencils, pens, laptops, smartphones, watches, jewelry, tablets, iPods, lunches, and so on). After all, taking others' things is not nice. *Be nice* also means students follow directions and raise their hand instead of blurting things out. Empathy is critical with this rule (see chapter 3, page 27).

If a student says something inappropriate, simply say, "In our class, we don't use those words. Hang on for just a second after class, please." Then, talk to him or her in private after class. The beauty of the *Be nice* rule is that you can apply it to nearly every circumstance. It shouldn't necessarily be your only rule. Although for some it is their only rule. Think it through using the five steps in figure 11.5 and then, only when you have a plan, make a decision to take action.

Student: _____ Occurrence: _____	
How can I rebuild the relationship?	Example: Listen, you're a good kid, and I like having you in my class. Your strategy:
How can I establish relevance?	Example: I asked you to stay after class, because I really want you to graduate. Remember that job you want? You need a degree for it. When you said what you said earlier in class, I got worried. Your strategy:
How can I create an ally?	Example: I'm on your side, and I know you're a good kid, but more importantly, other adults might not know you well. If they heard you say that, they'll go ballistic and maybe try to get you expelled. Your strategy:
How can I work toward a solution?	Example: What can you do next time, when you're really ticked off, that won't get you in trouble? Your strategy:
How can I reaffirm?	Example: Here's what I have. Can you do this? Now, just to make sure I said things right, tell me what you heard. Your strategy:
How can I exit the meeting?	Example: That sounds good. You're on the right track now. Hey, thanks for your time. We'll see you tomorrow. Have a good one. Your strategy:

Figure 11.5: Plan for intervention.

Visit go.SolutionTree.com/instruction for a free reproducible version of this figure.

Work Hard

Work hard is a simple but clear reminder that most good things require preparation, effort, and grit. To work hard means students come to school prepared with their supplies and expect to hit barriers and obstacles. It means switching tactics when you do hit roadblocks. Students may have to ask more questions in class, draw out their problems, ask a peer for help, work with a study buddy, or review their learning to look for clues. If someone else learns faster, the student needs to know he or she is not stupid.

Your framing of effort is critical. Make it clear the real goal of hard work: "The harder you try, the more you succeed" and "Working harder makes you smarter." When you introduce new learning tasks to your students, share the challenges as fun and cool. Always, dismiss the easy tasks as a bit boring and not very useful for the brain. Finally, dismiss the implications that our brains get tired easily. We do not run out of effort as quickly as most think we do (Job, Walton, Berneeker, & Dweck, 2015). Learning is supposed to be work; if it's not, they're not learning anything new.

Make No Excuses

The easy way out of every problem is to point fingers (lay blame on others) or play lame ("I'm a victim; it wasn't my fault"). But this path fails to promote personal responsibility. This rule is a way to teach students personal responsibility. No excuses means that when you don't do what you said you would, don't make excuses. Encourage students to state the truth, and then, if appropriate, apologize, and finally, fix the problem. To help a student lock in his or her own sense of accountability, have him or her fill out a simple form like the one in figure 11.6, and have both the student and you sign off on his or her solution. Then, ensure the student holds himself or herself accountable for that solution. This no-excuses approach can be a potentially harsh message for students to hear, and there's only one way for them to get this message from you: with love.

Student name: *Alex Steinmeir*	
What happened? *I didn't get my assignment done.*	
How have I taken responsibility for this? *I'm sorry I broke my promise to you.*	
What will I do to fix it? *I will get the assignment in to you on Friday instead.*	
Student signature: *Alex Steinmeir* Date: *1/10/2019*	Teacher signature: Eric Jensen Date: 1/10/2019

Figure 11.6: My responsibility plan.

*Visit **go.SolutionTree.com/instruction** for a free reproducible version of this figure.*

Again, your empathy is critical. Unless the teacher genuinely cares and looks out for every student, students will tune out. To pull this third rule off in your classroom, you'll need to model it in your own life. When you are tempted to complain, blame others, or play the victim, stop yourself. Remind yourself that your students need a strong role model. You don't need to be perfect; just remember to model this attribute and keep improving on it yourself by also letting students see you accept responsibility when you make mistakes.

Choose Well

This rule reminds students of the value of self-regulation and the power of choice. We are not responsible for everything that happens to us (such as a drunk driver who almost runs us off the road, a parent passing away, a hurricane or flood, a friend dying, or the loss of a job because of budget cuts), but we are responsible for how we respond.

Your references to having autonomy and choice are critical. Use the word *choice* in positive ways so students see it as a benefit: "You will get to choose the topic on this assignment" and "You made a good choice." If students see choosing as a heavy adult responsibility, they may back off of it. The fact is when students see more sense of autonomy in choice, they will engage more in the classroom (Hafen et al., 2012). We respond to our feelings by making choices. We respond to circumstances by making choices. We respond to pressure, deadlines, and emergencies with choices. The choices you make will reinforce your narrative or create a new one. Teach students that they always have a choice in life. *Choose well* is a reminder of that gift. Use figure 11.7 to pick an assignment you use with your students and consider three ways you can alter it to give them more choices.

Assignment or lesson:
Describe the existing process for the assignment.
Describe your first strategy for adding student choice:
Describe your second strategy for adding student choice:
Describe your third strategy for adding student choice:

Figure 11.7: Add student choice to an assignment.

*Visit **go.SolutionTree.com/instruction** for a free reproducible version of this figure.*

Quick Consolidation: Set Safe Classroom Norms

Creating an upbeat, emotionally positive class climate is no Pollyanna idea. The science is rock solid. This chapter reminds you to create and maintain norms in your classroom that foster a rich classroom climate that offers your students physical and emotional safety and a simple set of enforceable rules that encourage positive behavior, smart decision making, and dedicated effort. With this firmly in mind, answer the following reflection questions on how you can help make your classroom one that orchestrates the warm, uplifting climate that allows your students to flourish and bloom.

1. What do you know or understand about the importance of safe classroom norms to your students?

2. What physical safety concerns might your students have that are unique to your specific classroom environment? What new practices will you adopt in your classroom to ensure students understand a safety procedure?

3. Who are some students that show signs of feeling emotionally unsafe in your classroom? In the past, how have your responded to those signs, and how will you change your response to ensure they feel emotionally safe?

4. After reading and understanding the cool rules in this chapter, what changes will you make to your existing classroom rules to make them more effective?

5. What new and cool rules can you think of that you can use to replace existing rules that aren't effective?

CHAPTER 12

FOSTER ACADEMIC OPTIMISM

This chapter is all about creating a classroom climate where students *believe* they can achieve crazy high gutsy goals. In school, students understand quickly whether they are good at something (or not). Like most of us, they learn to predict how they'll do in class, based partially on past experiences. This prediction of expectations is important because it regulates how much effort they're willing to expend. As a teacher, you should know why you expend energy to create this type of class climate. Use the survey in figure 12.1 to assess the effort you currently expend.

What strategies or expectations do you set for your students, and what is your approach to helping achieve them?		
Do you feel like you engender in your students an expectation of success? (Circle one.)	Yes	No
What are some examples of ways you engaged a struggling student with this attitude?		
Do you go out of your way to create a sense of ownership by using words like *we*, *us*, and *together*? (Circle one.)	Yes	No
When there are discipline issues in your class, do you opt for a restorative approach rather than a punitive approach? (Circle one.)	Yes	No
Describe your strategies for handling discipline issues in your classroom.		

Figure 12.1: Consider how you foster an atmosphere of success.

Visit go.SolutionTree.com/instruction for a free reproducible version of this figure.

As we've seen previously, the effect size of having an expectation of success is sky-high at 1.44 (Hattie, 2009). That's why from day one highly effective teachers quickly take charge in each new class raising and creating strong, new, more optimistic expectations. If you fail to raise the mental and academic bar (with enthusiasm and gutsy goals), you'll allow students to expect and live out low expectations, and that action changes your climate (for the worse). This chapter builds on the positivity mindset of optimism and hope (see chapter 7, page 79) to establish five strategies for fostering that climate in your own classroom: (1) change the roles, (2) show the evidence, (3) change the game, (4) make mastery the endgame, and (5) create a sense of ownership.

Change the Roles

Many teachers find that the quickest way for students to think differently is to step into another role. In a high-poverty school in New Orleans, former English teacher Whitney Henderson (2012) got her students hooked in with a different tool: vision. To shift the student perspective, she asks students to write about two questions. First, they must answer, "Who do you want to be in life?" The *who* is a career label such as teacher, writer, or scientist. The change in student identity is critical. As we cover in chapter 10 (page 111), it invites students to begin to get inside the head of that occupation and prompts them to imagine and take on the character traits to be the dream occupation they want to be.

Second, they must answer, "What traits are important to being a _____?" These students are beginning the process of developing their psychological profile and new life narrative for thinking differently, as a successful role model. Have students use the worksheet in figure 12.2 to answer these questions.

Student name: *Rosa Lopez*
Who do you want to be in life? *Scientist*
What traits are important to being a *scientist* ? (Use your answer from the first question.)
A scientist must be curious and relentless in the search for answers.

Figure 12.2: Define your future.

Visit go.SolutionTree.com/instruction for a free reproducible version of this figure.

Having students answer these questions in this way gives them a clear understanding of the traits they must take on. This changing of roles can establish a powerful shift in mindsets that fosters academic optimism.

Show the Evidence

Katie Lyons, a former middle school history teacher from Chicago, wants her students to know that success is possible, and success can happen in her class. To do this, she records and plays student-produced documentaries and performances (Lyons, 2012). She displays exhibits that former students developed, navigates student-created websites, and shows papers that students have authored. She shows every class what students their own age can do when they reach for the stars. When it is time to ask students to do their best, every student knows this means to shoot for the stars. They can see real, detailed, and concrete examples of what quality work looks like. This kind of evidence gives students the vision and confidence that their goal is doable. Use figure 12.3 to brainstorm ideas you can use with students in your classroom.

Former students who have had professional success	What did they do?	How can you show or highlight this success for your students?

Figure 12.3: Identifying inspiring work of former students.

*Visit **go.SolutionTree.com/instruction** for a free reproducible version of this figure.*

Change the Game

Sometimes students feel that they cannot succeed at a certain task. When you have a sense students feel this way, change the game to improve classroom climate. That means you must identify a negative perception they have and change it—change who the students think they are, change what they think about a subject, or change how they see your role as a teacher in their lives.

Every teacher must sell students on the fact that what they are being asked to do in school is important, relevant, and urgent. For example, students' writing can tell a powerful story about themselves and, in so doing, maybe change the world. By using the Author's Chair activity, where students sit in front of the class in an "author's chair" and read their story, students form a comfort level among peers. Other students may also ask a question or share comments. They are becoming writers who are already changing the world, starting with themselves. The game was changed. When you have a topic or lesson coming up that you know will be challenging, use figure 12.4 to plan some strategies that will inspire students and change how they think about what they can do.

Lesson or topic: _____

What will make this difficult for my students?

_____

_____

_____

_____

What are some real-world examples of people using aspects of this lesson or topic to achieve great things?

_____

_____

_____

_____

What is an activity I can use to engage students that works in conjunction with these examples and will help them believe they can also achieve this task?

_____

_____

_____

_____

Figure 12.4: Changing the game.

*Visit **go.SolutionTree.com/instruction** for a free reproducible version of this figure.*

Make Mastery the Endgame

As we established in chapter 4, mastery is a process and destination. For instance, an effective teacher says, "I don't just want them to get it right. I want them to become so proficient that they rarely get it wrong. Only then, we'll move on." The mastery process is about developing a lifelong skill, such as perseverance, that makes complex, challenging learning worthwhile. This factor is not just good teaching. In mastery, there is no trying hard, doing your personal best, or being just good enough. The mastery process is a personal quest. There is no secret to mastery, but role modeling it does wonders. To do this, set gutsy goals (see page 41), and continually reinforce the big goal as well as the success made on the micro goals. Share examples of prior students reaching mastery, and point out who is on track to reach mastery. And, remember to celebrate small milestones (micro goals).

Create a Sense of Ownership

Remember to use the words *we* and *us* to say, "We're all in this together." This invites students to see the classroom experience as shared. That sharing invites them to be more likely to assert their sense of control over the classroom world (in a good way). They may embrace the opportunity of classroom responsibilities. When students own the climate, everything changes. Ownership comes in many forms.

Make discipline restorative instead of punitive (Riedl, Jensen, Call, & Tomasello, 2015). Make it about repairing relationships so that, if a student misbehaves, you give him or her the chance to come forward and make things right. For example, have the student sit down in a circle and talk out what happened with the teacher and the other involved parties. The mediator asks restorative questions like, "What happened? How did it happen? What can we do to make it right?" You can use the worksheet in chapter 11 (see figure 11.5, page 121) to help facilitate this process with students. Ultimately, it all leads to making a plan that all parties can live with, and the relationships are repaired and strengthened. Bottom line, the students are not disciplined.

At the grades K–5 level, you may also use cooperative learning and class jobs to empower students. Remember, all K–5 jobs should have recognizable titles that pay real money in the real world. At the grades 6–12 level, you could also have a classroom drawing, list jobs upfront, and have students complete resumes or applications, and use interviews to fill all the jobs available. These jobs would be for four to six weeks each. Students are welcome to trade jobs with another student if both parties agree. The key feature of ownership is that the job is necessary (and relevant) to help make the class work. Table 12.1 lists jobs for elementary students, with old and new classroom job titles. Table 12.2 lists more advanced jobs and descriptions for grades 6–12 students. You could, of course, come up with another dozen much-needed classroom jobs (using the real-world job titles is critical). Brainstorm other jobs you could use in class, and jot them down.

Regardless of the specific list, you can have students fill out an application like the one in figure 12.5 (page 130) to have them think and reflect about the class role they want and why they want it. Note in the figure that there is a spot for students to include a reference from someone else in the class. When you adopt the Fifty-Fifty Rule (see page 20) for increasing classroom collaboration, your students will get a lot of experience working together. The idea with using references in this context is to take advantage of this relationship building to ensure every student has a positive thing to say about a peer he or she has worked with.

Table 12.1: Class Jobs for Grades K–5 Students

Old Title	New Title
Line leader	Tour guide
Caboose	Security officer
Paper passer-outer	Materials handler
Pet monitor	Zookeeper
Bathroom monitor	Security
Teacher helper	Assistant teacher
Plant waterer	Botanist
Fish helper	Marine biologist
Messenger	FedEx or UPS worker
Lights	Electrician

Table 12.2: Class Jobs for Grades 6–12 Students

Title	Description
Chief learning officer (CLO)	The CLO ensures that no one snickers, laughs, makes fun of, or criticizes students in class. The CLO raises his or her hand and says "rerun" whenever there is an infraction, and the offending student apologizes and the student reoffers his or her contribution.
Chief safety officer (CSO)	The CSO says "rerun" for any instances of horseplay, grabbing, trash talking, or unsafe behavior. The offending student will back up and retrace his or her actions, apologizing if necessary.
IT specialist (ITS) or media specialist	The ITS or media specialist helps keep class technology running smoothly and supports other students (or the teacher) in effectively using it.
Key grip (KG)	The KG acts as a general-purpose handyman, responsible for setup, lighting, staging, and management.
Communications and publicity specialist (CAPS)	The CAPS shares news, weather reports, class progress on a project, team scores on a recent quiz, or class announcements.
Disk jockey (DJ)	The DJ is responsible for playing teacher-approved music at opportune times (such as when transitioning activities or entering and exiting the class), using the class iPod, computer, or radio. (Consider the following songs: "On Top of the World," Imagine Dragons; "Best Day of My Life, " American Authors; "Glad All Over," Carl Perkins; "Positive Vibration," Bob Marley; "Happy," Pharrell Williams; "Enjoy Yourself," The Jacksons.)
Environmental protection agent (EPA)	The EPA ensures that the physical environment is optimized—no trash or debris on the floor, waste gets recycled if possible, and the classroom is clean.

Class Job
APPLICATION

Name: _____

Job you are applying for: _____

Why do you want this job?

What prior jobs have you had in this class or in other classes?

What skills or prior experience do you already have that will help you succeed in this job?

Who is someone you've worked or partnered with in this class who can be your reference?

Figure 12.5: Application for class jobs.

*Visit **go.SolutionTree.com/instruction** for a free reproducible version of this figure.*

Quick Consolidation: Foster Academic Optimism

A rich classroom climate ensures students have a stake in the game and a reason to participate. Give them a sense of control over their daily experiences. It has to become "our class" and be an optimistic one. With this firmly in mind, answer the following reflection questions on how you will build and strengthen students' academic optimism.

1. What do you know or understand about the importance of ensuring students feel positive about their ability to succeed and master your class content?

2. When you use the Change the Roles strategy to get students thinking about their future, what are examples you can give them to help stimulate their imagination and broaden their thinking? What will help them to aim high?

3. What are some ways you can connect the Show the Evidence and Change the Game strategies in this chapter with your course content to help build up student attitudes of success?

4. How can you continue to revise and refine group and individual goals to inspire your students to achieve mastery?

5. What are some jobs with real-world names you can come up with that fit with your classroom needs? How will you implement them in your class?

Reflect on the Rich Classroom Climate Mindset

All meaningful and lasting change starts with a mirror. When you engage with this reflection remember that it's up to you to create the optimal conditions for learning; put people first and everything else second. Now that you understand the concept of the rich classroom climate mindset and have strategies to ensure your classroom fulfills its promise, it's time to self-assess and reflect on what comes next. Use the following questions to accomplish this.

1. When you look objectively at your classroom, do you see evidence that its climate fosters greatness? If not, reread these strategies to find the tool you need to move forward.

2. What strategy from part four will have the most impact on your classroom climate? When you put it into practice, how will you determine its effects?

3. What is the impact of your classroom's existing rules on its climate? What changes should you make that will help improve it?

4. What new activities can you implement that will help students believe in their ability to succeed in your class?

5. When your students struggle or show signs that they aren't buying into your climate-setting practices, how will you connect with them and raise them up?

PART FIVE

IMPLEMENTING THE ENRICHMENT MINDSET

Like many teachers at the beginning of the school year, I used to notice myself making instant judgments about my students as they arrived. I am embarrassed to admit thinking things like, "I'll bet she will do really well" or "He probably won't do that well." Even though I thought of myself as positive and encouraging to my students, in retrospect, I would bet that students could sense my small doubts. In fact, I'm sure they were hearing, "My teacher doesn't like me or believe in me." Take a moment to self-assess the assumptions you make about individual students when they enter your classroom. See figure P5.1 (page 134).

As you reflect on your answers, it may be tempting to think things like, "It's only human to think this way." Although you might be right, your goal is to maximize every student's potential, and this kind of thinking interferes with that. Think about how you respond when students struggle. How do your students respond to their own struggles? Your students respond to the smallest gesture—a smile, their name, a compliment, or encouragement on an assignment. Personalize the learning and use this to frame equity from the conversation to action steps.

The following chapters are all about building the enrichment mindset. The enrichment mindset rejects statements like, "He tried hard, but bless his heart; it's not going to happen," and takes the growth mindset further because adopting it changes the decisions you make, which in turn changes your behaviors. Behaviors over time become habits, and those habits become your character. The enrichment mindset says, "I know brains can change. I can grow and change myself first. Then, I can build powerful cognitive skills in my students."

1. How often do you find yourself judging students' abilities based on only initial impressions of their presence in your classroom? What is your best guess for the ratio of positive (this student will do well) and negative (this student will probably struggle) thoughts you have? What does this ratio tell you about your mindset about students' potential?

_____

_____

_____

_____

2. In what ways might your students pick up on your internal thoughts and motivations? How might this affect them? In particular, how might this affect students from poverty who may already experience overwhelming negativity about their capacity to learn?

_____

_____

_____

_____

3. Do you expect all students to approach their learning in the same way regardless of the experiences they bring into your classroom? How much effort do you devote to understanding the cognitive load students carry with them and how that might affect their learning?

_____

_____

_____

_____

4. How much time do you devote, in conjunction with your lessons, to helping students learn how to think about their work and their learning?

_____

_____

_____

_____

5. As part of your teaching, what strategies do you present to your students that could help them be more effective in their own studies?

_____

_____

_____

_____

Figure P5.1: Assess your understanding of how you perceive students' abilities and potential.

Visit go.SolutionTree.com/instruction for a free reproducible version of this figure.

> The enrichment mindset says, "I know brains can change. I can grow and change myself first. Then, I can build powerful cognitive skills in my students."

The enrichment mindset is critical. In short, it is often our mindsets and our internal narratives about why we were failing that shape our future. All of us fail at some point. The question to ask yourself is, "How do I respond to failure, both personally and as a teacher? I will learn and grow from my mistakes. Mistakes are feedback that helps me get better." Remember, the enrichment mindset broadens the growth mindset.

When we attribute our failures to the faults of others or a lack of our own ability, circumstances, IQ, genes, or talent, we get discouraged (Dweck, 2008). If we label our failures as normal, everyday setbacks, and we tie them to temporary (and changeable) variables, setbacks are likely to fuel us. Those variables include lack of effort, a poor attitude, inappropriate strategy, lack of tools, and insufficient experience.

Likewise, researchers commonly associate low socioeconomic status with differences in performance on a variety of academic endeavors (Farah et al., 2006; Gottfried, Gottfried, Bathurst, Guerin, & Parramore, 2003; Hackman & Farah, 2009). These differences usually involve three core neurocognitive systems: (1) language, (2) memory, and (3) cognitive control. These cognitive differences, which we explore in-depth in *Poor Students, Rich Teaching, Revised Edition* (Jensen, 2019), occur more among the poor (versus the middle class) and can reduce school performance. A variety of home, neighborhood, and school factors contribute to them. The good news is that strong teaching can moderate all of these differences. The variable here is relationships.

This part establishes the fundamentals for building an enrichment mindset in yourself and your students. The next three chapters offer the following strategies to help you enrich your students.

1. Manage the cognitive load.
2. Strengthen thinking skills.
3. Enhance study skills and vocabulary.

Make no mistake, this is your opportunity to show your own capacity to grow and help students graduate. Help your students develop the mindset they need to succeed. You'll never regret your decision.

Questions for Daily Reflection

Each day, consider your own mindset for helping students enrich their own academic experience by focusing on how you will help your students to better manage their cognitive load, develop their thinking skills, and refine their study habits. Then, answer the following questions.

1. Today, I will be on the lookout for students who appear to be stressed out to the point of distraction. How will I tailor my teaching approach to help them manage their cognitive load?

2. As part of my instruction, what strategy will I use today to help my students approach and think about their learning more effectively?

3. When assigning work and study topics to my students, what strategy will I give them to improve the effectiveness of their work?

CHAPTER 13

MANAGE THE COGNITIVE LOAD

Before we get started on enriching your students' brains, you should know what you're up against. Students with extremely difficult lives at home (such as those who face abuse, experience severe neglect, or must care for a younger sibling) will find their minds wandering as they ponder questions like, "What will it be like when I go home after school?" Thoughts on personal safety are strong and recurring, and they will compete with, or block out, thoughts about the class content. They may be hungry and unable to concentrate or can be wondering where they will sleep that night. A student with this much stress has a serious *cognitive load*. Use the survey in figure 13.1 to establish what you understand about how a high cognitive load affects outlook and behavior.

How often do you feel too overwhelmed in your personal life to focus on teaching? (Circle one.)	All the time	Sometimes	Rarely
Describe the ways it affects your teaching when you feel this way. What do you do to cope and stay focused?			
Do you have students who often seem disinterested in learning or unable to focus? (Circle one.)		Yes	No
What is your assessment of where these behaviors come from? How does your interpretation of these behaviors affect your view of those students?			
Do you adjust your teaching strategies or practices to address high stress levels in your students? (Circle one.)		Yes	No
What do you do to help students re-engage with classroom content when they appear overwhelmed by outside issues?			

Figure 13.1: Assess your approach to a high cognitive load.

*Visit **go.SolutionTree.com/instruction** for a free reproducible version of this figure.*

Cognitive load is the quantity of thoughts one has loaded in his or her brain at any given time. It's difficult for students from poverty to concentrate on homework when they have to think about daily survival. Students from poverty typically experience even greater cognitive load in learning environments than those in middle-class families (Siegler & Alibali, 2005). It's like having very slow internet speed. Unless you address this, you'll perceive such students as slow learners because they'll often appear distracted and forgetful and ask questions you just answered a moment ago. A student's cognitive ability has an over-the-top effect size on student achievement of 1.04 (Hattie, 2009). But students carrying a heavy cognitive load can't achieve great things when they are mentally consumed with survival (Jensen, 2019).

In this chapter, I offer some tools you can use to counter the cognitive load on the brain and another set of tools for strengthening students' knowledge retrieval skills.

Tools to Reduce Cognitive Load Issues

Cognitive load consumes students who worry about how their teacher or peers treat them. The key to offsetting it is to make sure that students know that their feelings are important to you and that you care about them. Many times students will check out because new content overwhelms them. Here are simple and powerful tools to help students succeed in demanding, sometimes stressful, content-rich classrooms.

- Chunk material.
- Hit the pause button.

- Stretch the content.
- Implement spaced relevance.

In addition to these strategies, having physically and emotionally safe classrooms (as we discussed in chapter 11, page 117) are also paramount in reducing students' cognitive load. You'll notice that each of these simple tools helps students care more, digest better, or remember longer.

Chunk Material

Why is chunking more important to students from poverty than nonpoor students? Chronic stress impairs working memory. Working memory is the skill of holding pictures or sounds in your head and manipulating them to come up with answers or opinions. When teachers cover content quickly, students are often overwhelmed. They may not have the background or the working memory to process it at the same pace, so they tune out. Break things into three- to six-minute chunks to produce sizable gains (Russell, Hendricson, & Herbert, 1984; Marzano, 2017), and invest more time in retrieving previous content, not adding more. Chunking your content into smaller, bite-sized pieces helps students digest more easily; avoid bigger chunks that they simply forget. Use figure 13.2 to help chunk out your lesson plans by breaking them up into pieces and establishing connections for retrieval of previous content.

Hit the Pause Button

On a micro scale, adding more pauses to the content is helpful (Jennings, 2015; Ruhl, Hughes, & Schloss, 1987). Preview the content you'll cover that day for the class, and then pause. After the opening of your class, summarize it in one to two sentences, and then pause. Pause after any strong statement. At the beginning of the year (or semester), be blunt; simply tell students, "Write this down; it's important." Invite students to lean in and listen closely. Pause before and after an important thought. Soon your students will realize that the pause is a cue: this is important; write this down! You can use figure 13.3 (page 140) to determine where the best chance for a quick pause lies within your lessons.

Lesson or unit topic:

Key component	Time to cover (in minutes)	Connected retrieval content

Notes and strategies:

Key component	Time to cover (in minutes)	Connected retrieval content

Notes and strategies:

Key component	Time to cover (in minutes)	Connected retrieval content

Notes and strategies:

Key component	Time to cover (in minutes)	Connected retrieval content

Notes and strategies:

Figure 13.2: Tool for chunking lesson plans.

*Visit **go.SolutionTree.com/instruction** for a free reproducible version of this figure.*

Lesson topic: _____

Date you will cover this lesson: __/__/__

Describe the scope and purpose of this lesson.

_____

_____

_____

List the lesson's key points.	Will you pause here before continuing? (circle one)
	Yes No
	Yes No
	Yes No
	Yes No
	Yes No

Figure 13.3: Find the pauses in your lesson plans.

*Visit **go.SolutionTree.com/instruction** for a free reproducible version of this figure.*

Unless you are building working memory daily, you'll need to adjust your teaching for students who are unable to manage their own cognitive load. Provide more time to make notes and point out when to do it. Say things like, "Grab your pens, and jot this down. You'll need to know it for later."

Stretch the Content

Research suggests that when teachers space learning out over time, students experience better quality of understanding and retrieval (Rohrer, Dedrick, & Stershic, 2015). *Spaced learning*, also known as distributed practice, is the process of using repeated learning experiences, separated by spaces or timed gaps, for processing and application. The concept is simple: "Too much, too fast, it won't last." This factor ranks high with a 0.71 effect size (Hattie, 2009). Learning is massed when there's little or no gap in the stream of content. Instead, prime students for future learning by introducing tough concepts days and weeks in advance with previews and advance organizers. Then, after the unit is finished, refer to the prior learning, using reviews a week later, and integrate it into the next unit. For example, if you think a unit will take two weeks to complete, adjust your schedule to allow it to take three to four weeks, and overlap it with the prior and upcoming units. Note that the best review is retrieval, not just looking at familiar content (see the next section). Give students time to think and figure out what they know instead of looking it up.

Of course, not all teachers have this sort of freedom or latitude with their planning. Although this may be a challenge, make it your goal to break your content areas up into four parts (periods) and teach 85 percent of the content during the middle periods, and 15 percent during the extended first and last periods. In my experience, the results are well worth the effort. You can also combine this strategy with the Chunk Material strategy. For example, use the chunking worksheets (see figure 13.2, page 139) to plan out three lessons, then use the worksheet in figure 13.4 to integrate them together in a way that spaces out the content.

Unit 1 (previous topic): _____	Days required to teach: _____
Unit 2 (current topic): _____	Days required to teach: _____
Unit 3 (next topic): _____	Days required to teach: _____

Period 1	
Time to spend on unit 1 (85 percent of available time): _____	Time to spend introducing unit 2 (15 percent of available time): _____
Key topic areas and notes:	Key topic areas and notes:

Period 2	
Time to spend on unit 2 (85 percent of available time): _____	Time to spend on unit 1 retrieval (15 percent of available time): _____
Key topic areas and notes:	Key topic areas and notes:

Period 3	
Time to spend on unit 2 (85 percent of available time): _____	Time to spend on unit 3 introduction (15 percent of available time): _____
Key topic areas and notes:	Key topic areas and notes:

Period 4	
Time to spend on unit 3 (85 percent of available time): _____	Time to spend on unit 2 retrieval (15 percent of available time): _____
Key topic areas and notes:	Key topic areas and notes:

Figure 13.4: Tool for stretching out lesson content.

*Visit **go.SolutionTree.com/instruction** for a free reproducible version of this figure.*

Tools to Strengthen Retrieval

When we teach well, we bring students into the content, and they understand it well. But there's another critical piece to the academic puzzle: recalling learning at test time. For many, learning and recall are the same. Many believe that if we learn it, we should be able to recall it. But a large amount of what we learn is implicit (not taught to us explicitly) so we only retrieve it with a cue. This can be especially true for students bearing a heavy cognitive load. "What's the name of the cross street near where you live?" That simple cue gives you the important difference: memory is what the brain stores; recall is what you can retrieve when you need it.

Frequency of use, relevance, and intensity of the memory are what mediate the gap between the two. You can recall a lot when the stress is low and there's friendly banter full of prompts and cues for prior memories. A family reunion or brainstorming in a classroom is a social vehicle that prompts our recall. But retrieval is different. Retrieval is the ability to generate the information without prompts such as social clues, multiple-choice tests, or verbal prompts. Retrieval practice at school is a huge yet enormously underused tool to strengthen recall, and it is far more effective than a simple study review (Jensen, 2019).

Spelling tests are a good example of familiarity versus retrieval. Students can think they know the words after rereading them several times, but when tested, they may not. It is the hard work of retrieval that helps cement the accurate memory. If a student looks up the right answer beforehand, he or she defeats the purpose of the activity.

In your classroom, retrieval practice can take the shape of any of the items listed in figure 13.5. Use the blank spaces to add some of your own.

Retrieval Tools	
Using self-quizzing time	Asking students to do the hard work of selectively remembering what they learned earlier (or the day before)
Letting students practice the learning several times using different strategies, such as flipcharts one day and verbal instruction the next	Using different problem types (such as for word and number problems, lists, narratives and characters, facts, inferences, and cause and effect)
Varying the process by making the retrieval social one day (with a partner or group) and independent the next (writing from memory)	

Figure 13.5: Ways to strengthen retrieval.

*Visit **go.SolutionTree.com/instruction** for a free reproducible version of this figure.*

Switching up the use of verbal and nonverbal strategies is effective. Using more nonverbal strategies helps to represent the learning differently (using the body, showing the learning, gesturing, or building it). Simply creating a visual map (graphic organizer) can boost retention high enough to contribute to student achievement from one to even two years of gains (Petty, 2009). Students can choose from among many ways to represent learning, so give them choice (such as from creating a cartoon, tree diagram, swim-lane chart, mind map, Venn diagram, bubble map, storyboard, cause-and-effect chart, flowchart, tables, or graphs).

Here are two nonverbal ways to enrich students' recall of your content—(1) using visual organizers and (2) gesturing the content.

Use Visual Organizers

Use visual organizers such as mind maps, time sequences, concept pattern organizers, target diagrams, cartoons, Venn diagrams, tree diagrams, flowcharts, cluster maps, spider webs, continuum diagrams, concept maps, or descriptive pattern organizers. David Hyerle's (1996) book *Visual Tools for Constructing Knowledge* is excellent. Use these first as a pretest. Ask students to show what they know in ten minutes. Then, use the visual organizer to preassess prior knowledge. You can also use them for a formative assessment or summative assessment. Using these can produce effect sizes on student achievement of up to 1.2 (Marzano, 1998). Figure 13.6 illustrates a sample visual organizer you can use with students.

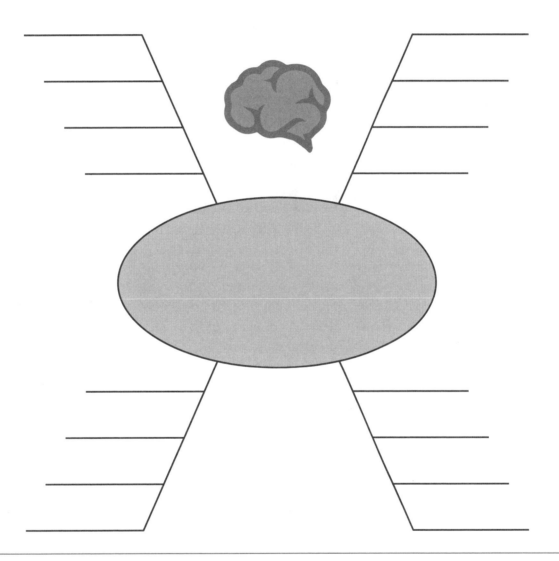

Figure 13.6: Sample visual organizer.

*Visit **go.SolutionTree.com/instruction** for a free reproducible version of this figure.*

Gesture the Content

When teachers gesture key concepts, it allows students to hear what they're saying without having to visualize it. This may mean acting out or showing something just through the use of expressions or hands alone. Gesturing reduces students' cognitive load and helps them learn (Ping & Goldin-Meadow, 2010). For example, you can use movement in mathematics to gesture the numbers, signs, equations, and answers (go to www.mathandmovement.com for ideas).

The idea is to avoid speaking or showing a picture. Here are two examples: (1) to illustrate a big idea, ask students to stretch their hands way out to either side, and (2) if one thing is way better than another, stand on a chair, point to the ceiling, and balance by touching a chair or student's shoulder. Another activity is to ask students to identify the two to three main concepts of the lesson. They can brainstorm a list of potential ideas first, and then vote on them within their teams. Next, take the top two and create a physical way to demonstrate them. See figure 13.7.

Brainstorm three concepts from the lesson.

1. _____

2. _____

3. _____

Choose the top two of these and describe a way to physically demonstrate these concepts.

Concept 1	Concept 2

Figure 13.7: Gesture key content.

*Visit **go.SolutionTree.com/instruction** for a free reproducible version of this figure.*

Quick Consolidation: Manage the Cognitive Load

Cognitive load issues are huge with students from poverty. You may see and hear students in class who often seem distracted, unfocused, inattentive, and impulsive. These are common symptoms of a stress disorder, because when the brain is consumed with survival, it uses up mental space it needs for academic excellence. You can either notice the issue and make the students the problem or change what you do and help them succeed. With this firmly in mind, answer the following reflection questions on what you've learned about helping students manage their cognitive load.

1. What do you know or understand about cognitive loads and how they affect student behavior and importance that you didn't know when you started this chapter?

2. What tools from this chapter can you use in your practice to help students manage their cognitive load?

3. What are some ways you can adapt these strategies to your specific instructional focus and needs?

4. What strategies from the relational or positivity mindsets can you use in conjunction with the strategies in this chapter to better recognize when a student has reached his or her cognitive limit and requires intervention to ease his or her load?

5. In what ways will you shift your instructional practices to make more time for students to learn retrieval skills? What will you do differently to ensure this time focuses specifically on sound retrieval practices instead of recall?

CHAPTER 14

STRENGTHEN THINKING SKILLS

Doing everything in your power to enrich students' brains means reviewing the effects of poverty and continuously making connections. Poverty commonly affects the cognitive skill base in students that schools value, which includes attentional skills, speed of processing, and memory. But what are thinking skills, and can we teach them? Use the survey in figure 14.1 to assess your current mindset toward thinking skills.

Do you have a strong grasp of what thinking skills are and why they're important? (Circle one.)	Yes		No
Describe how you define the concept of thinking skills. What makes these skills critical to learning?			
How much instructional time do you spend on helping students think more effectively about content? (Circle one.)	I build thinking skills into teaching.	I don't teach thinking skills, but they are important.	It's not my job to teach thinking skills.
Describe your strategy to teach students thinking skills as part of your instruction. If you don't address thinking skills as part of your teaching, why not?			
Are you aware of how poverty affects students' cognitive abilities? (Circle one.)	Yes		No
Describe how you believe poverty affects thinking. What strategies, if any, do you use to counteract these negative effects?			

Figure 14.1: Assess your knowledge of thinking skills.

*Visit **go.SolutionTree.com/instruction** for a free reproducible version of this figure.*

Thinking skills are a broad category. When we say that a student has good thinking skills, we often include the ability to pay attention; exert a strong locus of control; evaluate, process, prioritize, and sequence content; hold information in short-term memory; compare and contrast; extrapolate and use working memory while manipulating the content; and finally, defer gratification until the answers are necessary. That's more than half a dozen subskills and one reason why thinking skills are a challenge to teach.

Because it is nearly impossible to declare a universal thinking formula, the process of teaching students to think critically is far more effective if you empower students to do the right type of thinking at the right time. Cognitive expert Daniel Willingham (2008) asserts the thinking must be novel, not a memorized formula from a familiar situation. He also says critical thinking is self-directed; the thinker must be doing the thinking, not following a teacher's or coach's prompts. This understanding is what real enrichment is all about.

In fact, a good bit of evidence shows thinking skills can be taught, if you know how to do it right—and if you believe in the enrichment mindset, which says you can change and grow. In this chapter, we'll go through the evidence and supporting strategies for teaching these skills, and we'll examine some strategies to help you support top-flight thinking in your students. You can find additional strategies in *Poor Students, Rich Teaching, Revised Edition* (Jensen, 2019).

Strategies for Teaching Thinking Skills

Thinking skills are part of a student's clear path to graduation. Reasoning is an important thinking skill that can and should be taught with two specific rules in place: (1) having a high-performing teacher and (2) transferring the skill to dissimilar material weakens results (Barnett & Ceci, 2002; Reeves & Weisberg, 1994). When teaching tools for thinking skills to students, it's important to do so within the context of the content you have. In other words, these skills have moderate to low transfer. Use your own subject matter and foster the skills that apply to your class. A student may mount an argument against a nominal issue, missing the bigger point.

You can use the planning sheet in figure 14.2 to think about how you can connect your course content to a range of tools for optimal reasoning. Note that this list offers generic steps to teach and learn reasoning skills. It's not a formula but rather a set of reminders.

Over time, teach students to use every tool on this list so they'll be able to learn the right tools for the right problems. This means teaching thinking skills across the curriculum. In the following sections, I'll spell out some specific strategies.

Teach the Language of Thinking

Start with the basics of thinking—language—as some students need this background knowledge. Your students need consistent encouragement to learn and use the academic language of school. This is the foundation for reasoning. The words we choose represent the concepts and details of any reasoning we do. Without the correct word (or gesture, object, or other representation) to represent our thoughts, we cannot be accurate or complete in our thinking. Explain the following phrases, and then check for understanding.

- "Here's what this argument means."
- "What other words are similar to *means*?"
- "If I cut up a dessert into smaller pieces, what am I doing?" (Depending on the words your students use, question them: "Does *cut* mean *divide*, does *share* mean *divide*, does *split up* mean *divide*?")

Lesson plan or topic: _____

Choose three tools from the following list and write down your initial ideas for how you can connect some aspect of this topic with one of these tools.

Seek (read, listen, and experience).

Check claims, evidence, and biases.

Apply standards (discriminate input).

Use inductive and deductive reasoning.

Interpret and define the true problem.

Make predictions and inferences.

Analyze (by both whole and part).

Translate, explain, and take action.

Compare and contrast positions.

Tool 1: _____

_____

_____

_____

Tool 2: _____

_____

_____

_____

Tool 3: _____

_____

_____

_____

Figure 14.2: Assess your knowledge of thinking skills.

*Visit **go.SolutionTree.com/instruction** for a free reproducible version of this figure.*

Seek Out Information to Solve a Problem

First, encourage students to become curious learners and seek out relevant information. You can be a great role model for this process. In class every week, share something that fascinated you. If their role model is excited about learning, it will become contagious. Second, help them differentiate between various types of information and how they perceive it. Show them that the source of the material is key to understanding the type of reasoning to apply. The source may be a friend or a scholarly journal. Next, show students how to choose the correct problem to solve or argue. Use the seven-step framework for defining the true problem and honing students' reasoning skills featured in figure 14.3 (page 150).

To answer question 2, have students refer to the Business Insider infographic, *20 Cognitive Biases That Screw Up Your Decisions* (visit **go.SolutionTree.com/instruction** for a link to this infographic). Help them identify their own past biases to get to a clear-thinking pathway. Then, teach the many ways to approach a problem. Make a list of the types of problems to solve, and share how you would use different approaches with each. Model how to approach a problem, and have them use the seven-step framework worksheet to solve a similar problem.

Name: _____

1. Define the true problem.

_____
_____
_____

2. List personal biases you may have and how to overcome them.

_____
_____
_____

3. Generate two to five potential paths to take to solve the problem.

_____
_____
_____

4. Evaluate and select pathways, and then pick one to start.

_____
_____
_____

5. Implement your solutions.

_____
_____
_____

6. Analyze the results you obtained and try another, if needed.

_____
_____
_____

7. Summarize what you have learned.

_____
_____
_____

Figure 14.3: Framework to hone reasoning skills.

*Visit **go.SolutionTree.com/instruction** for a free reproducible version of this figure.*

Form Effective Arguments

Teach students that reasoning usually requires putting on different hats to see things from different points of view. Edward de Bono (1999) suggests six *thinking hats* (overview, information, benefits, creativity, feelings, and caution) to diversify thinking. You might also suggest using someone else's perspective ("I am going to look at this problem as a scientist, an ecologist, a businessperson, a mathematician, a politician, a church leader, or a school student"). There are endless ways to approach a problem. Your role is to help students get used to understanding any problem from more than one position.

As a thinking tool, walk through the five steps for forming an effective argument featured in figure 14.4. When students seem comfortable with the process, give them each a blank copy of this worksheet, have them pair up and take opposing views, and then describe their argumentative process using the worksheet.

Your name: _____ Your partner's name: _____	
Describe the argument. 	
Is your position for or against this argument? For ☐ Against ☐	

1. Describe your primary argument (for or against), and what you consider a valid alternative.

Your primary argument	Your alternative

2. Summarize the supporting evidence that backs up each argument.

For:	Against:

3. Analyze your partner's opposing views and supporting arguments.

4. Reflect on both your arguments and those of your partners and explain the reasoning for why one idea or bit of evidence is better than another.

5. Formulate your conclusions about the argument and what evidence would change a person's mind about it.

Figure 14.4: Form an effective argument.

*Visit **go.SolutionTree.com/instruction** for a free reproducible version of this figure.*

Use Argument Mapping

Next, it's time to illustrate and use visual thinking tools. Give students argument maps (such as a box-and-arrow or node-and-link diagram), which show the relationships, hierarchies, and links among all data pieces. (Rationale, www.rationaleonline.com, offers argument maps to support reasoning skills.) Argument mapping is semiformal, blending formal graph structure with natural language. You can think of it as addressing a design challenge: come up with a way to make a case and back it up with evidence. Researchers show that critical-thinking skills can be dramatically accelerated, with up to a 0.60 effect size, over one semester (van Gelder, 2015; van Gelder, Bissett, & Cumming, 2004). This suggests that argument mapping may foster college-prep thinking for K–12 students.

You might ask students to take their ideas and make a bubble map. They can put their key concept in the center. Ask them to make groups with new ways to divide up their words. When students add more concepts, it helps them see the breadth and depth of issues. Bubble maps help them start to identify the issues better based on relevance.

It's important to provide a model. What students need is not what you know (they can find that in a text or on the internet) but *how* you know what you know. This requires that you think like a beginner and literally write out the steps that one could follow to think like you. Teachers often post a model for the writing process or for solving word problems on the wall. Using models is a fantastic idea if you explain, refer to, and use them often. Use figure 14.5 to establish for students a basic problem-solving thinking model for arguments.

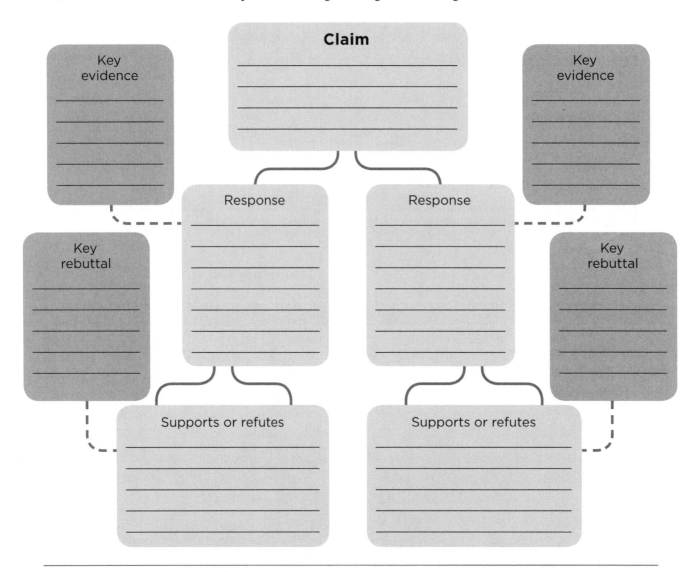

Figure 14.5: Basic problem-solving thinking model.

Visit ***go.SolutionTree.com/instruction*** *for a free reproducible version of this figure.*

Remember, a model is an outline of a procedure. Over time, a more advanced learner may embellish it or find shortcuts. But in the beginning, models can be priceless windows into the mental world of thinking skills. Using models is in my top-five list for smart cognitive skill building.

Use Powerful Questions

Teachers whose students struggle with reasoning typically ask one or two questions, often those that probe for answers like, "What is . . .?" or "Which of the . . .?" Teachers who excel at teaching reasoning use a sequence of questions to develop students' thinking. Figure 14.6 lists some powerful questions students can answer to examine and support their reasoning. They don't need to answer all the questions in this sheet. Depending on the context of their own questions, tell them which ones to focus on and come up with answers for.

Tell me, what claim are you making?

_____

_____

What's your evidence for saying _____?

_____

_____

Can you connect what another student has said to your comments? Do you feel different or the same; do you agree or disagree?

_____

_____

If _____ happened, what might happen next?

_____

_____

What are probable causes for _____?

_____

_____

Why did they do _____ this way, and can you think of other ways to do it?

_____

_____

Figure 14.6: Answer powerful questions.

Visit go.SolutionTree.com/instruction for a free reproducible version of this figure.

Whether you use a sheet like this or conduct a live conversation with your student, you should have your own process for using powerful questions. Here's mine.

- Provide sufficient wait time (five to ten minutes).

- Model how to answer (say, "That is true because of . . ."").

- Never accept easy answers (such as, "Yes," or "No," or "I don't know"). Challenge students to do more. Ask them to listen to the next two students and then make a fresh guess.

- Keep higher-order-question stems posted and refer to them often. Ensure everyone participates, and thank each student for contributing. Figure 14.7 (page 154) provides a series of these question stems with space to add more of your own.

Figure 14.7: Ask higher-order questions.

*Visit **go.SolutionTree.com/instruction** for a free reproducible version of this figure.*

You can say, "Thanks for jumping in" or "I love your ideas." The core understanding here is simple. Reasoning skills, one of the absolute basics of higher-order thinking and executive functioning, are a teachable process. If you fail to teach them, your students may miss out for the rest of their lives on the skills you take for granted. Now, let's take your students to an even higher cognitive level.

Support Top-Flight Thinking Skills

Over time, you'll become better at asking thinking questions that develop student brains. But to get to the highest levels, students also need to learn how to ask better questions. In *Making Thinking Visible: How to Promote Engagement, Understanding, and Independence for All Learners*, authors Ron Ritchhart, Mark Church, and Karin Morrison (2011) discuss the necessary scaffolding to enrich cognitive capacity.

The authors suggest and encourage using specific thinking routines every day to develop the skills. The three categories of routines are: (1) introducing and exploring ideas, (2) synthesizing and organizing, and (3) digging deeper. Have students use the worksheet in figure 14.8 to help support their deeper thinking into a specific topic or idea.

1. Describe the idea or topic you want to explore.

2. Describe your plan for exploring this idea.

3. Dig deeper into this exploration by answering the following questions.

What is a crucial point of view (that is not your own) for understanding the main idea? Describe the idea from that perspective.

What are five core assumptions you have about this topic? What is a question you could pose or problem about this assumption for which the answers could change your perspective?

What is the biggest problem from this list and how might solving it change your perspective?

What might critics be saying about this same topic and how might they be right?

How might people have viewed this idea twenty years ago, and what might people think about it twenty years into the future?

Figure 14.8: Think deeper about an idea or concept.

*Visit **go.SolutionTree.com/instruction** for a free reproducible version of this figure.*

This approach gives your students practice in writing, and you can further it by encouraging them to ask their peers questions. There's nothing new here, but it is the respect you show for your students, and hence, the culture of thinking, that gets fostered. Remind students that the questions they develop will bring the answers they want.

Teach your students thinking and questioning tools such as:

- Identifying what they know and what they need to ask more about

- Creating a circle of varied viewpoints and questions

- Employing statements like, "I used to think _____, and now I think _____."

- Fostering two opposing views and a verbal tug-of-war with questions

- Using sentence-phrase-word representation of meaning and new questions (students explain their thinking in one sentence, then shorten to a phrase, and then a word)

To develop top-flight thinking skills, you can also start with a simpler format, such as a three-step model like the worksheet in figure 14.9. Once students know the model, you'll be able to expand to use or add other models, such as the one in figure 14.8 (page 155).

What is your claim?

_____

_____

_____

What is your support for this claim?

_____

_____

_____

What questions do you still have? (Or, describe what else is true or not true.)

_____

_____

_____

Figure 14.9: A simple model for top-flight thinking.

*Visit **go.SolutionTree.com/instruction** for a free reproducible version of this figure.*

As you have seen, reasoning is actually a core cluster of skills, not just for school survival but, of course, for life. Students are not reasoning when they copy, recall, or complete simple tasks. Reasoning requires that students take information through a sequence of steps that allows them to understand it differently, find relevance, and change the representation of the information into a meaningful goal. You now have the tools to help them.

Quick Consolidation: Strengthen Thinking Skills

Any time a teacher complains that his or her students are not good at thinking, remember that the greatest probability is that no one has ever taught them to think. When teaching students to reason and think more effectively, different strategies fit different problems and situations. In this chapter, you saw a list of cognitive tools to use for any type of reasoning activity, although not all are mandatory for every situation. With this firmly in mind, answer the following reflection questions on what you've learned from this chapter and how you can integrate this new knowledge into your instructional practices.

1. What do you know or understand about the importance of the role of thinking skills in student learning that you didn't know when you started this chapter?

2. While teaching a unit, what new questions might you now ask students to gauge their learning? How will you change your process to give students time to develop and answer those questions?

3. What tools can you give to students to help them isolate and define a problem and the steps they can take to resolve it?

4. In what ways can you integrate the concept of asking powerful questions and forming effective arguments into your specific curriculum?

5. What new routines will you use to help your students develop top-flight thinking skills?

CHAPTER 15

ENHANCE STUDY SKILLS AND VOCABULARY

To develop the enrichment mindset, we must remember that the effects from poverty start early. From kindergarten on, the achievement gap widens between poor students and their middle-class peers, unless they catch up quickly—by the K–2 grades (Palardy & Rumberger, 2008). Most students from poverty end the K–5 experience right where they started it: behind grade level. Let me restate this: it is critical to teach students learn-to-learn skills (the steps and skills to start as a novice and become an expert), anything that builds cognitive capacity. Use the survey in figure 15.1 to assess your current mindset toward teaching learn-to-learn study skills.

Using your best estimate, what percentage of your students enter your classroom with a learning deficit that leaves them behind grade level? (Circle one.)	Less than one-third	About half	Two-thirds or more
Describe any strategies you use to help close this gap. (Or, what ideas can you think of that you haven't yet tried?)			
Do you consider the teaching of study skills and good study habits part of your teaching responsibilities? (Circle one.)		Yes	No
Describe some effective study skills you see your students use. How might you use these to aid students who show ineffective study skills or habits?			
How much time do you devote to helping students improve their vocabulary? (Circle one.)	I specifically teach new vocabulary every week.	I only teach new vocabulary when it connects to my teaching area.	I do not consider vocabulary a part of my teaching.
Describe the vocabulary deficits between your students from poverty and those with a healthier socioeconomic status. What could you do to close this gap?			

Figure 15.1: Assess your approach to developing students' study skills and vocabulary.

*Visit **go.SolutionTree.com/instruction** for a free reproducible version of this figure.*

Whatever your current approach to this topic, your thinking here should be simple; you must tell yourself, "If I don't better prepare my students, they may not make it." To that end, this chapter focuses on three brain builders—(1) contextual study skills, (2) relational study aids, and (3) vocabulary skill building—that are core for enriching students.

Contextual Study Skills

The use of specific study aids (such as study guides, study procedures, and advanced organizers like text outlines) shows very promising results with large effect sizes (0.77 and up; Petty, 2009). When the study process is fairly general (as in language arts) and more abstract, the research consensus is that direct teaching of all-purpose study skills is not highly effective—about a 0.45 effect size (Petty, 2009). Generic study skills can build confidence and improve attitude, but the effect size is unremarkable (Hattie, 2009).

Figure 15.2 lists the top study process achievement boosters (Petty, 2009) with space to write down your ideas for making use of them with the content you teach. These boosters should be in every student process for subject-specific study skills that you will develop, with help from your colleagues.

Achievement booster	Your ideas for helping students use these with your teaching
Relate the specific study method to the exact subject content. (Specifics work better than generalities.)	
Teach students metacognition skills to self-assess for depth and accuracy.	
Provide students thinking maps (bubble maps, flowcharts, or mind maps).	
When finished, debrief students with the questions, "How did you do that?" and "What can you do better?"	
Attribute student success to effort, attitude, and strategy.	
Practice content retrieval, not just a study review.	

Source: Petty, 2009.

Figure 15.2: Brainstorm ways to use high-impact study skills.

Visit **go.SolutionTree.com/instruction** for a free reproducible version of this figure.

Each high-impact study skill is powerful by itself. But when combined with the others, you will have the means to develop amazing learners. Walk students through each study step as a class. Then, let them do the step in pairs. Finally, when they have gained confidence, allow them to solve problems on their own.

Relational Study Aids

In addition to the establishing effective study skills, having students use study aids like summarizing and note taking can bump up progress with a 1.0 effect size (Marzano, 2001) or two years' worth of gains. Structural aids are strategies that show the specific framework of what students are learning. These aids, which might be an outline or other visual aid, have a strong effect size of 0.58 (but can go up to over 1.1), as 0.50 is one year's gain in academic achievement.

Relational study aids (bubble maps, mind maps, Venn diagrams, and so on) are highly contextual pending the course content and grade level, but done well, they help students see connections between the content and how to learn it. They are also underused and highly valuable. For example, figure 15.3 and figure 15.4 are two forms of a study aid for a mathematics class. The elementary flowchart in figure 15.3 is more student friendly, but both of these forms are helpful (versus using none at all), and a little creativity on your part can lead to a world of other possibilities for creating unique and beneficial study aids.

Mathematics Problem Solver

Figure 15.3: Sample mathematics study aid for elementary students.

Mathematics Problem Solving

1. **Begin with the right attitude.**
   "I can do this!"

2. **Determine the problem type.**
   Is the problem a word problem, an open problem, a closed problem, a logic problem, and so on?

3. **Analyze the problem.**
   What is known? What is unknown? What are the restrictions or limits? What can be estimated?

4. **Select a strategy.**
   Use an algorithm (a specific rule, procedure, or method); use formulas, graphic representations, or arithmetic operations; or turn it into a story with numeric or fictional characters.

5. **Check your work.**
   Look back and evaluate with reverse solving (use the answer to do the problem backwards), use a calculator, compare answers with an estimate, and check for common mistakes.

6. **Make a decision.**
   If your answer is not correct, retrace your steps and do steps 2, 3, and 4 again using a different approach. Try different solutions and eliminate those that don't work, or break the problem into smaller problems to solve. Ask a friend.

7. **Own the answer.**
   If the answer is correct, celebrate, and affirm your steps. Remember what to do next time.

Figure 15.4: Sample mathematics study aid for secondary students.

Work collaboratively with your school teams to create simple, five-to-seven-step grade-level study guides for your key content areas and incorporate them into the instructional process of retrieving the material a day or week later. These should include reading for depth, lower-level mathematics (addition, subtraction, multiplication, and division), and science. Making posters of the guides and referring to them in class are also helpful.

Vocabulary Skill Building

Students growing up in poverty often have a rich level of communication, especially in informal communication with peers and elders. However, although their informal communication is strong, a core component to predict academic achievement is academic vocabulary. Students with a low socioeconomic status often test low on academic vocabulary, meaning they have a harder time reaching academic success (Huttenlocher, Waterfall, Vasilyeva, Vevea, & Hedges, 2010).

When tested at age seven, high-performing students know and use an average of 7,100 root words, yet students in the lower quartile know and use 3,000 words. This gap (4,000-plus words) can be closed when the student learns five more words a day (in addition to those typically learned at grade level) for four to five years (Biemiller, 2003).

When you help students learn ten to twelve new words (relevant to tested material) per week, the gains over a year average 33 percentile points or a huge 0.95 effect size (Marzano, 2001). It's also imperative that teachers help students catch up and teach words that aren't specific to tested material but are academically general: like *rigorous*, *reflective*, or *assess*. Figure 15.5 provides a weekly planning sheet to help you come up with a list of words related the topic you are covering that week. At the end of the week, post this sheet in your classroom or share it with your students so they can refer to it when they need to.

Monday's lesson topic:	
New vocabulary word:	Definition:
Connection to topic:	
New vocabulary word:	Definition:
Connection to topic:	
Tuesday's lesson topic:	
New vocabulary word:	Definition:
Connection to topic:	
New vocabulary word:	Definition:
Connection to topic:	

Wednesday's lesson topic:	
New vocabulary word:	Definition:
Connection to topic:	
New vocabulary word:	Definition:
Connection to topic:	

Thursday's lesson topic:	
New vocabulary word:	Definition:
Connection to topic:	
New vocabulary word:	Definition:
Connection to topic:	

Friday's lesson topic:	
New vocabulary word:	Definition:
Connection to topic:	
New vocabulary word:	Definition:
Connection to topic:	

Reflect on this week.
What went well? What can you improve for next week?

Figure 15.5: Vocabulary-building planning sheet.

Visit go.SolutionTree.com/instruction for a free reproducible version of this figure.

When you ensure your students learn just ten extra words each week, that adds up to you exposing students to three hundred new vocabulary words a year. Over twelve years, this builds a 3,600-word database of academically relevant vocabulary. In the following sections, I offer three strategies to help you go even deeper with this strategy.

Role Model

Role model the use of the word. Use the word in a sentence, and then ask students to predict the meaning. Students can clarify their thinking by writing down the word in a worksheet like figure 15.6. If they don't get it, keep using it in new sentences, and let them work with others until they figure it out by consulting a thesaurus and a dictionary. Once you think they have a general idea of the definition, ask students to write or talk through a restated meaning in their own words with a partner. Then, they make their own interesting and accurate sentence using the word. Finally, ask them to draw the word and share the drawing.

Word	How did your teacher use it?	Based on this, what do you think it means?

Figure 15.6: Vocabulary role modeling.

*Visit **go.SolutionTree.com/instruction** for a free reproducible version of this figure.*

Use Big Words

Students whose teachers use more sophisticated vocabulary in class significantly improve their reading comprehension over the course of a semester or school year (Gámez & Lesaux, 2015). Given this, monitor the words you hear students using (or that you use yourself) that you can replace with bigger, more impressive synonyms, and use figure 15.7 to post them in your class. Whenever you catch a student or yourself using the simpler word, point to the poster and correct him or her (or yourself). You don't need to fill out the full sheet right away. As you identify common, too-simple words your students use, identify it with them, add it to the sheet, and brainstorm with them some bigger, better words.

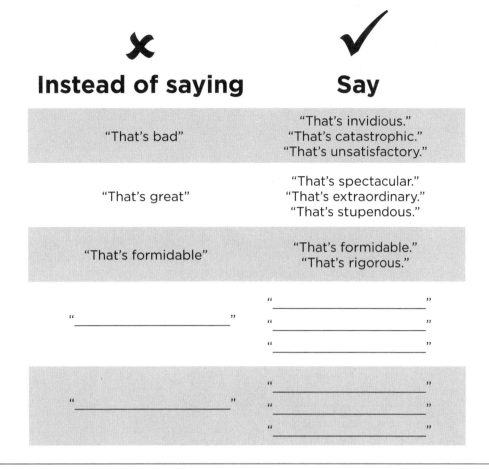

Figure 15.7: Use better, bigger words.

Visit go.SolutionTree.com/instruction for a free reproducible version of this figure.

Use Direct Vocabulary Instruction

Robert J. Marzano and Julia A. Simms (2014) suggest using direct vocabulary instruction with a research-based, six-step process. Use figure 15.8 (page 166) to brainstorm ways to use this process with up to six vocabulary words you plan to introduce.

Additionally, using gesturing and other nonverbal strategies (mind mapping, models, and so on) for learning and teaching vocabulary has a huge 2.27 effect size—over four years' worth of gains (Marzano, 1998). Ask students to pair up and demonstrate each new word, using words and gestures to help remember it.

Give students chances (through class discussion or assignments) to use all the words of the week. Teachers can use fun celebrations each time a student uses a word of the week. Use figure 15.9 (page 166) to brainstorm these celebrations. For example, every time it happens, the whole class stands up and says, "Oh, yes! I love this!" or add partner or team cheers to celebrate. In the following weeks, engage cooperative groups or student teams to review random vocabulary words from the comprehensive list.

List vocabulary terms you want to introduce.

_____   _____   _____

Step	Action
1. Demonstration	Provide a description, explanation, or example of the new terms. _____ _____ _____
2. Verbal	Ask students to restate the description, explanation, or example in their own words.
3. Nonverbal	Choose an activity for students to complete. Post their work on a word wall with rich adjectives for writing and content-related words the class is focusing on. (Circle one.) Draw a picture Create a symbol or graphic Design a gesture
4. Engagement	List other subject-related activities to help students add to their vocabulary knowledge. _____ _____ _____
5. Reciprocal teaching	When can you reuse or reintroduce these terms in future discussions? _____ _____ _____
6. Use of games	What are some games students can play that involve using this term? Involve students in games that allow them to play with these terms. _____ _____ _____

Figure 15.8: Process to introduce new vocabulary.

*Visit **go.SolutionTree.com/instruction** for a free reproducible version of this figure.*

Word of the week: _____

Who used the term correctly?	Celebration or reward

Figure 15.9: Celebrating proper vocabulary use.

*Visit **go.SolutionTree.com/instruction** for a free reproducible version of this figure.*

Quick Consolidation: Enhance Study Skills and Vocabulary

When it comes to learn-to-learn skills, study skills and vocabulary are two huge difference makers in the potential success of students from poverty. With study skills and vocabulary skills, your students can stand tall among the competition for a job. I am certain that you can understand the effect these strategies have on student achievement. With this firmly in mind, answer the following reflection questions on what you've learned and lock in on some strategies to make developing these skills in all your students part of your menu.

1. How has your understanding of the importance of teaching study skills and improving vocabulary evolved after reading this chapter?

2. What are some ways you can use the boosters in Contextual Study Skills to help students improve their study habits?

3. Brainstorm a relational study aid you can develop that is tailored to the content and your students' grade level. What does it look like? How will it benefit your students?

4. Why is building a strong vocabulary a highly beneficial strategy for closing the learning gap for students from poverty?

5. What strategies from this chapter can you use to help develop students' vocabulary? How might you adapt them to the specific content you teach?

Reflect on the Enrichment Mindset

All meaningful and lasting change starts with a mirror. Self-reflect first. How strong are your students' learn-to-learn skills? Use the following questions to help you grow the enrichment mindset in yourself and your students.

1. What new narrative about your students will you adopt that includes the enrichment mindset?

2. When students seem overwhelmed, how will you help them balance their cognitive load?

3. What new strategy in part five will you use to help students develop their cognitive skills? What support process can you create to ensure successful implementation? Will you engage colleagues, send notes to yourself, or create lesson plans that include fresh strategies and narratives?

4. What higher goals can you set for your students this year (or semester), and what will you do to help them adopt a strong learning approach matched with productive study skills?

The power of engaging the growth mindset is huge. Once you begin to say, "What else can I enrich?" a whole new world of teaching opens up for you. You can measure the strength of your enrichment mindset, not just in what you say to your students but also in what you teach them. That process speaks volumes and shows your students you believe in their potential.

PART SIX

IMPLEMENTING THE ENGAGEMENT MINDSET

You've cultivated a rich classroom climate, and you've enriched your teaching. Now it's time to think about how you engage your students with their learning. Engagement means different things to different people, especially those in academia who tend to think specifically about cognitive engagement. However, useful engagement happens on many levels. For example, just keeping your students in quality, alert emotional states is important. In this part, I introduce you to several levels of engagement and strategies to use immediately. Teachers who use high engagement and engage with relentless affirming interactions and thoughtful error correction usually have high-performing students (Valentine & Collins, 2011). Think of this mindset as building on the strategies for the enrichment mindset in part five.

Take a moment to consider your own strategies to keep students alert and engaged with their learning. See figure P6.1 (page 170).

Learning should tickle students' curiosity, inspire them with role models and heroes, grab them by the scruff of the neck, and serenade them through the highs and lows of emotions to something meaningful. Learning is something that students should feel, make, build, talk about, collaborate with others on, and write about. It is something that students need to debate, reflect on, and take positions on. Learning also must engage students in ways that make it worth doing. When you're not engaging students, achievement drops (Valentine, 2005). The engagement mindset says, "I can and will engage with purpose every student, every day, every nine minutes or less, guaranteed."

1. In your classroom, who carries the responsibility for ensuring students engage with your teaching? Do you feel that your approach to instruction is critical in holding students' attention or is it up to students to keep themselves focused?

_____

_____

_____

_____

2. What are your strategies for keeping students interested in your lessons? If you see students drifting, how do you approach getting them back on track?

_____

_____

_____

_____

3. How well do you understand the effects of poverty-driven stress on students' ability to remain focused on their learning? How do you recognize when a student is experiencing high stress and what do you do to help him or her cope with that and stay focused on learning?

_____

_____

_____

_____

4. How do you define the difference between learning for compliance and learning as a choice? What do you do to engage students in wanting to learn for its own sake as opposed to just pass the class?

_____

_____

_____

_____

5. Do you have an approach for getting students to buy into their learning as a group? What is that approach, and how well does making your students feel a part of a community drive their interest in learning?

_____

_____

_____

_____

Figure P6.1: Assess your strategies for engaging students.

*Visit **go.SolutionTree.com/instruction** for a free reproducible version of this figure.*

> The engagement mindset says, "I can and will engage with purpose every student, every day, every nine minutes or less, guaranteed."

Teachers with highly engaging classes have students who look forward to class every day, because there's always something they can do to keep them active and contributing. These teachers (and hopefully you too) see engagement at the heart and soul of learning. When you keep your students in constant states that are conducive to the work you do (curiosity, engagement, celebration, anticipation, and energy) you will bump up your odds for success (Erwin, Fedewa, Beighle, & Ahn, 2012). In fact, the effect size for an active classroom is a massive 1.51! That's over three years' worth of academic gains. Keep the bodies moving!

Speaking generally, most students from elementary to secondary are terrible at managing their own states of engagement. In the next three chapters, you'll read about the following strategies to keep them eager to learn.

1. Engage for maintenance and stress.

2. Engage students for a deeper buy-in.

3. Engage to build community.

Questions for Daily Reflection

Each day, consider your own mindset for how you will keep your students actively engaged in their own learning. Then, answer the following questions.

1. What strategy will I make time for in class today to help my students shake off some stress?

2. What will I do today to make my students' learning more relevant to them so that they buy in to their own learning and **choose** to learn?

3. How will I make time today to ensure my students feel a sense of community in my classroom?

CHAPTER 16

ENGAGE FOR MAINTENANCE AND STRESS

Your goal in the classroom is to maintain healthy student states of mind and body. If you don't influence their states, you're at the whim of random states or bad states. Students constantly seek something that will shift and help them manage their states (a text, a party, alcohol, a movie, a boyfriend or girlfriend, food, sports, and so on) because they rarely have strong self-regulation skills. Use figure 16.1 (page 174) to assess your current approach to student engagement as it pertains to maintenance and stress.

Understanding just a little of how the human brain functions at a chemical level is critically important to maintaining engagement in your students. Although engagement can affect other chemicals (cortisol, serotonin, and so on), simple activity bumps up the heart rate and nor-epinephrine and dopamine levels (Gillberg, Anderzén, Åkerstedt, & Sigurdson, 1986; Sutoo & Akiyama, 2003). An increased heart rate means greater circulation and oxygen to the brain. Increased norepinephrine in moderate amounts can bump up long-term memory and narrow attentional focus. Boost dopamine, and you get a better working memory, greater effort, and stronger neural plasticity to make changes.

While most teachers want more higher-order engagement, the reality is that although our brain works pretty fast (Buonomano, 2014), students still rarely go from a state of zero activity to high energy in a short amount of time (Halassa et al., 2014). It takes a classroom of constantly managed states to get the quality learning you want. As you know, you won't get higher-order thinking if students are drowsy, bored, and disconnected. To help drive this, the strategies in this chapter focus on ways to maintain engagement and to manage engagement-destroying stress levels. If you want to learn even more about how physical activity can produce engagement and improve learning, see the physical activity strategies for the graduation mindset in chapter 19 (page 206).

Engage to Maintain

The truth is, nothing will work in your class unless students are alert, focused, and in a receptive frame of mind. Without these states, you'll have to reteach content, and students will get bored. Use basic state-management tools to keep students active, focused, and interacting with you or their peers. These keep students in behaviorally flexible states and promote curiosity, attention,

Do you consider how students' emotional states affect their learning? (Circle one.)	Recognizing students' emotions is critical to teaching.	I care about my students, but I can't possibly monitor the emotions of every student.	I am a teacher, not a psychologist.
Describe what you know about how brain chemistry affects students' ability to engage with the content you teach.			
How do you approach students who seem disinterested in learning? (Circle one.)	I use strategies to re-engage them.	I criticize or chastise them.	I ignore them. I'm focused on students who are engaged.
Describe the strategies you use to engage students and hold their attention. If you notice their attention waning, what do you do to give them a quick jolt to bring back their focus?			
How do you approach stress levels for students in your classroom? (Circle one.)	I try to limit stress as much as possible.	I don't want students over-stressed, but they should feel a little pressure.	Students need to be responsible for learning to manage their own stress.
Write down what you know about stress and how it affects student behavior. Do you consider stress something that inhibits student performance or a strong motivator?			

Figure 16.1: Assess your approach to maintenance and engagement.

*Visit **go.SolutionTree.com/instruction** for a free reproducible version of this figure.*

and blood flow. They also maintain optimal brain chemistry by eliciting the appropriate levels of serotonin (for attention, behavioral flexibility, and comfort), noradrenaline (focus and memory), dopamine (mood, effort, and neural plasticity), and cortisol (for memory and energy).

Many students, particularly the poor, have had adverse home-life experiences, which foster the biological residue of chronic and acute stress known as allostasis (Evans & English, 2002). These students often feel hopeless, depressed, or hypervigilant (Landis et al., 2007). Even physical movement alone can enhance blood flow and productive neurochemicals that enhance cognition (Tomporowski, Davis, Miller, & Naglieri, 2008).

To that end, figure 16.2 highlights seven short and physical activities to influence the mind and body in the easiest and quickest way possible. I've set it up to work as a weekly checklist. Whenever you use one of these activities in your class, put a tick in the tracking box. This will help you rotate through the different strategies without over-relying on one strategy or another. Although they are easy, as a group, they are quite powerful because each focuses on a simple goal, such as arousal, to maintain states of alertness.

Strategy	Times Used This Week				
	Mon	Tues	Wed	Thurs	Fri
1. **Repeat after me:** Students repeat what the teacher says—"Today we focus on two core ideas. How many are we focusing on?" (Class responds: "Two!")					
2. **Turn to:** This strategy occurs after a student success—"Turn to your neighbor and say, 'Great effort.'"					
3. **Clap-boom-clap:** Students pay attention to listen to each clap and participate—"Follow along with me. I clap once, and you repeat. Every time I double clap, you say 'Boom!' That tells me you're ready for something big! Are you ready?"					
4. **Physical acts:** Students are usually eager to move around—"Quick! Let's find a new partner. Slide your chair a foot to the side, and rotate it to find a new neighbor."					
5. **Attention-getters:** This strategy especially appeals to students who are bored or have lost focus—"If you're ready for something new, clap twice, and say, 'Yes!'" Or, "If you want to try out an experiment, stomp your feet twice, and please stand up."					
6. **Ownership strategies:** Students want to feel ownership over their work—"If you've got your handout, hold it up high, and say, 'I got mine.' Now, put your name on it. Great. Now, look on your neighbor's paper, and if he or she doesn't have a name on it, wake him or her up."					
7. **Call and response:** This strategy creates quick refocus routines—"Class up!" (The students respond, "That's us!") Or, "Mind up!" (The students respond, "That's me!")					

Figure 16.2: Weekly usage of engagement strategies.

*Visit **go.SolutionTree.com/instruction** for a free reproducible version of this figure.*

You can modify these activities for developmental age and, over time, your students can lead them. Incorporating a simple activity every ten to fifteen minutes (or less) will keep students engaged. Without engagement strategies, students may feel lethargic, and it becomes harder to engage them the longer that state sets in. However, if students are experiencing high or low stress, you might instead use any of the strategies in the next section.

Engage to Manage Stress

To help students manage their own stress, keep the relevance high, and give students some sense of control over the process. This feeling of being in control is critical (Santiago, Etter, Wadsworth, & Raviv, 2012), and you can learn some additional strategies to give students this feeling in chapter 10 (page 111). Following are three quick activities that help students connect and control their stress with the one thing closest to them—their body. First, do these with your class and describe how and why they work. Then, over time, allow students to lead groups or the whole class. These are stress-lowering tools you can use every day for both your students and yourself.

1. **Extend, compact, and release series:** Students stand up and complete a series of movements that either stretch out their limbs (stand on tiptoes and then relax, extend each leg forward and then release, then move a step backward with one leg and then relax, or press palms tightly together and then release). These activities can help with boosting well-being and lowering stress (Carlson, Collins, Nitz, Sturgis, & Rogers, 1990).

2. **Fluid movements:** Students stand with knees slightly bent, and move arms in slow, grand, sweeping, circular movements, creating swirls or shaping images (as is done with tai chi or hula) with their hands. When done purposefully, they'll reduce stress and gain attention and creativity (Slepian & Ambady, 2012).

3. **Mindful breathing:** Students stand up and practice a series of inhales and exhales on a slow ascending path of deeper breathing. First, they'll inhale through the nose and hold it to the count of two and exhale. This has shown to benefit students at every education level (Kim et al., 2002; Mason, Rivers Murphy, & Jackson, 2019; Noggle, Steiner, Minami, & Khalsa, 2012; Terjestam, Jouper, & Johansson, 2010).

Alternatively, how do you raise the good stress with your students? The good stress goes up when we feel a sense of control and excitement at the same time. Here are some of your potential good stress–inducing strategies: engaging in physical activity (walk, stomp, act out, dance, or role-play), involving music (making it or listening to it), building cooperation (or competition), establishing deadlines (to create urgency), and designating a leader (student, teacher, or soundtrack).

Some specific ideas for activities to engage students in these ways include the following.

- **Simon says:** This common game can improve self-regulation. First, do the typical starter format to show students how to behave. Then, mix up Simon's commands. Say, "Only do the first of the two commands." Then, give two quick back-to-back directions such as, "Simon says, 'Clap your hands.' Simon says, 'Stomp your feet.'" This is perfect for younger students at the K–3 level, and, with modifications, can be very tough for secondary students too. For example, say, "You will get three commands from Simon; only do the middle one of the three."

- **Walk to the music:** Select five to seven pieces of music with very different pacing, style, and genre. Have students stand up and listen for directions. Students' assignment is to move to each song's beat or pacing. Play each song for about fifteen to twenty seconds, and then go to the next one. On the last song, all students head back to their seats.

- **Head-to-toes and head-toes-knees-shoulders:** These familiar activities, in which teachers instruct students to touch their head, toes, knees, or shoulders and also perform an opposite action, are helpful when introducing literacy and mathematics. The head-to-toes task (for elementary students) and the head-toes-knees-shoulders task (for secondary students) require students to integrate attention, working memory, and inhibitory control.

- **Drumbeats:** Use drumbeats to trigger different actions that students do while sitting (like clapping or stomping) or walking. For example, students walk quickly to fast drumming and slowly to slow drumming and freeze when the drumming stops. You may also ask students to respond to opposite cues, such as walking slowly to fast drumbeats or stomping their feet for slow drumming.

- **Orchestra conductor:** In this simple activity, every student uses his or her own musical instrument (real or imagined). The leader uses a drumstick or pencil as a conducting baton. When the conductor waves the baton, students play their instruments at the same rate as the speed of the baton. Then, the teacher can reverse the directions, asking students to move slowly when the baton goes fast. Establish a baseline of expected cues, then reverse them and speed them up. At first, the teacher should role model with students how to use a baton to lead the orchestra with the song blasting out over the classroom. Once the teacher models this, students will get the idea.

- **Touch and go:** In this activity, the teacher plays music and gives students simple, easy tasks. For example, he or she may ask students to circle two tables, touch three walls, touch two objects made of wood, or touch the backs of eleven chairs. Students return to their seats when the music stops. The teacher can also give them a specific amount of time to do the tasks, such as sixty seconds.

To avoid having any of these stress-relieving activities get stale for your students, keep a record of the activities you use and any relevant details about how you implemented them or how students responded. (Did the activity appear to lower student stress levels or increase engagement?). Figure 16.3 offers a four-week record sheet for tracking your usage and results.

Week 1 dates:				
Monday	**Tuesday**	**Wednesday**	**Thursday**	**Friday**
Activities to connect with and control stress:	Activities to connect with and control stress:	Activities to connect with and control stress:	Activities to connect with and control stress:	Activities to connect with and control stress:
Activities to raise the good stress:	Activities to raise the good stress:	Activities to raise the good stress:	Activities to raise the good stress:	Activities to raise the good stress:
Notes:	Notes:	Notes:	Notes:	Notes:
Weekly reflection:				

Figure 16.3: Log your stress-maintenance activities.

continued ⇨

Week 2 dates:

Monday	Tuesday	Wednesday	Thursday	Friday
Activities to connect with and control stress:	Activities to connect with and control stress:	Activities to connect with and control stress:	Activities to connect with and control stress:	Activities to connect with and control stress:
Activities to raise the good stress:	Activities to raise the good stress:	Activities to raise the good stress:	Activities to raise the good stress:	Activities to raise the good stress:
Notes:	Notes:	Notes:	Notes:	Notes:

Weekly reflection:

Week 3 dates:

Monday	Tuesday	Wednesday	Thursday	Friday
Activities to connect with and control stress:	Activities to connect with and control stress:	Activities to connect with and control stress:	Activities to connect with and control stress:	Activities to connect with and control stress:
Activities to raise the good stress:	Activities to raise the good stress:	Activities to raise the good stress:	Activities to raise the good stress:	Activities to raise the good stress:
Notes:	Notes:	Notes:	Notes:	Notes:

Weekly reflection:

Week 4 dates:				
Monday	**Tuesday**	**Wednesday**	**Thursday**	**Friday**
Activities to connect with and control stress: Activities to raise the good stress:	Activities to connect with and control stress: Activities to raise the good stress:	Activities to connect with and control stress: Activities to raise the good stress:	Activities to connect with and control stress: Activities to raise the good stress:	Activities to connect with and control stress: Activities to raise the good stress:
Notes:	Notes:	Notes:	Notes:	Notes:
Weekly reflection:				

*Visit **go.SolutionTree.com/instruction** for a free reproducible version of this figure.*

Quick Consolidation: Engage for Maintenance and Stress

All learning is state dependent, so if your students are in poor states for learning (such as apathy, boredom, frustration, anger, or distrust), you're wasting their time and yours. Too much and too little stress is ineffective for learning. Once you become more purposeful about maintaining healthy student states and managing stress, you'll have more time in your classroom because you'll spend less time reteaching and more time celebrating the learning. With this firmly in mind, answer the following reflection questions on what you've learned about engaging for maintenance and stress.

1. After reading this chapter, how has your perception of your role changed in terms of maintaining students' engagement and helping them manage their stress?

2. What are some ways that using quick attention-getting activities can change students' arousal states?

3. How does achieving arousal impact students' level of engagement?

4. Why is it important to put students in a state of moderate stress (as opposed to trying to eliminate it)? What are some indicators that students are feeling over-stressed?

5. What are some ways you can adapt the strategies in this chapter for engagement and stress management to fit your specific teaching style and curriculum?

CHAPTER 17

ENGAGE STUDENTS FOR A DEEPER BUY-IN

If you're tired of reteaching over and over, it's time for a change in strategy that fosters student buy-in and sustains durable learning. The effectiveness of activities or content blocks typically depend on how well you prepare learners *before* you begin instruction. Remember, relevance is everything to students' brains. Use the survey in figure 17.1 to assess how you currently engage students for setup and buy-in.

How do you view the responsibility for learning? (Circle one.)	I actively attempt to get buy-in from all students.	I tell students why content is important. I don't focus on buy-in.	Buy-in depends on the students. I can't make them be interested.
Explain your thinking behind the answer you chose. Why do you feel achieving buy-in is or isn't your responsibility?			
What factors go into students buying into your teaching? (Circle all that apply.)	Personal interest Cultural relevancy	Career or college ambitions Problem-solving or project-based work	My enthusiasm for the content Novelty
Explain how the answers you selected reflect your beliefs in how students learn. Is learning a choice or something students do to comply with expectations?			
Do you deliberately engage in questioning activities or strategies to achieve buy-in? (Circle one.)			Yes No
What are some ways you use questioning to engage students? If you don't use any strategies, what are some ways you could use questions to engage them?			

Figure 17.1: Assess your approach to setup and buy-in.

*Visit **go.SolutionTree.com/instruction** for a free reproducible version of this figure.*

Part four (page 107) introduced the power of relevance and the essentialness of using student voice and vision in a culturally responsive classroom. However, the tools in this chapter are at the apex of learning, so lean in and lock in because buy-in is priceless for any learning activity. Without it, even good activities will die. Buy-in practically ensures the next task you do will work and the lesson will be more effective because students will pay close attention and save the learning in their brain.

In this chapter, I examine the difference between compliance learning and choice learning, then you'll learn how to distinguish between setup (arousal) and full buy-in, and finally you'll learn how to ask the right questions to achieve buy-in.

Move From Compliance Learning to Choice Learning

There are two types of classroom learning: (1) compliance ("OK, I guess I can do this") and (2) choice learning ("This sounds good; I'm gonna jump in and give it a go!"). Over fifty million U.S. students attend school, and many are compliant learners.

Compliance learning invites reteaching in your classroom. Why? Unless the brain perceives the task to be behaviorally relevant, it usually does not save or remember the learned task (Green & Bavelier, 2008). Compliance learning means students go through the motions, but they rarely recall learning. When that happens, more students will need reteaching. Motivated, choice learning is more likely to stick (be remembered). If you find that you are reteaching content just ten extra minutes a day for up to four days a week, that squanders forty minutes a week. Over a year, that's twenty hours of valuable classroom time flushed down the toilet.

A teacher who opens a lesson with a problem to solve, a puzzle, a game, or a joke is likely building up and hoping for *student arousal*. "Get that brain going," is the mantra. Those are not bad ideas, they are just not quality buy-in. Arousal, which we covered in detail in chapter 16 (page 173), means the student is awake, alert, and in a good metabolic state for learning something. But that is not the same as a biological state of relevant buy-in, which is a yearning, hungry state that must be fulfilled (Adcock, Thangavel, Whitfield-Gabrieli, Knutson, & Gabrieli, 2006).

Use figure 17.2 to write down some key points in your process for teaching a specific lesson plan. What activities do you use to engage students and teach the material? How do you relate the content to your students so they understand why it's important to them? Then, ask yourself if you've successfully framed this content or activity as choice learning or compliance learning. If it's the latter, write down any ideas you have to shift your focus from compliance to choice.

I cannot emphasize this enough: unless you get buy-in from your students every single time you introduce new content, an activity, or anything you want their brain to save, you risk students forgetting it. The human brain is driven by behavioral relevance. It is as if the brain says, "Why should I care about this? Because if I really should care about it, I'll remember it!" To help you do this in your classroom, you must be able to distinguish between the three stages for preparing students to learn: (1) setup, (2) buy-in, and (3) relevance.

Learn Setup, Buy-In, and Relevance

It's easy to confuse the three stages of learner preparation with each other. Trust me, it happens to most every teacher, and it did to me, too. The success of these three tools is partially dependent on the relationship you have with your students, the classroom climate, the hope students have for success, and your relationships with them. Think of these three strategies as layers of persuasion to achieve a full, encompassing buy-in through deep, compelling relevance.

Lesson topic:	
Key component or activity:	
Describe the process:	Is this choice learning? Yes ☐ No ☐
What changes can you help students choose to learn this content?	
Key component or activity:	
Describe the process:	Is this choice learning? Yes ☐ No ☐
What changes can you help students choose to learn this content?	
Key component or activity:	
Describe the process:	Is this choice learning? Yes ☐ No ☐
What changes can you help students choose to learn this content?	

Figure 17.2: Move from compliance learning to choice learning.

Visit go.SolutionTree.com/instruction for a free reproducible version of this figure.

Setup

The first layer is the setup to prepare the soil for learning. It says, "*Wake up!* This will be *good!*" The setup may be done with arousal (energizers), questions that get students curious (like, "How would you like to try a really cool experiment?") or sheer excitement from teacher enthusiasm (like, "Wow! I am so pumped about this. Everybody up please!"). Figure 17.3 offers a pair of sample statements with room for you to add more of your own.

Setup statement	Hook:
"Oh! I've got a great idea; it'll only take a moment. First, stand up please."	Curiosity
"I'm going to share something that will totally boggle your mind!"	Anticipation

Figure 17.3: Establish setup (arousal).

Visit go.SolutionTree.com/instruction for a free reproducible version of this figure.

If students are not "aroused" (if they are sleepy, tired, disconnected, and so on), the next two layers may not work at all. That's why these initial lay-the-groundwork strategies are quick, to the point, and work the majority of the time. Plus, right after a class energizer is a great time to introduce new learning; blood flow is up and so are the brain's chemicals for learning (dopamine, norepinephrine, and some cortisol).

Buy-In

Establishing buy-in also means using hooks, but in this case the purpose is to help students know the point of what you are asking them to do or learn in class. Establishing buy-in may seem new (or one more thing) to you, but it meets an important need in your students. It answers the question, "*Why* are we doing this?" When you offer a strong buy-in right after an energizer, it is almost *guaranteed* to get your students moving, mentally engaged, and ready for the next step.

Figure 17.4 offers some examples of a quick "Why?" inserted into your teaching. Use the space provided to add some of your own.

Buy-in statement	Hook
"First, take in a deep breath. Now, if you're ready to learn something amazing, that will help your grade, stomp your feet twice."	(The hook is the new learning.)
"How about if we try out a way to help your brain remember more things at test time, with less study time? Are you willing to give it a go?"	(The hook is an easier time on tests while saving on study time.)

Figure 17.4: Establish buy-in (the "Why?").

Visit go.SolutionTree.com/instruction for a free reproducible version of this figure.

The idea is to get students to nibble at a good idea until they want to eat up the rest of the learning.

Relevance

The third and final layer is establishing relevance that is both compelling and deep. Notice the stages we've covered so far: (1) wake up the brain and body with an arousal for setup, (2) then evoke curiosity, anticipation, or challenge to start the process of getting students to start leaning in to the learning. Most teachers will use either setup (for arousal) or buy-in, but not purposefully. They often stumble upon this third layer.

Relevance can take some time to settle in and become meaningful. That said, it is stickier because, once students acknowledge and buy in to it, it has more lasting power than the setup or hooks. Why? Deep relevance taps into our values. But, like many things, it is something you need to re-invoke over time, using different looks, angles, and descriptions.

There are two lists of drivers that have helped me better serve students, and they may help you, too. See figure 17.5. The left column lists behavior drivers that are internal and self-referencing. The right column lists external drivers that require others to be a part of the experience.

Internal drivers	External drivers
Create security (have economic, social, and personal safety)	Social status (to feel respected as special within one's group)
Generate autonomy (be able to choose, control, and do something oneself)	Connection (to belong to or have affiliation with a person or chosen group)
Foster identity (believe and act like one's authentic self)	Worthiness (to matter to, be worthy of, and be accepted by others)
Establish a sense of mastery (get very good at something)	Mission (to be part of something greater than oneself)
Provide a deeper meaning (connect to personal, cultural, and spiritual beliefs)	Validation (to be right or to prove one's goodness or potential through a strongly held belief or an action, choice, or strategy one takes)

Figure 17.5: Drivers of relevance.

*Visit **go.SolutionTree.com/instruction** for a free reproducible version of this figure.*

When you see students acting out, you'll see the driver in action. One sixteen-year-old may be seeking autonomy or even social status. Another may be seeking control or fostering an identity of being a behavior problem. An eight-year-old may be most concerned about security in his or her neighborhood or having a parent's validation. The take-home message here is simple: while many things can nudge us to make a decision in the moment (like participating in an energizer), over the long haul, we are more willing to act out of what is deeply relevant to us.

Use Hooks

As you have seen, there are critical stages to achieving full buy-in, each with a variety of approaches you can take toward achieving it. All achieve at least some level of arousal and get students learning with energy and momentum, but the lasting one is the culminating step of achieving *compelling, deep relevancy.* (It's the holy grail for buy-in.) Let's explore some strategies you can use to make the layers of the process happen.

You could divide your classroom hooks into sections such as kinesthetic (what students can make, toss, play, catch, and act out), props (what you can show or pass around), safari (take your students outside the classroom or go on short field trips), music (set the tone, create an effect, highlight a concept, and use song lyrics), or visual arts (create a poster or lighting change). You could also use theater (become a character or act out an idea or event), hobbies (have a student or you share a hobby, then tie it into the content), or autonomy (allow students to create their own sources for connections). You might use current events (tie in news or pop culture), mystery bag or box (create a special bag or box with a content-relevant item inside), interior design (change the room by altering setup, clearing out chairs, or making it a theme party), and costumes (wear a scarf, hat, or full outfit to portray a character).

Using the lesson plans you reflected on and ideas you wrote down in figure 17.2 (page 183), you can use figure 17.6 (page 186) to take those initial ideas and shape them by targeting different specific hooks you want to use and describing specifically how you will implement them with your students. If you want more hook ideas, there are at least fifty or more hooks you can use that are perfect for K–12 teachers. See *Teach Like a Pirate* (Burgess, 2012) for elementary students and *How to Motivate Reluctant Learners* (R. Jackson, 2011) for specific secondary ideas.

Lesson component:
Hook:
Section (describe the activity):

Elementary social hooks	Secondary social hooks
• Next grade level as a challenge or draw • Simple privilege • Fun • Raw teacher enthusiasm • Deep curiosity • Positive affirmation • Grossness • Friendship • Physical activity • Cool mystery	• Edgy and risky activities • Peer pressure • A strong challenge • Stair-stepping activity • Collaboration with friends • Social status • Experiments • Voice development (being heard) • Local problems • Huge projects • College • Competition • New relationships

What other ideas do you have for hooks?

Figure 17.6: Add hooks to your instruction.

*Visit **go.SolutionTree.com/instruction** for a free reproducible version of this figure.*

Use Questions

Good questions can evoke curiosity, relevance, and reflection. Great questions can change class climate or even student lives. A whole-class question and answer session, when done well, has a strong effect size of 0.81, contributing nearly two years' worth of student achievement (Hattie, 2009), but it is no easy task. It requires participation, inquiry with safety, and a clear goal of deeper understandings while maintaining relationships.

To get started, post the following questions on the board, a screen, or a flipchart. Then, start calling on everyone. If you want to mix up the process a bit, put a jar, basket, or bowl up front filled with student names, and then call on someone to pick a name (students are immune if they pick their own name). If a student is called on and doesn't know the answer, ask him or her to say, "I don't know, but I'd like to know. Give me a minute, and call on me again." Then, come back to the student a minute later, when he or she is ready. Here are powerful questioning groups you can pull from.

- **Discovery questions:** When students begin a unit or are initially behind, help them find some cognitive footing with discovery questions. Find out their prior knowledge by learning the labels, facts, fragments, and assumptions they have. For example, you might ask, "What do you already know about the Civil Rights Movement in the 1960s?"

- **Essential questions:** These questions elevate the quality and depth of learning by embracing and using relevant interests (McTighe & Wiggins, 2013; Watanabe-Crockett, 2019). There are two types of essential questions: (1) broad (the point goes beyond a unit to a larger, transferable idea such as "What defines a great leader?") and (2) content specific (answerable through a unit's content, such as "After reading *Catch-22*, how do you think you would cope in another world of earlier wars—Yossarian's—and why?").

- **Summarizing-the-content questions:** Students grasp the content and make some statements about it. For example, "What is this about? What is the key understanding? What are two or three key points here? What is a good title for this text? How would you describe the learning in one or two sentences?"

- **Elaborative questions:** Before asking elaborative questions, establish a basic understanding of the content with students. Students should be clear on the talking points and able to summarize the content. Elaborative questions detail unique features or properties of the learning ("What makes tectonic plates so unpredictable?") and potential conflicts ("Why did the Occupy Wall Street group protest? What is its position, and what do the opposing arguments say?").

- **Evidence-gathering questions:** Here, students use reasoning and argumentation to support claims that they make about any statements, arguments, or positions. For example, "Tell me why you feel that your position is a valid one. What makes it any different than the opposition's? What would your opponent say and why? How would you rebut them? What facts support your position that others don't have?"

Use the worksheet in figure 17.7 to highlight parts of your lessons where you can use some form of questioning to increase buy-in. Write down the type of questions best suited to the learning and your ideas for using those questions with your students.

Lesson topic: _____

What are the key points of instruction?

What are some key discovery questions you can pose?

What are some key essential questions you can pose?

What are some key elaborative questions you can pose?

What are some key evidence-gathering questions you can pose?

Figure 17.7: Determine questions for buy-in.

*Visit **go.SolutionTree.com/instruction** for a free reproducible version of this figure.*

For those who do contribute, expect more. Ask students, "How do you know that is true (or false)?" When students respond to any answer, say, "Thank you. I appreciate you jumping in and enjoyed hearing your contributions. Now tell me a bit more." Keep the conversation alive by asking more questions: "How do you know that might be true?"

Remember to do this process with love; respect student concerns for how their peers see and hear them. Never, ever embarrass a student in class. The idea here is simple: discover, probe, and push in a respectful way that appreciates what every student knows and how each can grow.

Quick Consolidation: Engage for Setup and Buy-In

Establishing setup (arousal states) and achieving buy-in (behavioral relevancy) are critical to the work you do. Buy-in is particularly fundamental to all classroom learning, or students might not learn (or at the least, they won't recall it). With this firmly in mind, answer the following reflection questions on what you've learned and become more purposeful about implementing setup and buy-in.

1. What did you learn in this chapter that you didn't know before about the importance of arousing students' interest in what you're teaching and the importance of making their learning a choice?

2. What is the difference between setup and buy-in, and what are some ways can you use hooks to move from one to the other?

3. What strategies will you use to achieve deeper relevance with your students? How will you recognize when students have made that connection with the content they're learning?

4. What are some ways you can use questioning with the specific content areas you teach to achieve buy-in?

5. What are some ways you can combine different aspects of this chapter's strategies (choice learning, hooks, and questioning) with your teaching curriculum to shift the level of students' buy-in into overdrive?

CHAPTER 18

ENGAGE TO BUILD COMMUNITY

We are all unique, with different needs, motivations, and comfort zones, and the same applies to your students. Some students are in their element interacting with and working with their peers. Others feel more comfortable with more isolation, being left to their own devices. But the truth is, regardless of tendencies toward extroversion or introversion, students learn better with social interaction (when teaching others, for example) than if their focus is just on individually preparing for the next test (Lieberman, 2014). Use the survey in figure 18.1 (page 192) to assess the communal traits present in your classroom.

Each of us has some need to belong to a community, and many students from poverty lack any sense of this outside of school. So make no mistake in understanding that your classroom is a community, and for many of your students, it may be the only real, supportive community they have. The goal of this chapter is to build a classroom community of engaged learners. Building a sense of community fosters academic optimism and reduces inappropriate student behavior. In this chapter, I discuss solving common problems, using reciprocal teaching, and celebrating small whole-class victories.

Solving Common Problems

Brainstorm some common recurring classroom problems. Examples include starting class on time, having students be quiet, and finishing up on time. To automate a solution to these problems, introduce a special type of community-building activity—a ritual. How is a ritual different from any other classroom activity? Class routines, or rituals, are short preplanned events that help solve recurring problems with positive energy. These activities build camaraderie and promote an inclusive culture. Class rituals have just five criteria to make them work. They must (1) solve a recurring problem (or students won't see the relevancy), (2) include and engage all students (or you'll lose the participation), (3) be simple and easy to do (students must be able to automate them), (4) be predictable (students should be ready for them every time), and (5) end on a positive emotional state (or students won't keep doing them). Most teachers have procedures that may meet some of these criteria, but rituals meet every single one. They are so simple that it's as if you simply press play to solve a problem when you initiate a ritual.

Teachers design rituals to engage more of the class socially and build community. How? It is something everyone in the class does together (even if they are in a team doing it) to solve a

How do you view your classroom environment? (Circle one.)	My classroom is a place for everyone to come together to learn.	My classroom is a place where students succeed or fail on their own merits.
What are some examples of ways you've fostered a sense of community in your classroom? If you don't see your classroom as a community, explain why not.		

Do you have any rituals you use to bring your students together when it's time to start learning? (Circle one.)	Yes No
Describe some of your rituals and why you use them. What problems do they solve? If you have no rituals, what are some common classroom problems a daily ritual might solve?	

How important are celebrations to your classroom? (Circle one.)	We celebrate both minor and major milestones and events.	We take time to celebrate only major accomplishments.	My classroom is only for learning activities.
Describe some of the things you celebrate and why you celebrate them. If you don't use celebrations in your classroom, reflect on why not.			

Figure 18.1: Assess your approach to engagement through community.

*Visit **go.SolutionTree.com/instruction** for a free reproducible version of this figure.*

common problem. You can start one during the first week of class, and then use it semesterlong or yearlong. Use figure 18.2 (page 193) as a checklist to ensure your classroom rituals meet each of the five criteria.

Here are some priceless classroom routines that help the whole class solve problems together.

- **Callbacks:** Start class in the morning, after recess, or after a task with a callback—"If you made it to your seat on time, raise your hand and say, 'Yes!' Now, turn to your neighbor and say, 'Welcome back!'"

- **End-of-class celebrations:** End the class with a celebration. Students stand and share a learning highlight from the class with another teammate. Then, they put both hands far out to their left and right sides and bring them together with a big clap and say, "Yes!"

- **Attention-getters:** Use a whistle and say, "Students, when I have a *really important* idea, I want to know if you're on board. When I blow my train whistle, everyone says, 'All aboard!' Now, let's try it out."

Notice these rituals meet the five criteria from figure 18.2. How can you use them in your classroom? When you do, within three to five weeks, you'll notice that your students may habituate to an activity, a song, or a ritual, and you'll need to change it. The beauty of these is that everyone does them at the exact same moment, on cue, every time. Every student goes into the same state, saying the same words. This is a unity builder, and these are priceless

Describe the ritual:		
1. Does this ritual solve a recurring problem?	Yes ☐	No ☐
How?		
2. Does this ritual include and engage everyone?	Yes ☐	No ☐
How?		
3. Is this ritual simple and easy to do?	Yes ☐	No ☐
How?		
4. Is this ritual predictable?	Yes ☐	No ☐
How?		
5. Does this ritual enable the class to end on a positive emotional state?	Yes ☐	No ☐
How?		

Figure 18.2: Design highly effective rituals.

*Visit **go.SolutionTree.com/instruction** for a free reproducible version of this figure.*

in your classroom. Do not dismiss these because they seem too simple or may not be for older students. I have used them with all K–12 students.

Using Reciprocal Teaching

Reciprocal teaching is a strong complementary factor that can strengthen engagement and, ultimately, student achievement (Rosenshine & Meister, 1994). When done well, it is a very powerful learning tool in the top 20 percent of all classroom strategies (Petty, 2006). Reciprocal teaching involves teaching students specific comprehension-fostering strategies. Students learn four strategies: (1) asking questions about the text, (2) summarizing what was read, (3) predicting what might happen next, and (4) attempting to clarify words and phrases they did not understand. Using reciprocal teaching, you gradually release responsibility, so the student gets better and better.

To build comprehension, consider using the following key strategies after exposing students to the content (Palincsar & Brown, 1984). First, ask students to find a partner. Their partner can be a long-term study buddy or a temporary one (see chapter 2, page 21). The roles are simple but quality social activities with cognitive benefits. Once they have a partner, do a buy-in as we described in the previous chapter. Then, they are ready for one of the following tasks.

- **Clarifying the content:** When content is either tough, higher level, or obscurely written, this step is critical to use. Ask questions such as, "Can you rephrase that in your own words? What questions does that passage bring to you? How would you explain that to a student who knew nothing about this topic?"

- **Modeling teaching:** Students teach another how to do something, directions for an upcoming task, or how something works, unfolds, or develops.

- **Taking sides:** Give partners a topic, and have each pick a side. They get one minute to think through or write out a couple of talking points. Then, they argue their side (either pro or con on a topic). They can either switch sides or offer a rebuttal to their partner's arguments.

- **Taking a role:** Students take on a role (famous person in history, mathematician, leader, writer, scientist, or activist) and then add a bit of that person's character and make a policy speech (content summary). The other partner serves as a skeptic (or a reporter) and asks up to three questions.

- **Creating a quiz:** Two partners work together for nine minutes to create three questions each. When the time is up, ask them to remove the easiest question from each list, so they have two left. Then, they stand up and walk to find another twosome and trade quiz questions. A third person can act as the arbiter of the quizzes.

Use the worksheet in figure 18.3 to help students with their reciprocal teaching.

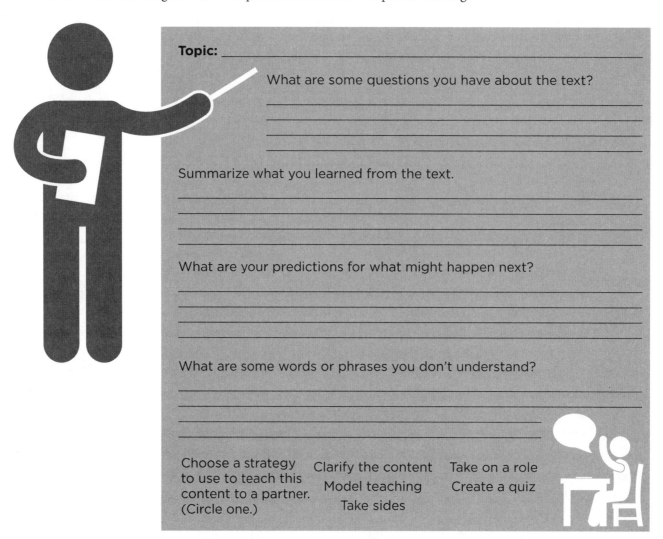

Figure 18.3: Use reciprocal teaching.

Visit *go.SolutionTree.com/instruction* for a free reproducible version of this figure.

When you get students up and moving, it invigorates blood flow and important chemicals like dopamine and noradrenaline. That's why any activity that lets students get up, walk, meet others, or even go outside is a good idea if it's done well. It is the activity that engages better brain chemicals (Gillberg et al., 1986).

Celebrating Small Whole-Class Victories

In chapter 4, I wrote about the value of setting gutsy goals, but small victories matter too. Set class goals and milestones (such as attendance, percentage of turned-in papers, or participation). Then, as the class gets close to the goal, ramp up the interest and the focus. This is the place to teach the value of keeping your macro goal in mind while still focusing on the moment. Use figure 18.4 to plan your micro goals and keep morale high.

List some full-class micro goals and keep track of when the class meets them.

Micro goal:	Goal met?	Goal met on:	Celebration
		__/__/__	
		__/__/__	
		__/__/__	
		__/__/__	

Figure 18.4: Brainstorm full-class goals.

Visit *go.SolutionTree.com/instruction* for a free reproducible version of this figure.

There's power in the timing and purpose of celebrating by managing student states with affirmations, celebrations, and emotional rewards. There are multiple ways to do this. For example, make the celebration a team activity. Teams will plan out their fifteen-second celebration and lead the whole class in it. Alternatively, you may create a class ritual for celebration by using a happy dance or rhythm-clap plus "We did it!" affirmations. The social side of this engagement strategy is key.

Quick Consolidation: Engage to Build Community

When you create a classroom community through activities, it fosters camaraderie and reduces inappropriate student behavior. Moreover, by ensuring your classroom feels like a functioning, healthy community, you will find you consistently have continuously engaged learners. If you already use these classroom activities like rituals, reciprocal teaching, and celebrations, I invite you to sharpen them to get the most value. If you don't already use them, please give them a try. With this firmly in mind, answer the following reflection questions on ways you can make your classroom a thriving, engaging community for your students.

1. What did you learn in this chapter about the importance of building a classroom community that you didn't already know?

2. Think about some of the common problems you listed at the start of this chapter. What new rituals could you create (or what existing rules could you change) to help the whole class buy in to addressing them?

3. What are some lessons you already teach that would benefit students to learn from reciprocal teaching?

4. Which of the reciprocal teaching strategies present in this chapter would be perfect for engaging students with those lessons?

5. Think of some of the small, whole-class success stories you've witnessed in the past year. What could you do differently to ensure those successes don't go unrecognized?

Reflect on the Engagement Mindset

All meaningful and lasting change starts with a mirror. Self-reflect first. Take a moment and ask yourself a few questions about what you do to build student engagement by considering their existing levels of buy-in, mobility, and metabolic states.

1. Do you bring a strong engagement mindset into your class every day? Either way, what is your evidence?

2. When things are going well, what percentage of the class is right in the palm of your hand? What can you do to improve this number?

3. When you're struggling, what percentage of your class has tuned out? What strategies from this chapter can you use to boost this number?

4. What are some stress indicators you see in your classroom, and what activities will you engage them in to reduce that stress?

5. What are some choices you can make to help you and your students have a good day every day?

When you make choices and plan a time for implementing strategies to get buy-in from your students and keep them engaged every day, you will find that your own enthusiasm and energy for teaching soar to new heights.

PART SEVEN

IMPLEMENTING THE GRADUATION MINDSET

This part begins with my own personal mission for college and career readiness standards. I am committed to helping 100 percent of K–12 students graduate job or college ready. When I share this mission with others, some feel like kindred spirits and like my gutsy goal. But others simply smile, and I suspect they silently say to themselves, "Right; like *that's* going to happen." What do you consider successful when it comes to graduating your students? See figure P7.1 (page 200).

Your mindset must be that every single student deserves a great education that leads to graduation for college and the workplace. This is a way to frame equity from the conversation to action steps.

Every day, when you go to work, remind yourself, "Our students need every minute I can invest in each and every day." Yes, it's hard work, and you must accept that up front. Without focus, the amount of distracting noise out there can make you, and students, feel crazy and leave you saying to yourself, "These students may have it tough, but they're so often tardy, truant, or absent. I don't think they even want to graduate." Tune it out. Stop listening to the negativity. Fill your mind with the dreams that you and your students have for graduation and future success.

The graduation mindset adopts a bold, laser-like focus intent on helping all students become college and career ready. The graduation mindset says, "Focus on what matters. Be an ally to help students graduate college and career ready."

1. What percentage of your students go on to graduate? What do you take from that number? Do you consider this percentage a success story for your school or district, or something that demands improvement?

_____

_____

_____

_____

2. What factors do you think most impact a student from poverty's ability to graduate? What do you do to mitigate these factors?

_____

_____

_____

_____

3. Do you believe it is possible for high-poverty school districts to achieve sky-high graduation rates? Why or why not?

_____

_____

_____

_____

4. How do you perceive the importance of arts education and physical activity in contributing to student graduation rates?

_____

_____

_____

_____

5. Do you feel all students should graduate ready to go to college? Is it just as important that students graduate with the ability to immediately enter the workforce in a promising career?

_____

_____

_____

_____

Figure P7.1: Assess your strategies for helping students graduate.

Visit **go.SolutionTree.com/instruction** for a free reproducible version of this figure.

> The graduation mindset says, "Focus on what matters. Be an ally to help students graduate college and career ready."

When you can adopt this mindset, you're ready to do the kind of work that has led to success at many other high-performing schools. It's a mindset that says, "At our school, every teacher is totally committed to helping students succeed. In fact, I would go so far as to say, 'We simply won't let them fail.'"

High-performing schools do things differently; that's why they succeed. The difference has nothing to do with broken students and more to do with broken spirits among the staff. The high-performing school staff don't make excuses, nor do they talk about the schools that fail. They roll up their sleeves and go to work.

What do high-performing schools do? Figure P7.2 lists five major building blocks and five core practices based on policy analysis from the Center for Public Education (2005).

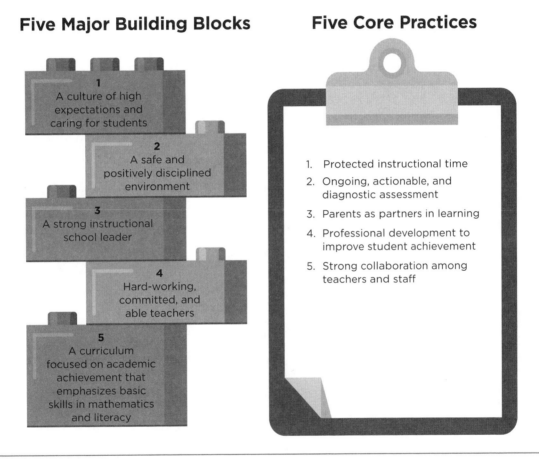

Five Major Building Blocks

1. A culture of high expectations and caring for students
2. A safe and positively disciplined environment
3. A strong instructional school leader
4. Hard-working, committed, and able teachers
5. A curriculum focused on academic achievement that emphasizes basic skills in mathematics and literacy

Five Core Practices

1. Protected instructional time
2. Ongoing, actionable, and diagnostic assessment
3. Parents as partners in learning
4. Professional development to improve student achievement
5. Strong collaboration among teachers and staff

Figure P7.2: Learn to manage the noise.

*Visit **go.SolutionTree.com/instruction** for a free reproducible version of this figure.*

How did you respond to these lists? Did you think, "Those sound good," then just keep reading without starting to think about what you could accomplish at your school? High-poverty, high-performing schools consider every option. They hold discussions, look at their data, listen to students via surveys, and are fanatic about patching any gaps that hurt students' chances for graduation. Use the building blocks and core practices as a checklist as you work toward implementing a graduation mindset in every student—and in yourself.

The two chapters in this part offer strategies to help your students prepare for graduation—no matter what grade they're in. These strategies include the following.

1. Support alternative solutions.
2. Prepare for college and careers.

In these chapters, you'll begin a new narrative, one all about reaching a school goal of 100 percent graduation. You have the skills, and the outcome can become real.

Questions for Daily Reflection

Each day, consider your own mindset for how you can best help students achieve the ultimate goal of graduating college or career ready. Then, answer the following questions.

1. What is one thing I will do today to communicate to my students that their graduation is my ultimate goal and that I will do whatever I can to help them reach this goal?

2. While reflecting on today's lesson plan, how could I include music or physical activity to boost student performance?

3. What strategies can I include in my teaching to empower students to get ready for future college or career work?

CHAPTER 19

SUPPORT ALTERNATIVE SOLUTIONS

Let's start with a simple question: If you knew of a program that kept students in school, reduced student discipline problems, strengthened cognitive capacity, reduced dropouts, and improved graduation rates, would you support it? Of course you would!

Researchers have studied programs that do those things for decades and yet, we have to beg, plead, fight, and scream for their implementation. Take a moment, and use the survey in figure 19.1 to assess how you and your school approach these issues.

Does your school have programs designed specifically to help students graduate and succeed in post-graduate life? (Circle one.)	Yes No
Describe some of these programs. What do they focus on, and how effective have they been? What could improve them?	
Is education related to the arts and physical education a priority at your school? (Circle one.)	Yes No
Describe the opportunities students have to engage in arts and physical education programs. Are these well- or under-funded?	
Regardless of what you teach, do you put an emphasis on the arts and physical activity in your instruction? (Circle one.)	Yes No
Describe what you do to connect the arts (such as music) and physical activity to your teaching. What could you do?	

Figure 19.1: Assess your approach to alternative solutions.

Visit go.SolutionTree.com/instruction for a free reproducible version of this figure.

Across the United States, fewer and fewer schools include arts programs and physical fitness programs (Parsad & Spiegelman, 2012). Seven in ten parents say their child's school has zero physical education (NPR, Robert Wood Johnson Foundation, & Harvard School of Public Health, 2013). Somehow, other new curricula with far less evidence to support their contribution to student achievement seem to push them out of the public eye.

This chapter reviews two strong ways to keep students in school and help them graduate college or career ready: (1) arts and (2) physical activity.

Tools to Support the Arts

Here we define arts as the big four: musical arts (playing an instrument), performing arts (theater, choir, dance, tap dance, and comedy), kinetic arts (handiwork, tapestry, and sculpture), and visual arts (drawing, painting, and digital arts). There are brain systems, which I refer to as the *academic operating system* (see figure 19.2), that are developed in precise and lasting ways from long-term exposure to arts, and students are more likely to be successful when they excel at these skills (Skoe & Kraus, 2012).

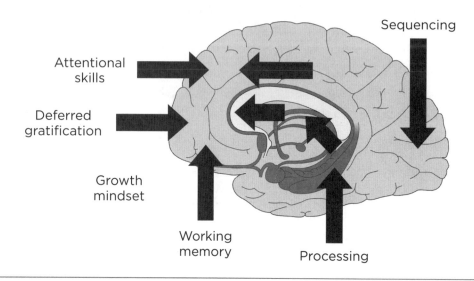

Figure 19.2: How arts build the academic operating system.

For example, schools that have music programs have significantly higher attendance rates than do those without muisc programs (93.3 percent as compared to 84.9 percent) and have significantly higher graduation rates than do those without music programs (90.2 percent as compared to 72.9 percent). I posit this is the case in part because musical training enhances memory (Ho, Cheung, & Chan, 2003), academic achievement (Southgate & Roscigno, 2009), and social development (Catterall, 2003).

Maybe most critically, a U.S. longitudinal aggregate of four databases with thousands of low–socioeconomic status students found clear positive differences (Catterall, 2009). As I explore more deeply in *Poor Students, Rich Teaching, Revised Edition* (Jensen, 2019), the arts have a particularly strong effect on low-income students, making them more likely to graduate and post higher scores in high school writing, science, and mathematics.

In my experience, the arts influence the following five factors when students participate in them three to five days a week for at least thirty to ninety minutes at a time.

1. **Effort:** Motivation and the ability to defer gratification
2. **Processing skills:** Auditory, visual, and tactile
3. **Attentional skills:** Engage, focus, and disengage as needed
4. **Memory capacity:** Short-term and working memory
5. **Sequencing skills:** Knowing the order of a process

With an eye toward these five factors, there are multiple ways you can use music and drama in your school. If at all possible, your ideal strategy is to have a certified arts teacher work with your students for fifteen to thirty minutes for three days a week at both the elementary and secondary level. When there are not enough art teachers, teachers can use arts in their own way (drawings, gestures, dance, and energizers).

Maybe the quickest way for students to get music training (without a music instructor) is by learning to play on an iPad. Consider the use of these apps: Tiny Piano, Nota, Musical Touch, Pro Keys, and Twelve Tone. These will get a student hooked on being a musician! There are many YouTube videos that teach introductory music lessons. That's not as good as a qualified music teacher, but it is better than no music exposure at all.

To support drama, allow students to role-play a topic. Students can do this in science (to show how an experiment will work, a reaction of chemicals, or an ecological outcome). They can do it in mathematics (to show a key formula, how each part of an equation plays out, or a memorable way to store the formula), or in language arts (to tell a story, explain a review, or show relevance to student lives). Performing and learning the skills of drama will build a large group of transferrable skills. Movement, often part of drama, can affect cognition in many ways.

Use figure 19.3 to rebuild one of your lesson plans to include music or drama components.

Topic or lesson:	
List up to five key aspects of this lesson:	**How might you use the arts to connect to this?**
	Connect to effort:_____ Connect to processing skills: _____ Connect to attention skills: _____ Connect to memory capacity: _____ Connect to sequencing skills: _____
	Connect to effort:_____ Connect to processing skills: _____ Connect to attention skills: _____ Connect to memory capacity: _____ Connect to sequencing skills: _____
	Connect to effort:_____ Connect to processing skills: _____ Connect to attention skills: _____ Connect to memory capacity: _____ Connect to sequencing skills: _____
	Connect to effort:_____ Connect to processing skills: _____ Connect to attention skills: _____ Connect to memory capacity: _____ Connect to sequencing skills: _____
	Connect to effort:_____ Connect to processing skills: _____ Connect to attention skills: _____ Connect to memory capacity: _____ Connect to sequencing skills: _____

Figure 19.3: Integrate the arts into your lessons.

Visit go.SolutionTree.com/instruction for a free reproducible version of this figure.

Tools to Support Physical Activity

Previous chapters have provided strategies for adding physical activity to classroom instruction and with good reason. A third of students from poverty suffer from chronic stress and depression (Pratt & Brody, 2014). However, there is increasing evidence that voluntary gross motor exercise is a viable preventive and treatment strategy for depression (Yau, Li, Xu, & So, 2015). New brain cells contribute to better mood, memory, weight management, and cognition (Marin-Burgin & Schinder, 2012; van Praag, Fleshner, Schwartz, & Mattson, 2014). Another long-term study finds that overall physical fitness is a strong predictor of academic achievement, and the lack of fitness begins as early as fourth grade (London & Castrechini, 2011). You can learn much more about the evidence behind the connection to physical activity and improved learning in *Poor Students, Rich Teaching, Revised Edition* (Jensen, 2019).

With these benefits in mind, it's critical for you to support a full twenty- to thirty-minute physical activity break, in any way that you can, at the K–5 level. Do not, under any circumstances, punish a student by keeping him or her in the classroom during recess. There are dozens of alternatives (for example, stand last in line for lunch, lose privileges, stay after school for five minutes, and so on). You could also keep students more engaged to reduce behavioral issues and teach students the behaviors you want, rather than only punishing bad behavior (refer to part six, page 169).

For example, are you giving students constant stretch breaks and energizers to burn off energy? If not, include out-of-seat activities every ten to twenty minutes during your class. Take students outside, and let them do laps around a fitness or walking area. A great way to support physical activity in your classroom is to form teams for energizers that get the body moving. Assign a personal trainer to keep each team (four per team for grades K–5 and five per team for grades 6–12) engaged in the activity. Give personal trainers a cue every fifteen to twenty-five minutes to get the team moving, and rotate the trainers every two weeks. Use the planning sheet in figure 19.4 to organize your class into these teams.

Class or period:	
Start and end dates (change teams after two weeks):	
Team number:	
Leader:	Team members:

Figure 19.4: Form class exercise teams.

*Visit **go.SolutionTree.com/instruction** for a free reproducible version of this figure.*

Also, try the following activities with your class.

- **Invite students to run in place for one minute:** Once you begin, students will get excited, especially if you encourage some friendly competition or collaboration. Students who are extra active, bored, or just need to release a little steam will find this is a jewel.

- **Integrate movement with subject areas:** For example, check out activities at Action Based Learning (http://actionbasedlearning.3dcartstores.com).

- **Do whole-group activities that bring students together:** For example, allow a student to teach the class a dance step.

- **Allow student volunteers to be leaders:** Everyone follows as he or she walks, marches, and dances around the classroom for forty-five seconds.

- **Play an imaginary sport:** Students within a team all stand up, and each picks a favorite sport. One at a time, that person goes through the kinesthetic motions of that sport, while the other team members mimic the motions for thirty seconds. Rotate to the next team member, and everyone follows that student too. This is great fun and goes quickly.

At the secondary level, students still need to move their bodies. This means physical education is critical, but so are classroom activities that allow students to move. Use figure 19.5 to plan physical activities for the week.

Day	Activity
Monday	
Tuesday	
Wednesday	
Thursday	
Friday	

Figure 19.5: Planning sheet for physical activity.

Visit **go.SolutionTree.com/instruction** *for a free reproducible version of this figure.*

Quick Consolidation: Support Alternative Solutions

Use the arts and physical activity every day to enrich every student and move him or her toward graduation. Remember, graduation is not an accident; it is a hard, long-term process that takes its toll on students. When you provide the tools, hope, and relationships and go above and beyond, the students will feel it. They will feel that graduation is indeed that important. Once they are on board, success belongs to everybody. With this firmly in mind, answer the following reflection questions on ways you can use the arts and physical activity to bring out the graduation mindset in your students.

1. What did you learn about the connections between the arts and activity, and their connection to graduation rates, that you didn't know when you started this chapter?

2. What are some strategies from this chapter you can use to increase your use of music or drama in your teaching practices?

3. What are some strategies from this chapter you can use to increase your students' exposure to physical activity in your classroom?

4. With this new learning in mind, what other alternative practices can you come up with or refine that you believe might help your students adopt a graduation mindset?

5. In what ways could you take a whole-school approach to improving connections to physical activity and the arts for all students?

CHAPTER 20

PREPARE FOR COLLEGE AND CAREERS

There have always been some students who struggle or fail in nearly every area of school until they get to do something with their hands, participate in something physical, or get outdoors and learn. Some students practically live for these activities that may include vocational training, outdoor learning, project-based work, field trips, apprentice learning, and service learning. This makes it important for schools and teachers to offer students opportunity to explore the full range of what they can do and what avenues for their future speak most to them. Use the survey in figure 20.1 to assess how you and your school approach these factors.

What is your school's focus for students' lives after graduation? (Circle one.)	College	Career	Both
Describe your school or district's goals for and approach to preparing students for life after high school. What does it do well? What could it do better?			
Does your school have programs to help students enter college or get career training? (Circle all that apply.)	College-preparatory programs	Career-training programs	Neither
Describe the strategies these programs use. Do they have the resources necessary to achieve their goals? How could they improve?			
How often do you bring up graduation, college, and career in your day-to-day teaching? (Circle one.)	At least once a week	At least once a month	Rarely or never
Describe your strategies for addressing graduation and post-graduate life in your teaching. What could you do to make these a larger emphasis?			

Figure 20.1: Assess your approach to college and career prep.

Visit go.SolutionTree.com/instruction for a free reproducible version of this figure.

As you consider how to approach preparing students for life after school, it's critical that you choose activities and programs suited to their age level. As a generalization, keep your younger students closer to school. The novelty of outside experiences is more likely to overwhelm elementary students, depending on their previous at-home experiences. They'll remember the field trip but will likely learn less from it than if you just use a simple outdoor science activity within the school grounds. But what else can you do to help students graduate career or college ready? The key here is to put yourself in your students' shoes. What will move them forward in life? What can you do immediately? How can you best facilitate the process? Use the following list to help guide your answers to these questions.

- **College ready:** Do they have the life skills to deal with college life? Do they have solid study skills for each subject? Do they have a mentor to contact for support? If a student does not get a scholarship, here's what to do. Remind your students that college really can be free. The University of the People (http://uopeople.edu) is an accredited and tuition-free college (although there are some fees involved, up to $4,000 for tests).

- **Career ready:** Does every graduate have a resume? Does every graduate have interviewing skills through constant practice and feedback? Does each graduate have either a confirmed job or at least five leads to follow up on? Does he or she have a mentor to contact for support?

There are also some great websites that may help students avoid uncertainty, stress, or confusion about the college process. Work with students on college help sites like the National Association for College Admission Counseling (www.nacacnet.org) and the BigFuture College Board (https://bigfuture.collegeboard.org/get-started). Remember, community colleges can be a great stepping stone to either a job or a four-year degree elsewhere.

In the rest of this chapter, we examine some strategies that high-performing schools have found successful and follow that with a look the power of career and technical education programs

Strategies to Prepare for College and Career

Let's explore some of the strategies from high-performing schools I have worked with that helped prepare students for college and career. These are from highly successful elementary and secondary schools that discovered how to make the magic happen.

- **Increase exposure:** Help all students get exposure to college and jobs. Help all students get exposure to college and jobs. For example, for an elementary school, have all fifth graders partner up with one other student. They pick one college within driving distance and research it well (costs, scholarships, areas of specialization, location, demographics, and so on). Then, they prepare a fifteen-minute poster session to share with second graders. All fourth graders do the same with a career that only needs a high school degree.

- **Link behaviors and outcomes:** Help students link current behaviors and outcomes with a goal. "Your extra time on the homework really paid off. That effort will help you get into the college you want."

- **Link the content:** Use classroom content areas to talk about professions. For example, for high school science, media arts, language, or mathematics classes, mention jobs that require mastery of these subjects (biologist, graphic designer, translator, and engineer). Keep sharing the occupations that tie into the class you teach. You can even get your students involved this by having them do a little research into the careers and applications your teaching content extends to. See figure 20.2.

- **Assume the attribution:** Use the "when" phrase, not the "if" phrase. Instead of "If you graduate," say "When you graduate." Instead of "If you go to college," say "When you go to college."

Career	In what way does this career require this mastery?
First:	
Second:	
Third:	

Name: _____ Topic or skill: _____

Research this topic's application in the professional world, and list three careers that require mastery of this topic.

Figure 20.2: Connect content with career.

*Visit **go.SolutionTree.com/instruction** for a free reproducible version of this figure.*

- **Boost system knowledge:** Ensure that all students in high school, starting at the ninth-grade level, get a personalized scholarship committee. This group may comprise three to four counselors, teachers, or office staff. The role of this committee is to assess the student's interests, find schools that are strong in these areas, discover the entry requirements (such as grades and classes), find scholarship pathways, and help him or her make a plan to take the classes, get the grades, and earn a scholarship. To simplify this process, have students fill out the first half of figure 20.3 (page 212) and then have the scholarship committee use the student's answers to record preliminary information about schools that fit with that student's interests and career ambitions. Using this form, you can then prepare a full plan for the student you can use to motivate his or her learning and adopt a graduation mindset.

- **Offer supplemental programs:** Is your secondary school really committed to student success? Consider the following secondary strategies.

  - Provide a daily forty-five-minute after-school session with tutors from a nearby university (at zero cost to the school) to ensure that every student gets 100 percent of assigned homework done right.

  - Offer a strong mentorship program for all new students.

  - Provide language translation opportunities for families.

  - Raise money to ensure students have the transportation they need.

  - Have all students take honors classes (through the Advancement Via Individual Determination [AVID] program [www.avid.org]).

  - Require all students starting in seventh grade to participate in a schoolwide exhibition and the school science fair.

  - Provide college-level workshops for parents to involve them in supporting their students in the college journey.

Student (Fill out top section.)

Name: _____

What are some of your favorite interests or hobbies?

_____

_____

What have been your favorite classes or subjects? Why are these your favorites?

_____

_____

What do you picture yourself doing after you graduate high school?

_____

_____

_____

— —

Scholarship committee (Fill out bottom section.)

Committee member	Role

List three schools that fit with this student's interests and aspirations.

School	Applicable program	Notable entry requirements	Notable scholarship pathways

Notes on recommendations for this student:

Figure 20.3: Form to boost system knowledge.

Visit go.SolutionTree.com/instruction for a free reproducible version of this figure.

One of the schools that uses these strategies, Preuss School UCSD (https://bit.ly/2pIETW7), is a 100 percent–poverty public school that sends over 90 percent of its students to college. It raises students' expectations and goals, and then delivers the support to help students make their goals happen.

Strategies to Empower Career and Technical Education

In addition to strategies that focus on college advancement, it's also important to find ways to promote career and technical education at your school. Provide mentors, since we know the research supports this action step (Chan et al., 2013). There are thousands of jobs waiting for skilled workers, but we have not prepared students for them (Bartash, 2018). Figure 20.4 lists a series of jobs for which we should be offering skill sets.

Skill or program	Yes	No
Computer coding and software development		
Industrial services (welding, construction, and plumbing)		
Audio and video technology, information technology support, and electronic data processing (systems operations)		
Food and nutrition science, culinary arts		
Business development and marketing		
Agricultural development		
Animal production, science, and business		
Hospitality and tourism		
Plant science, natural resources, and ecology		
Corrections, law enforcement, and security		
How many programs does your school or district offer?		
What could your school or district do to expand its offerings?		

Figure 20.4: Identify career offerings your school supports.

Visit go.SolutionTree.com/instruction for a free reproducible version of this figure.

Your school can offer coursework in these areas by fostering career and technical education programs within the school, not just as an after-graduation choice. Here are three options for starting a career and technical education program in your school.

1. Contact your state department of education for more information on what is available for blending career and technical education into your school.

2. Start slow and implement one program a year.

3. Do miniprograms that take less time. The following are some suggestions for effective miniprograms at your school.

    a. Students research and create a simulation for dealing with fire drills, bullying, hostage situations, or floods.

    b. Students establish ties with local businesses for apprentice work.

    c. Students develop field trips within the school to see staff, vegetation, or design elements.

    d. Students set up a tour of a local business during slow times—such as weeks with no testing or holidays.

    e. Students form partnerships with Boy Scouts or Girl Scouts, 4-H club, or local camping facilities.

    f. Students work with local museums, cultural exhibits, and art galleries for field trips.

Although I am college educated, I don't feel that college is for everybody. Any time you push students too hard in any direction, you'll get resistance. Here are options for students who are not ready for college. Introduce them to the following resources.

- *Better Than College: How to Build a Successful Life Without a Four-Year Degree* by Blake Boles
- *40 Alternatives to College* by James Altucher
- TED and TEDx Talks that make great introductions to careers (search through the education category)

The more options students see, the better the likelihood that they'll find the right fit.

Quick Consolidation: Prepare for College and Careers

There is typically a sense of community among students and the teacher as they work toward a common goal. Focus on what matters: be an ally to help students graduate job or college ready. With this firmly in mind, answer the following reflection questions on ways you can ensure all your students graduate ready for college or career.

1. What did you learn in this chapter that you didn't already know about the importance of ensuring all students approach the graduation mindset with a college or career in mind?

2. What are some strategies for helping students identify a future college pathway that suits their interests and goals? What can you do to ensure your school adopts these strategies?

3. In thinking about some of the potential career and technical education pathways that would benefit your students, what are some specific ways your school could increase or improve its offerings?

4. If you have a student approach you with no ambition toward preparing for a college or career, what will you do to help him or her foster a stronger mindset toward graduation?

5. Think about students who've left your school and found success after graduation. What can you do to demonstrate their example for your existing students in a way that motivates them?

Reflect on the Graduation Mindset

All meaningful and lasting change starts with a mirror. Self-reflect first. Take a moment and ask yourself a few questions about what you do to help your students graduate.

1. What changes will you make to your teaching mindset to focus on achieving 100 percent student graduation?

2. What are some ways you can use music or physical activity in your classroom to benefit student learning?

3. What is a strategy you can implement to help students decide whether to focus on graduating college ready or career ready?

4. What strategies in this part could you work on with leadership and colleagues to adopt as a whole-school approach? Who are the key motivators you need on board to make this happen?

5. What is another mindset in this book you can use in conjunction with the graduation mindset to help ensure all your students graduate?

No one is telling you this is easy. You are in a tough profession. All you can ask of yourself is to be true to yourself and your students. At any point in your work, if you're uncommitted and on the fence, your students will sense it. If you're just waiting for retirement, how many students will you adversely influence before you call it quits? Your students need a teacher who is all in.

Epilogue

The mindsets and tools in this book are critical because high-performing teachers (those who achieve at least two years of academic gains for each year in the classroom) succeed with students from poverty. Likewise, high-performing schools progress because of one major theme: no excuses. We see students working hard and knowing they will succeed in these schools precisely because the staff won't let them fail. So in closing out this handbook, consider your next steps. What decisions will you make? What are your action steps? How you can access and use the tools in this book to improve your practices across each mindset?

To help you with this process, this epilogue provides two valuable resources that will help clarify your approach to this book's mindsets and do the leg work necessary to *transfer* your good intentions (your plans) into productive practice in your classroom.

Clarify Your Vision

A good place to start in establishing your approach to altering your mindsets is to print and fill out separate copies of figure E.1 (page 218), one for each of the seven mindsets: (1) relational, (2) achievement, (3) positivity, (4) rich classroom climate, (5) enrichment, (6) engagement, and (7) graduation. Answer, do you buy into each mindset fully or halfway, or do you reject it? Do you have ideas for taking it further? If you see places for improvement, how will you take action to make change happen? What will be the evidence procedure for tracking the changes you make?

Do not be quick to dismiss the importance of this activity. It is powerful and an important part of learning, using formative evaluation (0.90 effect size), developing teacher clarity (0.75 effect size), and professional development and reflection (0.62 effect size; Hattie, 2009). To be exemplary, it takes a continual process of learning, reflection, decision making, planning, action steps, and feedback. You must repeat this cycle of excellence again and again for your whole career. This is the path of excellence, but it is also a choice.

Real, daily excellence is a choice. It is a choice to grow. It is a choice to embrace change. Real, positive change comes from the development of true expertise in a life filled with purposeful workplace practice and integration of high-level personal beliefs. You'll have to be the change first before you see it in your students. Figure E.2 (pages 219–220) offers a concise reflection on the choices before you, one for each mindset. Consider these choices and print out and use the online version as a poster to keep these mindsets and choices firmly in your thinking as you teach and work to support your students.

Mindset: _____

Do you buy into this mindset?   Fully ☐   Halfway ☐   Reject ☐

Why?

How could you take this mindset or its strategies further?

How will you track and respond to the evidence from the changes you make?

Respond to the following four questions, or share them with a colleague, and collaborate on the answers.

1. What has happened in the past in your classroom on this topic? (This speaks to your track record.)

2. Where do you see a place (if any) for making a change in regard to this mindset? (This speaks to your skills in reflection and the ability to be honest and actionable with yourself.)

3. For each change you'd like to make, what will be the evidence of success? How will you know when you succeed at it? (This speaks to your prediction skills and knowledge of your own limitations.)

4. When you have successfully implemented the changes from this activity, would you consider sharing your experiences (what you learned or did well) with colleagues? (This speaks to your social skills, school culture building, teamwork, and comfort with yourself.)

Figure E.1: Your changing mindset.

Visit go.SolutionTree.com/instruction for a free reproducible version of this figure.

You Are Your Mindset: Which Is Yours?

Preparing to Make Choices

"It's not my fault. We teachers get kicked around, plus the parents and students don't care. No wonder everybody is stressed and students drop out."

"My greatest power is the power of choice. I have a great deal of influence over how I run my own brain. I remember this every day: I have a choice."

The Relational Mindset

"I was hired for the content I know, and I don't have enough time to teach social skills! I wasn't hired to be their parent!"

"We are all connected in this life together. Always connect first as a person (and an ally) and second as a teacher."

The Achievement Mindset

"It's not my fault. Parents should motivate their own kids, not me."

"I can build student effort, motivation, and attitudes to succeed. They are all teachable skills."

The Positivity Mindset

"I try to be positive, but look at what I'm up against. Positivity is for the deluded. I'm real with my students. I tell things like they are."

"I am an optimistic and grateful ally who helps students build a successful narrative of their future."

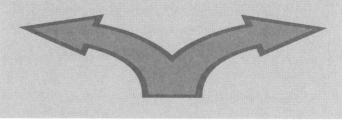

The Rich Classroom Climate Mindset

"My job is teaching content. Students must wake up and enter the real world. Learning does not need to feel good!"

"I focus on what students need to succeed and build it into the learning and social environment every day."

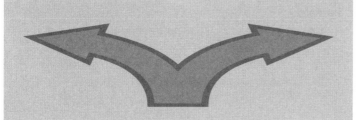

The Enrichment Mindset

"Some kids got it, and others don't. If they're ready, they'll learn it. If they haven't learned how to do this by now, they'll never get it."

"I know brains can change. I can grow and change myself first. Then, I can build powerful cognitive skills in my students."

Figure E.2: You are your mindset.

continued ⇨

The Engagement Mindset

"We have a ton of content to cover and usually lecture is the best way to do it. Besides, the engagement strategies are all a bunch of fluff."

"I can and will engage with purpose every student, every day, every nine minutes or less, guaranteed."

The Graduation Mindset

"I try to be a positive person, but realistically, these kids have come from pretty bad homes. I am not expecting much good to happen."

"I will focus on what matters. I will be an ally to help students graduate college and career ready."

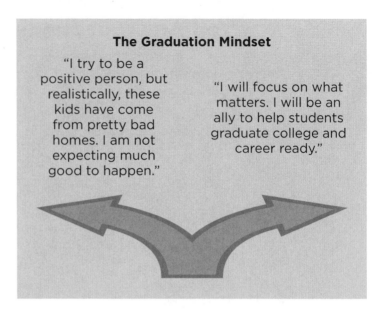

Visit go.SolutionTree.com/instruction for a free reproducible version of this figure.

Many consider making the choice to get started the hardest part of any new initiative or new thinking, but ultimately, it's about sustaining that choice. As you reflect on each of the decisions on the poster in figure E.2, use the content in the next section to help you do the work of going from motivation to change to a solid plan for implementing that change.

Transfer Good Things to Your Classroom

On a broad scale, there are at least three steps to growing your students and helping them graduate. Let's unpack them: (1) *motivation* to make a change (the why), (2) the *growth* and *learning* necessary to make a change (the what), and (3) the *implementation* of that change (the how and when).

The first of the three may also be labeled as having affect, caring, desire, or of course, motivation. Because you have gotten this far, it is likely you are already motivated to make a difference in your work. The growing and learning process typically means you are gaining resources that foster greater skill or knowledge. You might start this process in a discussion group, attend a conference, or learn and reflect at home. In this case, you've read a book and hope to get strategies of value. But of course, those strategies are useless if left on the page or in your head.

That's why I am most concerned about that last (and crucial) step: the implementation of the new learning. This transfer process (from notions to commitments to lesson plans to using it in a classroom) is different for everyone. For some, it starts with a grade-level or subject-level team meeting. For others, it begins with asking colleagues or doing research on a recurring problem. For others, it starts with a scrap of paper.

For you, in this moment, you've got a resource in front of you, and now it's time to get what you found of value *into your workplace*. Life is too short to have wasted your time reading without getting the real goodies from the book: better students.

Let's explore how to make that happen with the least amount of grief and the greatest likelihood of success. Why? Commonly at schools, the rate of implementation is far less than what it could be if only just a few simple strategies are put into play.

As soon as someone (like me) suggests to you that there may be more work ahead for this last step (called *transfer*), it can be discouraging. But it all comes back to who you are. Are you a teacher—someone who tries your best each day? Or, are you a change agent—someone who is committed every day to improving student learning? If you are serious about improving student outcomes, *you have to be* serious about making the changes.

Typically, educators rely on two things, such as *make a decision* and *use willpower*. If that was all that was necessary, all the teachers in the country would be well above average! As a professional developer, I have learned to hold up a mirror often to learn from what I do well and where I need to change. I am pretty good (as likely you are) at the first two steps (motivated to learn and doing the learning). But the implementation has been a weak spot, and I am committed to supporting those who use my work to become more successful at helping students grow and graduate.

Is it possible for you to succeed with just the first two steps I established at the beginning of this section? Of course! A small percentage of teachers do find a way to make that happen. But after doing a deep dive into the science of implementation behaviors, I have found that you can guarantee your implementation by deploying the following seven steps.

1. **Make a clear choice:** You chose the habit, so never think, "I have to do this." Instead say, "I get to do this!" Write the choice out, visualize it, and share it with others (make it real). Shift and strengthen your identity by ensuring that you think of yourself as the kind of person who does this kind of action (Murty, DuBrow, & Davachi, 2015).

   For example: Tell yourself, "My goal is to ensure my students receive better feedback, so I'm going to make sure I say things, like, 'Your effort was amazing; you stayed with that for a long time!' instead of offering vague feedback, such as 'Good job.' I will remind myself that I am a change agent who can and does change to help my students grow."

2. **Boost intention with a strong why:** Tie the new behavior to what matters most to you (your core drivers). Your motivators may be personal, such as those that will help you foster security (economic, social, and personal), foster autonomy (being able to choose and do it yourself), foster identity (believe and act like your authentic self), gain mastery (get very good at something), or find deeper meaning (by refining personal, cultural, or spiritual beliefs).

   Your motivators may also be external, such as those that help you improve social status by gaining respect from those in your culture, establish a sense of belonging and affiliation to a group you choose, feel validation and worthiness through others' acceptance, gain a sense of mission by being a part of something greater than yourself, or demonstrate that you have something to prove (your potential, a strongly held belief, or an action or strategy you take).

   For example: Say to yourself, "Getting better at this formative assessment will help me feel more confident, gain a bit more mastery, and help me keep my job. It will also help me feel a bit more respected by my peers and plug into the school mission better."

3. **Script the behavior:** Be clear about what you'll be doing; describe the new action in detail, including what you will do and when. Turn the behavior prompt into index cards, lesson plans, or a digital format to use.

   For example: "I will give my students *more specific* feedback. ('Your effort was amazing; you stayed with that for a long time!') instead of vague feedback ('Good job'). If I forget or fail to live up to this plan, I will correct it by engaging the SEA strategy ('Did I see a strong strategy, effort, or attitude?') and using those things to *add on* to my initial feedback with what I *wanted* to say ('Good job . . . and, your attitude was super positive the whole time, which helped you keep others on your team motivated')" (Gollwitzer & Sheeran, 2006).

4. **Create cues:** You have several ways to prompt the behavior. You could make the environment the place for the cue. You could set up a nudge to remind yourself using visual, sound, and environmental cues. You could tell your students about the habit, and give them a signal to use it with you if you forget. You could use habit stacking (where you automatically add this new action onto another habit you already do methodically). Acknowledge that, without some kind of a trigger, it will be tough to remember.

   For example: "I will add a classroom cue that every time I walk up to a student and it's time for feedback, students will know to raise their hand to their head and tap it. I will explain to them this is a cue to me to use my plan. I will also put a reminder poster in my classroom that reads 'Enjoy the SEA of change' to ensure I have a constant visual reminder around me."

5. **Do the new behavior:** Stick to the script or the plan. The more you do it right from the start, the fewer the mistakes and the stronger the outcomes. The more you plan out and critique the behavior and fine-tune it, the better the acquisition of skill.

   For example: "Each day I will assess my successes and failures at implementing this plan. I will put pieces in the form of index cards, lesson plans, and digital reminders to ensure I'm growing this behavior every day."

6. **Enjoy a reward:** The reward comes two ways: now and later. First, there is the satisfaction of seeing, hearing, and feeling the success in your students as the new behavior makes a difference in the class. The other is just a small dose of hedonistic happiness—a checked box on your habit app, applause from students, a snack packet of M&Ms, and so on. When you accumulate an appropriate number of these little successes, grant yourself something bigger, like buying yourself something special or taking the day off.

   For example: "Every time I successfully use my new behavior, I will put a button in a jar. When I get to twenty-five buttons, I'll treat myself to a copy of that movie I've been wanting to buy."

7. **Renew yourself:** Most habit changes take time (not days, but months). The average time for solid habit formation is about *ten weeks* (or sixty-six days). Research indicates the range among all the tasks it studied was *18 to 254* days (Lally, van Jaarsveld, Potts, & Wardle, 2010). In the study, those who chose to add drinking a glass of water to their morning routine took twenty days to form the habit. But to add fifty sit-ups a day, it took *over* ten weeks. Be ready to tweak, modify, and be patient with yourself. Plan to edit, revise, and improve as you go.

   For example: "Every time I start a new behavior, I will keep a small paper pad near my classroom desk. At the top of it, I will write a key word to describe my new habit and then draw a line under it for notes." You might go a couple of days with no notes, then have two notepads to fill after a day. The idea is to notice what you did well, and always ask if you could do it better next time. That's all you can ask of yourself.

For most educators, reflecting, having discussions, and making plans for implementation is a different kind of work to put into the job. But it may be the most important new part of the job. Why? It is what matters most. After all, if you are not implementing the changes, what exactly are you doing? My request of you is to please just do this once. Think of it as my free trial offer to you. Figure E.3 provides a useful tool to help you establish, detail, and reflect on your plan using these seven steps.

My Plan for Moving From Concept to Reality

1. Choose a concept or idea to make real. (This step works best if it is your idea.)

   _____

   _____

   _____

2. Establish intention. (Reflect on why you want to make this happen.)

   _____

   _____

   _____

3. Script the behavior and add plan B. (Be clear about what you'll be doing. Expect setbacks, and have an alternative if plan A doesn't work out.)

   _____

   _____

   _____

4. Create cues. (Expect that you will forget to carry out certain key behaviors, and set up cues and prompts to remind you to engage in them.)

   _____

   _____

   _____

5. Do the behavior. (Stay as close as you can to the script in step 3.)

   _____

   _____

   _____

6. Reward yourself. (Your brain needs something to look forward to; make sure you have a reward in mind for accomplishing your goal. Have both now and later rewards.)

   _____

   _____

   _____

7. Renew yourself. (Reflect on what you achieved. Ask yourself, "What worked, and what could I improve?")

   _____

   _____

   _____

Figure E.3: The implementation process for creating transfer.

Visit **go.SolutionTree.com/instruction** for a free reproducible version of this figure.

With your structured approach to implementing the high-impact mindsets in this book, you can make miracles happen in your life. Scattered, random positive things in your classroom will have little lasting effect. But make one small change, take one micro step, or try a mini attitude booster, and if you stick with it, you'll see miracles happen over time.

Can you start today?

References and Resources

Aas, M., Henry, C., Andreassen, O. A., Bellivier, F., Melle, I., & Etain, B. (2016). The role of childhood trauma in bipolar disorders. *International Journal of Bipolar Disorders, 4*(1), 2.

Adair, J. K., Colegrove, K. S-S., & McManus, M. E. (2017). How the word gap argument negatively impacts young children of Latinx immigrants' conceptualizations of learning. *Harvard Educational Review, 87*(3), 309–334.

Adcock, R. A., Thangavel, A., Whitfield-Gabrieli, S., Knutson, B., & Gabrieli, J. D. (2006). Reward-motivated learning: Mesolimbic activation precedes memory formation. *Neuron, 50*(3), 507–517.

Adelabu, D. H. (2007). Time perspective and school membership as correlates to academic achievement among African American adolescents. *Adolescence, 42*(167), 525–538.

Adler, A. D., Conklin, L. R., & Strunk, D. R. (2013). Quality of coping skills predicts depressive symptom reactivity over repeated stressors. *Journal of Clinical Psychology, 69*, 1228–1238.

Aikens, N. L., & Barbarin, O. (2008). Socioeconomic differences in reading trajectories: The contribution of family, neighborhood, and school contexts. *Journal of Educational Psychology, 100*(2), 235–251.

Algina, J., & Olejnik, S. (2003). Conducting power analyses for ANOVA and ANCOVA in between-subjects designs. *Evaluation and the Health Professions, 26*(3), 288–314.

Algoe, S. B. (2012). Find, remind, and bind: The functions of gratitude in everyday relationships. *Social and Personality Psychology Compass, 6*, 455–469.

Algoe, S. B., & Fredrickson, B. L. (2011). Emotional fitness and the movement of affective science from lab to field. *American Psychologist, 66*(1), 35–42.

Algoe, S. B., Haidt, J., & Gable, S. L. (2008). Beyond reciprocity: Gratitude and relationships in everyday life. *Emotion, 8*(3), 425–429.

Allen, J. P., McElhaney, K. B., Kuperminc, G. P., & Jodl, K. M. (2004). Stability and change in attachment security across adolescence. *Child Development, 75*(6), 1792–1805.

Alliance for Excellent Education. (n.d.). *The high cost of high school dropouts: The economic case for reducing the high school dropout rate.* Accessed at https://all4ed.org/take-action/action-academy/the-economic-case-for-reducing-the-high-school-dropout-rate on September 13, 2018.

Alloway, T. P., & Alloway, R. G. (2010). Investigating the predictive roles of working memory and IQ in academic attainment. *Journal of Experimental Child Psychology, 106*(1), 20–29.

Almeida, D. M., Neupert, S. D., Banks, S. R., & Serido, J. (2005). Do daily stress processes account for socioeconomic health disparities? *Journals of Gerontology: Series B, 60,* 34–39.

Altucher, J. (2012). *40 alternatives to college.* Seattle, WA: CreateSpace.

Amat, J., Paul, E., Zarza, C., Watkins, L. R., & Maier, S. F. (2006). Previous experience with behavioral control over stress blocks the behavioral and dorsal raphe nucleus activating effects of later uncontrollable stress: Role of the ventral medial prefrontal cortex. *Journal of Neuroscience, 26*(51), 13264–13272.

American Institute for Economic Research Staff. (2012). *The everyday price index.* Accessed at www.aier.org/sites /default/files/Files/Documents/Research/3631/EB201202.pdf on May 22, 2015.

Amodio, D. M., Harmon-Jones, E., Devine, P. G., Curtin, J. J., Hartley, S. L., & Covert, A. E. (2004). Neural signals for the detection of unintentional race bias. *Psychological Science, 15*(2), 88–93.

Amy Purdy. (n.d.). In *Wikipedia.* Accessed at https://en.wikipedia.org/wiki/Amy_Purdy on May 14, 2016.

Appleton, J. J., Christenson, S. L., & Furlong, M. J. (2008). Student engagement with school: Critical conceptual and methodological issues of the construct. *Psychology in the Schools, 45,* 369–386.

Arakaki, M. (2010, November 4). *Mr. Irish's classroom football theme* [Video file]. Accessed at www.youtube.com /watch?v=Y6kp11hMTIk on May 22, 2015.

Asbury, C., & Rich, B. (Eds.). (2008). *Learning, arts, and the brain: The Dana Consortium report on arts and cognition.* New York: The Dana Foundation. Accessed at www.dana.org/uploadedFiles/News_and_Publications/Special _Publications/Learning,%20Arts%20 and%20the%20Brain_ArtsAndCognition_Compl.pdf on January 6, 2016.

Au, J., Sheehan, E., Tsai, N., Duncan, G. J., Buschkuehl, M., & Jaeggi, S. M. (2015). Improving fluid intelligence with training on working memory: A meta-analysis. *Psychonomic Bulletin and Review, 22*(2), 366–377.

Aydin, K., Ucar, A., Oguz, K. K., Okur, O. O., Agayev, A., Unal, Z., et al. (2007). Increased gray matter density in the parietal cortex of mathematicians: A voxel-based morphometry study. *American Journal of Neuroradiology, 28*(10), 1859–1864.

AZ Quotes. (n.d.). *You may not be responsible for being down, but you must be responsible for getting up.* Accessed at www.azquotes.com/quote/765869 on July 25, 2015.

Azer, S. A. (2011). Learning surface anatomy: Which learning approach is effective in an integrated PBL curriculum? *Medical Teacher, 33*(1), 78–80.

Bailey, T. C., Eng, W., Frisch, M. B., & Snyder, C. R. (2007). Hope and optimism as related to life satisfaction. *Journal of Positive Psychology, 2*(3), 168–175.

Bankrate. (2012). *Financial Security Index down slightly.* Accessed at www.bankrate.com/finance/consumer-index /financial-security-charts-1112.aspx on January 6, 2016.

Banks, J., Cochran-Smith, M., Moll, L., Richert, A., Zeichner, K., LePage, P., et al. (2005). Teaching diverse learners. In L. Darling-Hammond & J. Bransford (Eds.), *Preparing teachers for a changing world: What teachers should learn and be able to do* (pp. 232–274). San Francisco: Jossey-Bass.

Baratta, M. V., Zarza, C. M., Gomez, D. M., Campeau, S., Watkins, L. R., & Maier, S. F. (2009). Selective activation of dorsal raphe nucleus-projecting neurons in the ventral medial prefrontal cortex by controllable stress. *European Journal of Neuroscience, 30*(6), 1111–1116.

Barbarin, O., Iruka, I. U., Harradine, C., Winn, D. M., McKinney, M. K., & Taylor, L. C. (2013). Development of social-emotional competence in boys of color: A cross-sectional cohort analysis from pre-K to second grade. *American Journal of Orthopsychiatry, 83*(2), 145–155.

Barnett, S. M., & Ceci, S. J. (2002). When and where do we apply what we learn? A taxonomy for far transfer. *Psychological Bulletin, 128*(4), 612–637.

Bartash, J. (2018, July 19). *Screaming labor shortage forcing firms to get creative to fill job openings.* Accessed at www.marketwatch.com/story/screaming-labor-shortage-forcing-firms-to-get-creative-to-fill-record-job -openings-2018-07-18 on September 13, 2018.

Bastian, B., Kuppens, P., De Roover, K., & Diener, E. (2014). Is valuing positive emotion associated with life satisfaction? *Emotion*, *14*(4), 639–645.

Baumeister, R. F., Bratslavsky, E., Finkenauer, C., & Vohs, K. D. (2001). Bad is stronger than good. *Review of General Psychology*, *5*(4), 323–370.

Baumeister, R. F., & Leary, M. R. (1995). The need to belong: Desire for interpersonal attachments as a fundamental human motivation. *Psychological Bulletin*, *117*(3), 497–529.

Behnke, A. O., Piercy, K. W., & Diversi, M. (2004). Educational and occupational aspirations of Latino youth and their parents. *Hispanic Journal of Behavioral Sciences*, *26*(1), 16–35.

Beierholm, U., Guitart-Masip, M., Economides, M., Chowdhury, R., Düzel, E., Dolan, R., et al. (2013). Dopamine modulates reward-related vigor. *Neuropsychopharmacology*, *38*(8), 1495–1503.

Belfield, C. R., Levin, H. M., & Rosen, R. (2012, January). *The economic value of opportunity youth*. Washington, DC: Civic Enterprises. Accessed at www.serve.gov/sites/default/files/ctools/econ_value_opportunity_youth.pdf on May 3, 2014.

Berger, J., Heinrichs, M., von Dawans, B., Way, B. M., & Chen, F. S. (2016). Cortisol modulates men's affiliative responses to acute social stress. *Psychoneuroendocrinology*, *63*, 1–9.

Berger, M., & Sarnyai, Z. (2015). "More than skin deep": Stress neurobiology and mental health consequences of racial discrimination. *Stress*, *18*(1), 1–10.

Berghorst, L. H., Bogdan, R., Frank, M. J., & Pizzagalli, D. A. (2013). Acute stress selectively reduces reward sensitivity. *Frontiers in Human Neuroscience*, *7*(133), 1–15.

Berns, G. S., Blaine, K., Prietula, M. J., & Pye, B. E. (2013). Short- and long-term effects of a novel on connectivity in the brain. *Brain Connectivity*, *3*(6), 590–600.

Best, J. R. (2010). Effects of physical activity on children's executive function: Contributions of experimental research on aerobic exercise. *Developmental Review*, *30*(4), 331–351.

Bezold, C. P., Konty, K. J., Day, S. E., Berger, M., Harr, L., Larkin, M., et al. (2014). The effects of changes in physical fitness on academic performance among New York City youth. *Journal of Adolescent Health*, *55*(6), 774–781.

Bhullar, N., Schutte, N. S., & Malouff, J. M. (2013). The nature of well-being: The roles of hedonic and eudaimonic processes and trait emotional intelligence. *Journal of Psychology*: *Interdisciplinary and Applied*, *147*(1), 1–16.

Biemiller, A. (2003). Vocabulary needed if children are to read well. *Reading Psychology*, *24*, 323–335.

Biffle, C. (2013). *Whole brain teaching for challenging kids*. San Bernardino, CA: Whole Brain Teaching.

Black, P., & Wiliam, D. (1998). Inside the black box: Raising standards through classroom assessment. *Phi Delta Kappan*, *80*(2), 139–148.

Blackwell, L. S., Trzesniewski, K. H., & Dweck, C. S. (2007). Implicit theories of intelligence predict achievement across an adolescent transition: A longitudinal study and an intervention. *Child Development*, *78*(1), 246–263.

Blake, D. T., Heiser, M. A., Caywood, M., & Merzenich, M. M. (2006). Experience-dependent adult cortical plasticity requires cognitive association between sensation and reward. *Neuron*, *52*(2), 371–381.

Blokland, G. A., McMahon, K. L., Thompson, P. M., Martin, N. G., de Zubicaray, G. I., & Wright, M. J. (2011). Heritability of working memory brain activation. *Journal of Neuroscience*, *31*(30), 10882–10890.

Bogdan, R., & Pizzagalli, D. A. (2006). Acute stress reduces reward responsiveness: Implications for depression. *Biological Psychiatry*, *60*(10), 1147–1154.

Bolte, A., Goschkey, T., & Kuhl, J. (2003). Emotion and intuition: Effects of positive and negative mood on implicit judgments of semantic coherence. *Psychological Science*, *14*(5), 416–421.

Bouffard, S. (2014). A new role for guidance counselors. *Harvard Education Letter*, *30*(6). Accessed at http://hepg .org/hel-home/issues/volume-30,-number-6/helarticle/a-new-role-for-guidance-counselors on May 22, 2015.

Boushey, H., Bernstein, J., & Mishel, L. (2002). *The state of working America 2002–03.*Washington, DC: Economic Policy Institute.

Boykin, A. W., Tyler, K. M., Watkins-Lewis, K., & Kizzie, K. (2006). Culture in the sanctioned classroom practices of elementary school teachers serving low-income African American students. *Journal of Education for Students Placed at Risk, 11*(2), 161–173.

Branham, M. (2017). *Massachusetts program the 'Cadillac of CTE.'* Accessed at www.csg.org/pubs/capitolideas/sep _oct_2011/MassRegional.aspx on October 9, 2018.

Brennan, T. (2004). *The transmission of affect.* Ithaca, NY: Cornell University Press.

Bridgeland, J. M., DiIulio, J. J., Jr., & Morison, K. B. (2006, March). *The silent epidemic: Perspectives of high school dropouts.* Washington, DC: Civic Enterprises. Accessed at www.ignitelearning.com/pdf/TheSilentEpidemic3 –06FINAL.pdf on February 4, 2013.

Brockman, J. (Ed.). (2012). *This will make you smarter: New scientific concepts to improve your thinking.* New York: Harper Perennial.

Brody, G. H., Lei, M. K., Chen, E., & Miller, G. E. (2014). Neighborhood poverty and allostatic load in African American youth. *Pediatrics, 134*(5), 1362–1368.

Brown, B. (2012). *Daring greatly: How the courage to be vulnerable transforms the way we live, love, parent, and lead.* New York: Gotham Books.

Brown, B. (2015). *Rising strong.* New York: Spiegel & Grau.

Brown, J., Cooper-Kuhn, C. M., Kempermann, G., van Praag, H., Winkler, J., Gage, F. H., et al. (2003). Enriched environment and physical activity stimulate hippocampal but not olfactory bulb neurogenesis. *European Journal of Neuroscience, 17*(10), 2042–2046.

Bruckheimer, J. (Producer), Oman, C. (Producer), & Washington, D. (Director). (2001). *Remember the Titans* [Motion picture]. United States: Walt Disney Home Video.

Bruininks, P., & Malle, B. F. (2005). Distinguishing hope from optimism and related affective states. *Motivation and Emotion, 29*(4), 324–352.

Brummelman, E., Thomaes, S., Overbeek, G., Orobio de Castro, B., van den Hout, M. A., & Bushman, B. J. (2014). On feeding those hungry for praise: Person praise backfires in children with low self-esteem. *Journal of Experimental Psychology: General, 143*(1), 9–14.

Budde, H., Voelcker-Rehage, C., Pietrabyk-Kendziorra, S., Ribeiro, P., & Tidow, G. (2008). Acute coordinative exercise improves attentional performance in adolescents. *Neuroscience Letters, 441*(2), 219–223.

Bui, Q. (2015, February 5). Map: The most common* job in every state. *Planet Money: The Economy Explained.* Accessed at www.npr.org/sections/money/2015/02/05/382664837/map-the-most-common-job-in-every-state on January 6, 2016.

Bull, R., Espy, K. A., & Wiebe, S. A. (2008). Short-term memory, working memory, and executive functioning in preschoolers: Longitudinal predictors of mathematical achievement at age 7 years. *Developmental Neuropsychology, 33*(3), 205–228.

Buonomano, D. V. (2014). Neural dynamics based timing in the subsecond to seconds range. In H. Merchang & V. de Lafuente (Eds.), *Neurobiology of interval timing: Advances in experimental medicine and biology 829* (pp. 101–117). New York: Springer.

Burgess, D. (2012). *Teach like a pirate: Increase student engagement, boost your creativity, and transform your life as an educator.* San Diego, CA: Dave Burgess Consulting.

Butler-Barnes, S. T., Williams, T. T., & Chavous, T. M. (2012). Racial pride and religiosity among African American boys: Implications for academic motivation and achievement. *Journal of Youth and Adolescence, 41*(4), 486–498.

Caeyenberghs, K., Leemans, A., Heitger, M. H., Leunissen, I., Dhollander, T., Sunaert, S., et al. (2012). Graph analysis of functional brain networks for cognitive control of action in traumatic brain injury. *Brain, 135*(4), 1293–1307.

Caldwell, C. H., Zimmerman, M. A., Bernat, D. H., Sellers, R. M., & Notaro, P. C. (2002). Racial identity, maternal support, and psychological distress among African American adolescents. *Child Development*, *73*(4), 1322–1336.

Campbell, P. (2018, January 30). Trucks headed for driverless future. *Financial Times*. Accessed at www.ft.com /content/7686ea3e-e0dd-11e7-a0d4-0944c5f49e46 on August 14, 2018.

Canfield, J. (2015). *The success principles*: How to get from where you are to where you want to be (10th anniv. ed.). New York: William Morrow.

Canfield, J., & Hansen, M. V. (2013). *Chicken soup for the soul* (20th anniv. ed.). Cos Cob, CT: Chicken Soup for the Soul.

Carlson, C. R., Collins, F. L., Jr., Nitz, A. J., Sturgis, E. T., & Rogers, J. L. (1990). Muscle stretching as an alternative relaxation training procedure. *Journal of Behavior Therapy and Experimental Psychiatry*, *21*(1), 29–38.

Carlson, S. A., Fulton, J. E., Lee, S. M., Maynard, L. M., Brown, D. R., Kohl, H. W., III., et al. (2008). Physical education and academic achievement in elementary school: Data from the early childhood longitudinal study. *American Journal of Public Health*, *98*(4), 721–727.

Carney, D. R., Cuddy, A. J. C., & Yap, A. J. (2010). Power posing: Brief nonverbal displays affect neuroendocrine levels and risk tolerance. *Psychological Science*, *21*(10), 1363–1368.

Carter, S. C. (2001). *No excuses*: Lessons from 21 high-performing, high-poverty schools. Washington, DC: Heritage Foundation.

Catalino, L. I., Algoe, S. B., & Fredrickson, B. L. (2014). Prioritizing positivity: An effective approach to pursuing happiness? *Emotion*, *14*, 1155–1161.

Catalino, L. I., & Fredrickson, B. L. (2011). A Tuesday in the life of a flourisher: The role of positive emotional reactivity in optimal mental health. *Emotion*, *11*(4), 938–950.

Catt, M. (Producer), & Kendrick, A. (Director). (2006). *Facing the giants* [Motion picture]. United States: Samuel Goldwyn Films.

Catterall, J. S. (2003). Research and assessment on the arts and learning: Education policy implications of recent research on the arts and academic and social development. *Journal for Learning Through Music*, *3*, 103–109.

Catterall, J. S. (2009). *Doing well and doing good by doing art*: The effects of education in the visual and performing arts on the achievements and values of young adults. Los Angeles: Imagination Group.

Catterall, J. S., Chapleau, R., & Iwanaga, J. (1999). Involvement in the arts and human development: General involvement and intensive involvement in music and theater arts. In E. Fiske (Ed.), *Champions of change*: The impact of the arts on learning (pp. 1–18). Washington, DC: Arts Education Partnership.

Catterall, J. S., Dumais, S. A., & Hampden-Thompson, G. (2012). *The arts and achievement in at-risk youth*: Findings from four longitudinal studies (Research Report No. 55). Washington, DC: National Endowment for the Arts.

Ceballo, R. (2004). From barrios to Yale: The role of parenting strategies in Latino families. *Hispanic Journal of Behavioral Sciences*, *26*(2), 171–186.

Ceci, S. J., & Williams, W. M. (1997). Schooling, intelligence, and income. *American Psychologist*, *52*(10), 1051–1058.

Center for Public Education. (2005). *High-performing, high-poverty schools*: Research review. Accessed at www.center forpubliceducation.org/Main-Menu/Organizing-a-school/High-performing-high-poverty-schools-At-a-glance -/High-performing-high-poverty-schools-Research-review.html on May 18, 2016.

Centre for Confidence and Well-Being. (n.d.). *Glasgow University mindset research*. Accessed at www.centreforconfi ce.co.uk/information.php?p=cGlkPTE1NQ== on May 22, 2015.

Cepeda, N. J., Coburn, N., Rohrer, D., Wixted, J. T., Mozer, M. C., & Pashler, H. (2009). Optimizing distributed practice: Theoretical analysis and practical implications. *Experimental Psychology*, *56*(4), 236–246.

Chan, C. S., Rhodes, J. E., Howard, W. J., Lowe, S. R., Schwartz, S. E., & Herrera, C. (2013). Pathways of influence in school-based mentoring: The mediating role of parent and teacher relationships. *Journal of School Psychology*, *51*(1), 129–142.

Chetty, R., Friedman, J. N., Hilger, N., Saez, E., Schanzenbach, D. W., & Yagan, D. (2011). How does your kindergarten classroom affect your earnings? Evidence from Project STAR. *Quarterly Journal of Economics, 126*(4), 1593–1660.

ChildStats. (2015). *America's children: Key national indicators of well-being, 2015—Child poverty.* Accessed at www.childstats.gov/americaschildren/eco1.asp on October 14, 2015.

Choi, J., Jeong, B., Rohan, M. L., Polcari, A. M., & Teicher, M. H. (2009). Preliminary evidence for white matter tract abnormalities in young adults exposed to parental verbal abuse. *Biological Psychiatry, 65*(3), 227–234.

Chung-Do, J., Filibeck, K., Goebert, D. A., Arakawa, G., Fraser, D., Laboy, J., et al. (2013). Understanding students' perceptions of a high school course designed to enhance school connectedness. *Journal of School Health, 83*(7), 478–484.

Cimpian, A., Arce, H.-M., Markman, E. M., & Dweck, C. S. (2007). Subtle linguistic cues affect children's motivation. *Psychological Science, 18*(4), 314–316.

Clamp, M., Fry, B., Kamal, M., Xie, X., Cuff, J., Lin, M. F., et al. (2007). Distinguishing protein-coding and noncoding genes in the human genome. *Proceedings of the National Academy of Sciences of the United States of America, 104*(49), 19428–19433.

Coe, D. P., Peterson, T., Blair, C., Schutten, M. C., & Peddie, H. (2013). Physical fitness, academic achievement, and socioeconomic status in school-aged youth. *Journal of School Health, 83*(7), 500–507.

Coe, D. P., Pivarnik, J. M., Womack, C. J., Reeves, M. J., & Malina, R. M. (2006). Effect of physical education and activity levels on academic achievement in children. *Medicine and Science in Sports and Exercise, 38*(8), 1515–1519.

Coe, R. (2002, September). *It's the effect size, stupid: What effect size is and why it is important.* Paper presented at the annual conference of the British Educational Research Association, University of Exeter, England.

Cohen, G. L., Garcia, J., Purdie-Vaughns, V., Apfel, N., & Brzustoski, P. (2009). Recursive processes in self-affirmation: Intervening to close the minority achievement gap. *Science, 324*(5925), 400–403.

Cohler, B. J. (1980). Personal narrative and life course. In P. Baltes & O. G. Brim, Jr. (Eds.), *Life span development and behavior* (Vol. 4, pp. 205–241). New York: Academic Press.

Cohn, M. A., & Fredrickson, B. L. (2010). In search of durable positive psychology interventions: Predictors and consequences of long-term positive behavior change. *Journal of Positive Psychology, 5*(5), 355–366.

Cohn, M. A., Fredrickson, B. L., Brown, S. L., Mikels, J. A., & Conway, A. M. (2009). Happiness unpacked: Positive emotions increase life satisfaction by building resilience. *Emotion, 9*(3), 361–368.

Coller, R. J., & Kuo, A. A. (2014). Youth development through mentorship: A Los Angeles school-based mentorship program among Latino children. *Journal of Community Health, 39*(2), 316–321.

Commission on Children at Risk. (2003). *Hardwired to connect: The new scientific case for authoritative communities.* New York: Institute for American Values.

Conway, A. R., Kane, M. J., & Engle, R. W. (2003). Working memory capacity and its relation to general intelligence. *Trends in Cognitive Sciences, 7*(12), 547–552.

Conzemius, A. E., & O'Neill, J. (2014). *The handbook for SMART school teams: Revitalizing best practices for collaboration.* Bloomington, IN: Solution Tree Press.

Cook, J. E., Purdie-Vaughns, V., Garcia, J., & Cohen, G. L. (2012). Chronic threat and contingent belonging: Protective benefits of values affirmation on identity development. *Journal of Personality and Social Psychology, 102*(3), 479–496.

Cook, S. W., Mitchell, Z., & Goldin-Meadow, S. (2008). Gesturing makes learning last. *Cognition, 106*(2), 1047–1058.

Coplan, J. D., Andrews, M. W., Rosenblum, L. A., Owens, M. J., Friedman, S., Gorman, J. M., et al. (1996). Persistent elevations of cerebrospinal fluid concentrations of corticotropin-releasing factor in adult nonhuman primates exposed to early-life stressors: Implications for the pathophysiology of mood and anxiety disorders. *Proceedings of the National Academy of Sciences of the United States of America, 93*(4), 1619–1623.

Covey, S. R. (2013). *The 7 habits of highly effective people: Powerful lessons in personal change.* New York: Simon & Schuster.

Cowan, N. (2010). The magical mystery four: How is working memory capacity limited, and why? *Current Directions in Psychological Science, 19*(1), 51–57.

Crocker, R. (2015). Emotional testimonies: An ethnographic study of emotional suffering related to migration from Mexico to Arizona. *Frontiers in Public Health, 3,* 177.

Crone, E. A., Wendelken, C., Donohue, S., van Leijenhorst, L., & Bunge, S. A. (2006). Neurocognitive development of the ability to manipulate information in working memory. *Proceedings of the National Academy of Sciences of the United States of America, 103*(24), 9315–9320.

Davis, O. S., Butcher, L. M., Docherty, S. J., Meaburn, E. L., Curtis, C. J. C., Simpson, M. A., et al. (2010). A three-stage genome-wide association study of general cognitive ability: Hunting the small effects. *Behavior Genetics, 40*(6), 759–767.

de Bono, E. (1999). *Six thinking hats* (Rev. and updated ed.). Boston: Back Bay.

De La Paz, S. (2005). Teaching historical reasoning and argumentative writing in culturally and academically diverse middle school classrooms. *Journal of Educational Psychology, 97*(2), 139–158.

De Smedt, B., Janssen, R., Bouwens, K., Verschaffel, L., Boets, B., & Ghesquière, P. (2009). Working memory and individual differences in mathematics achievement: A longitudinal study from first grade to second grade. *Journal of Experimental Child Psychology, 103*(2), 186–201.

Delgado, M. R., Nearing, K. I., LeDoux, J. E., & Phelps, E. A. (2008). Neural circuitry underlying the regulation of conditioned fear and its relation to extinction. *Neuron, 59*(5), 829–838.

DeNavas-Walt, C., Proctor, B. D., & Smith, J. C. (2011). *Income, poverty, and health insurance coverage in the United States: 2010* (Current Population Reports). Washington, DC: U.S. Government Printing Office.

DePaoli, J., Bridgeland, J., Atwell, M., & Balfanz, R. (2018). *2018 Building a Grad Nation: Progress and challenge in raising high school graduation rates.* Accessed at http://gradnation.americaspromise.org/2018-building-grad-nation-report on September 13, 2018.

Dexter, C. A., Wong, K., Stacks, A. M., Beeghly, M., & Barnett, D. (2013). Parenting and attachment among low-income African American and Caucasian preschoolers. *Journal of Family Psychology, 27*(4), 629–638.

Dharmadhikari, A. S. (2013). Six degrees of separation: Use of social network analysis to better understand outbreaks of nosocomial transmission of extensively drug-resistant tuberculosis. *Journal of Infectious Diseases, 207*(1), 1–3.

Disabato, D. J., Goodman, F. R., Kashdan, T. B., Short, J. L., & Jarden, A. (2015). Different types of well-being? A cross-cultural examination of hedonic and eudaimonic well-being. *Psychological Assessment, 28,* 471–482.

Doan, S. N., & Evans, G. W. (2011). Maternal responsiveness moderates the relationship between allostatic load and working memory. *Development and Psychopathology, 23*(3), 873–880.

Dolcos, S., Hu, Y., Iordan, A. D., Moore, M., & Dolcos, F. (2016). Optimism and the brain: Trait optimism mediates the protective role of the orbitofrontal cortex gray matter volume against anxiety. *Social Cognitive and Affective Neuroscience, 11,* 263–271.

Dougherty, S. M. (2018). The effect of career and technical education on human capital accumulation: Causal evidence from Massachusetts. *Education Finance and Policy, 13*(2), 119–148.

Douglas-Hall, A., & Chau, M. (2007). *Most low-income parents are employed.* New York: National Center for Children in Poverty.

Draganski, B., Gaser, C., Busch, V., Schuierer, G., Bogdahn, U., & May, A. (2004). Neuroplasticity: Changes in grey matter induced by training. *Nature, 427*(6972), 311–312.

Dubois, L., Ohm Kyvik, K., Girard, M., Tatone-Tokuda, F., Pérusse, D., Hjelmborg, J., et al. (2012). Genetic and environmental contributions to weight, height, and BMI from birth to 19 years of age: An international study of over 12,000 twin pairs. *PLOS ONE, 7*(2).

Duckworth, A. L., Kirby, T. A., Oettingen, G., & Gollwitzer, A. (2013). From fantasy to action: Mental contrasting with implementation intentions (MCII) improves academic performance in children. *Social Psychological and Personality Science, 4*(6), 745–753.

Duckworth, A. L., Peterson, C., Matthews, M. D., & Kelly, D. R. (2007). Grit: Perseverance and passion for long-term goals. *Journal of Personality and Social Psychology, 92*(6), 1087–1101.

Duckworth, A. L., Quinn, P. D., Lynam, D. R., Loeber, R., & Stouthamer-Loeber, M. (2011). Role of test motivation in intelligence testing. *Proceedings of the National Academy of Sciences of the United States of America, 108*(19), 7716–7720.

Duckworth, A. L., Quinn, P. D., & Seligman, M. E. P. (2009). Positive predictors of teacher effectiveness. *Journal of Positive Psychology, 4*(6), 540–547.

Dunning, D. L., Holmes, J., & Gathercole, S. E. (2013). Does working memory training lead to generalized improvements in children with low working memory? A randomized controlled trial. *Developmental Science, 16*(6), 915–925.

Dusek, J. A., Otu, H. H., Wohlhueter, A. L., Bhasin, M., Zerbini, L. F., Joseph, M. G., et al. (2008). Genomic counter-stress changes induced by the relaxation response. *PLOS ONE, 3*(7).

Duyme, M., Dumaret, A.-C., & Tomkiewicz, S. (1999). How can we boost IQs of "dull children"? A late adoption study. *Proceedings of the National Academy of Sciences of the United States of America, 96*(15), 8790–8794.

Dweck, C. S. (1999). *Self-theories: Their role in motivation, personality, and development.* Lillington, NC: Edwards Brothers.

Dweck, C. S. (2002). The development of ability conceptions. In A. Wigfield & J. S. Eccles (Eds.), *Development of achievement motivation* (pp. 57–88). New York: Academic Press.

Dweck, C. S. (2008). *Mindset: The new psychology of success (how we can learn to fulfill our potential).* New York: Ballantine Books.

Eamon, M. K. (2001). The effects of poverty on children's socioemotional development: An ecological systems analysis. *Social Work, 46*(3), 256–266.

Economic Policy Institute. (2014). *Real median household income, all households and working-age, 1979–2013 (2013 dollars).* Accessed at www.stateofworkingamerica.org/charts/real-median-household-income on January 6, 2016.

Edcoogle. (2014, September 24). *5 amazing kids who changed the world. This is inspirational.* Accessed at www.edcoogle.com/blog/2014/09/5-amazing-kids-changed-world-inspirational on October 21, 2015.

Eichenlaub, J. B., Ruby, P., & Morlet, D. (2012). What is the specificity of the response to the own first-name when presented as a novel in a passive oddball paradigm? An ERP study. *Brain Research, 1447*, 65–78.

Eldridge, B., Galea, M., McCoy, A., Wolfe, R., & Graham, H. K. (2003). Uptime normative values in children aged 8 to 15 years. *Developmental Medicine and Child Neurology, 45*(3), 189–193.

Elliot, A. J., & Dweck, C. S. (Eds.). (2005). *Handbook of competence and motivation.* New York: Guilford Press.

Elliott, E. S., & Dweck, C. S. (1988). Goals: An approach to motivation and achievement. *Journal of Personality and Social Psychology, 54*(1), 5–12.

Emmons, R. A. (2007). *Thanks! How the new science of gratitude can make you happier.* Boston: Houghton Mifflin.

Emmons, R. A., & Stern, R. (2013). Gratitude as a psychotherapeutic intervention. *Journal of Clinical Psychology, 69*, 846–855.

Engel de Abreu, P. M., Abreu, N., Nikaedo, C. C., Puglisi, M. L., Tourinho, C. J., Miranda, M. C., et al. (2014). Executive functioning and reading achievement in school: A study of Brazilian children assessed by their teachers as "poor readers." *Frontiers in Psychology, 10,* 550.

Engineer, N. D., Engineer, C. T., Reed, A. C., Pandya, P. K., Jakkamsetti, V., Moucha, R., et al. (2012). Inverted-U function relating cortical plasticity and task difficulty. *Neuroscience, 205,* 81–90.

Engle, R. W. (2001). What is working memory capacity? In H. L. Roediger III, J. S. Nairne, I. Neath, & A. M. Suprenant (Eds.), *The nature of remembering: Essays in honor of Robert G. Crowder* (pp. 297–314). Washington, DC: American Psychological Association.

Epel, E. S., Blackburn, E. H., Lin, J., Dhabhar, F. S., Adler, N. E., Morrow, J. D., et al. (2004). Accelerated telomere shortening in response to life stress. *Proceedings of the National Academy of Sciences of the United States of America, 101*(49), 17312–17315.

Erickson, K. I., Voss, M. W., Prakash, R. S., Basak, C., Szabo, A., Chaddock, L., et al. (2011). Exercise training increases size of hippocampus and improves memory. *Proceedings of the National Academy of Sciences of the United States of America, 108*(7), 3017–3022.

Eriksson, P. S., Perfilieva, E., Björk-Eriksson, T., Alborn, A. M., Nordborg, C., Peterson, D. A., et al. (1998). Neurogenesis in the adult human hippocampus. *Nature Medicine, 4,* 1313–1317.

Erwin, H., Fedewa, A., Beighle, A., & Ahn, S. (2012). A quantitative review of physical activity, health, and learning outcomes associated with classroom-based physical activity interventions. *Journal of Applied School Psychology, 28*(1), 14–36.

Esquith, R. (2007). *Teach like your hair's on fire: The methods and madness inside room 56.* New York: Penguin Books.

Evans, G. W. (2003). A multimethodological analysis of cumulative risk and allostatic load among rural children. *Developmental Psychology, 39*(5), 924–933.

Evans, G. W. (2004). The environment of childhood poverty. *American Psychologist, 59*(2), 77–92.

Evans, G. W., & Cassells, R. C. (2014). Childhood poverty, cumulative risk exposure, and mental health in emerging adults. *Clinical Psychological Science: A Journal of the Association for Psychological Science, 2*(3), 287–296. Accessed at http://doi.org/10.1177/2167702613501496 on October 9, 2018.

Evans, G. W., & English, K. (2002). The environment of poverty: Multiple stressor exposure, psychophysiological stress, and socioemotional adjustment. *Child Development, 73*(4), 1238–1248.

Evans, G. W., & Fuller-Rowell, T. E. (2013). Childhood poverty, chronic stress, and young adult working memory: The protective role of self-regulatory capacity. *Developmental Science, 16,* 688–696.

Evans, G. W., & Kantrowitz, E. (2002). Socioeconomic status and health: The potential role of environmental risk exposure. *Annual Review of Public Health, 23,* 303–331.

Evans, G. W., & Kim, P. (2007). Childhood poverty and health: Cumulative risk exposure and stress dysregulation. *Psychological Science, 18*(11), 953–957.

Evans, G. W., & Kim, P. (2012). Childhood poverty and young adults' allostatic load: The mediating role of childhood cumulative risk exposure. *Psychological Science, 23,* 979–983.

Evans, G. W., & Schamberg, M. A. (2009). Childhood poverty, chronic stress, and adult working memory. *Proceedings of the National Academy of Sciences of the United States of America, 106*(16), 6545–6549.

Farah, M. J., Shera, D. M., Savage, J. H., Betancourt, L., Giannetta, J. M., Brodsky, N. L., et al. (2006). Childhood poverty: Specific associations with neurocognitive development. *Brain Research, 1110*(1), 166–174.

Farr, S. (2010). *Teaching as leadership: The highly effective teacher's guide to closing the achievement gap.* San Francisco: Jossey-Bass.

Federal Interagency Forum on Child and Family Statistics. (2011). *America's children: Key national indicators of well-being, 2011.* Washington, DC: U.S. Government Printing Office. Accessed at www.childstats.gov/pdf/ac2011/ac_11.pdf on May 22, 2015.

Ferguson, R. F. (1998). Can schools narrow the black-white test score gap? In C. Jencks & M. Phillips (Eds.), *The black-white test score gap* (pp. 318–374). Washington, DC: Brookings Institution Press.

Fernald, A., Marchman, V. A., & Weisleder, A. (2013). SES differences in language processing skill and vocabulary are evident at 18 months. *Developmental Science, 16*(2), 234–248.

Finerman, W. (Producer), Starkey, S. (Producer), Tisch, S. (Producer), & Zemeckis, R. (Director). (1994). *Forrest Gump* [Motion picture]. United States: Paramount Pictures.

Fishman, S. (2012). *The first five: Maximizing the opening minutes of class.* Accessed at http:// tntp.org/assets/documents /TNTP_FishmanPrizeSeries_2012.pdf on October 22, 2015.

Flores, D., Lemons, A., & McTernan, H. (2011). *The correlation between student growth mindset and conceptual development in physics.* Accessed at http://modeling.asu.edu/modeling/Mindset&Physics-McT,L,F.pdf on January 6, 2016.

Forgeard, M., Winner, E., Norton, A., & Schlaug, G. (2008). Practicing a musical instrument in childhood is associated with enhanced verbal ability and nonverbal reasoning. *PLOS ONE, 3*(10).

Fredrickson, B. L., & Branigan, C. A. (2005). Positive emotions broaden the scope of attention and thought-action repertoires. *Cognition and Emotion, 19*(3), 313–332.

Fredrickson, B. L., Grewen, K. M., Coffey, K. A., Algoe, S. B., Firestine, A. M., Arevalo, J. M. G., et al. (2013). A functional genomic perspective on human well-being. *Proceedings of the National Academy of Sciences of the United States of America, 110*(33), 13684–13689.

Fredrickson, B. L., & Losada, M. F. (2005). Positive affect and the complex dynamics of human flourishing. *American Psychologist, 60*(7), 678–686.

Fredrickson, B. L., Tugade, M. M., Waugh, C. E., & Larkin, G. R. (2003). What good are positive emotions in crises? A prospective study of resilience and emotions following the terrorist attacks on the United States on September 11th, 2001. *Journal of Personality and Social Psychology, 84*(2), 365–376.

Froh, J. J., Sefick, W. J., & Emmons, R. A. (2008). Counting blessings in early adolescents: An experimental study of gratitude and subjective well-being. *Journal of School Psychology, 46*(2), 213–233.

Fry, R. (2013, August). *A rising share of young adults live in their parents' home.* Washington, DC: Pew Research Center. Accessed at www.pewsocialtrends.org/files/2013/07/SDT-millennials-living-with-parents-07–2013.pdf on May 2, 2014.

Gabe, T. (2010, April). *Poverty in the United States: 2008.* Washington, DC: Congressional Research Service. Accessed at http://assets.opencrs.com/rpts/RL33069_20100421.pdf on May 22, 2015.

Gaither, S. E., Chen, E. E., Corriveau, K. H., Harris, P. L., Ambady, N., & Sommers, S. R. (2014). Monoracial and biracial children: Effects of racial identity saliency on social learning and social preferences. *Child Development, 85,* 2299–2316. Accessed at www.ncbi.nlm.nih.gov/pubmed/25040708 on October 9, 2018.

Galatzer-Levy, R. M., & Cohler, B. J. (1993). *The essential other: A developmental psychology of the self.* New York: Basic Books.

Galla, B. M., Plummer, B. D., White, R. E., Meketon, D., D'Mello, S. K., & Duckworth, A. L. (2014). The Academic Diligence Task (ADT): Assessing individual differences in effort on tedious but important schoolwork. *Contemporary Educational Psychology, 39*(4), 314–325.

Gámez, P. B., & Lesaux, N. K. (2015). Early-adolescents' reading comprehension and the stability of the middle school classroom-language environment. *Developmental Psychology, 51*(4), 447–458.

Garner, P. W. (1996). The relations of emotional role taking, affective/moral attributions, and emotional display rule knowledge to low-income school-age children's social competence. *Journal of Applied Developmental Psychology, 17*(1), 19–36.

Garner, R. (1990). When children and adults do not use learning strategies: Toward a theory of settings. *Review of Educational Research, 60*(4), 517–529.

Gay, G. (2010). *Culturally responsive teaching: Theory, research, and practice* (2nd ed.). New York: Teachers College Press.

Gazzaniga, M. S. (1998). *The mind's past.* Los Angeles: University of California Press.

Getahun, D., Jacobsen, S. J., Fassett, M. J., Chen, W., Demissie, K., & Rhoads, G. G. (2013). Recent trends in childhood attention-deficit/hyperactivity disorder. *Journal of the American Medical Association Pediatrics, 167*(3), 282–288.

Gillberg, M., Anderzén, I., Åkerstedt, T., & Sigurdson, K. (1986). Urinary catecholamine responses to basic types of physical activity. *European Journal of Applied Physiology and Occupational Physiology, 55*(6), 575–578.

Ginsborg, J. (2006). The effects of socioeconomic status on children's language acquisition and use. In J. Clegg & J. Ginsborg (Eds.), *Language and social disadvantage: Theory into practice* (pp. 9–27). San Francisco: Wiley.

Glaze, L. E., & Parks, E. (2012, November). *Correctional populations in the United States, 2011.* Washington, DC: Bureau of Justice Statistics. Accessed at www.bjs.gov/content/pub/pdf/cpus11.pdf on May 22, 2015.

Godfrey, K. M., Costello, P. M., & Lillycrop, K. A. (2015). The developmental environment, epigenetic biomarkers and long-term health. *Journal of Developmental Origins of Health and Disease, 5,* 399–406.

Goldin, A. P., Hermida, M. J., Shalom, D. E., Elias Costa, M., Lopez-Rosenfeld, M., Segretin, M. S, et al. (2014). Far transfer to language and math of a short software-based gaming intervention. *Proceedings of the National Academy of Sciences of the United States of America, 111,* 6443–6448.

Goldin, P. R., McRae, K., Ramel, W., & Gross, J. J. (2008). The neural bases of emotion regulation: Reappraisal and suppression of negative emotion. *Biological Psychiatry, 63*(6), 577–586.

Goldin-Meadow, S., Cook, S. W., & Mitchell, Z. A. (2009). Gesturing gives children new ideas about math. *Psychological Science, 20*(3), 267–272.

Gollnick, D. M., & Chinn, P. (2013). *Multicultural education in a pluralistic society.* Boston: Pearson.

Gollwitzer, P. M., & Sheeran, P. (2006). Implementation intentions and goal achievement: A meta-analysis of effects and processes. *Advances in Experimental Social Psychology, 38,* 69–119.

Gonzalez-Mena, J., & Pulido-Tobiassen, D. (1999). *Teaching diversity: A place to begin.* Accessed at www.scholastic .com/teachers/article/teaching-diversity-place-begin-0 on October 14, 2015.

Good, C., Aronson, J., & Inzlicht, M. (2003). Improving adolescents' standardized test performance: An intervention to reduce the effects of stereotype threat. *Journal of Applied Developmental Psychology, 24*(6), 645–662.

Goodyear, D. (2009, October 26). Man of extremes: The return of James Cameron. *The New Yorker.* Accessed at www.newyorker.com/reporting/2009/10/26/091026fa_fact_goodyear on October 14, 2015.

Gorski, P. (2008). The myth of the culture of poverty. *Educational Leadership, 65*(7), 32–36.

Gottfried, A. W., Gottfried, A. E., Bathurst, K., Guerin, D. W., & Parramore, M. M. (2003). Socioeconomic status in children's development and family environment: Infancy through adolescence. In M. H. Bornstein & R. H. Bradley (Eds.), *Socioeconomic status, parenting, and child development* (pp. 189–207). Mahwah, NJ: Erlbaum.

Governing. (2015). *Bankrupt cities, municipalities list and map.* Accessed at www.governing. com/gov-data/municipal -cities-counties-bankruptcies-and-defaults.html on January 14, 2016.

Graham, S., & Perin, D. (2007). *Writing next: Effective strategies to improve writing of adolescents in middle and high schools.* Washington, DC: Alliance for Excellent Education.

Grant, H., & Dweck, C. S. (2003). Clarifying achievement goals and their impact. *Journal of Personality and Social Psychology, 85*(3), 541–553.

Green, C. S., & Bavelier, D. (2008). Exercising your brain: A review of human brain plasticity and training-induced learning. *Psychology and Aging, 23*(4), 692–701.

Grissom, J. B. (2005). Physical fitness and academic achievement. *Journal of Exercise Physiology, 8*(1), 11–25.

Hackman, D. A., & Farah, M. J. (2009). Socioeconomic status and the developing brain. *Trends in Cognitive Sciences, 13*(2), 65–73.

Hafen, C. A., Allen, J. P., Mikami, A. Y., Gregory, A., Hamre, B., & Pianta, R. C. (2012). The pivotal role of adolescent autonomy in secondary school classrooms. *Journal of Youth and Adolescence, 41*(3), 245–255.

Halassa, M. M., Chen, Z., Wimmer, R. D., Brunetti, P. M., Zhao, S., Zikopoulos, B., et al. (2014). State-dependent architecture of thalamic reticular subnetworks. *Cell, 158*(4), 808–821.

Hall, C. C., Zhao, J., & Shafi, E. (2014). Self-affirmation among the poor: Cognitive and behavioral implications. *Psychological Science, 25*(2), 619–625.

Hammack, P. L., & Toolis, E. (2014). Narrative and the social construction of adulthood. *New Directions for Child and Adolescent Development, 145,* 43–56.

Hamre, B. K., & Pianta, R. C. (2001). Early teacher–child relationships and the trajectory of children's school outcomes through eighth grade. *Child Development, 72*(2), 625–638.

Hamre, B. K., & Pianta, R. C. (2005). Can instructional and emotional support in the first-grade classroom make a difference for children at risk of school failure? *Child Development, 76*(5), 949–967.

Hamre, B. K., & Pianta, R. C. (2006). Student-teacher relationships. In G. C. Bear & K. M. Minke (Eds.), *Children's needs III: Development, prevention, and intervention* (pp. 59–71). Washington, DC: National Association of School Psychologists.

Hanson, J. L., Chandra, A., Wolfe, B. L., & Pollak, S. D. (2011). Association between income and the hippocampus. *PLOS ONE, 6*(5).

Hanushek, E. A. (2005). The economics of school quality. *German Economic Review, 6*(3), 269–286.

Hanushek, E. A. (2011). Valuing teachers: How much is a good teacher worth? *Education Next, 11*(3), 40–45.

Harrell, E., Langton, L., Berzofsky, M., Couzens, L., & Smiley-McDonald, H. (2014). *Household poverty and nonfatal violent victimization, 2008–2012.* Washington, DC: U.S. Department of Justice.

Harris, B., Ravert, R. D., & Sullivan, A. L. (2015). Adolescent racial identity self-identification of multiple and "other" race/ethnicities. *Urban Education, 52*(6), 774–794. Accessed at https://doi.org/10.1177/0042085915574527 on October 9, 2018.

Hart, B., & Risley, T. R. (1995). *Meaningful differences in the everyday experiences of young American children.* Baltimore: Brookes.

Hart, B., & Risley, T. R. (2003). The early catastrophe: The 30 million word gap by age 3. *American Educator, 27,* 4–9.

Hasenstaub, A., Sachdev, R. N., & McCormick, D. A. (2007). State changes rapidly modulate cortical neuronal responsiveness. *Journal of Neuroscience, 27*(36), 9607–9622.

Hattie, J. A. (2009). *Visible learning: A synthesis of over 800 meta-analyses relating to achievement.* New York: Routledge.

Hattie, J. A., Biggs, J., & Purdie, N. (1996). Effects of learning skills interventions on student learning: A meta-analysis. *Review of Educational Research, 66*(2), 99–136.

Hattie, J. A., & Timperley, H. (2007). The power of feedback. *Review of Educational Research, 77*(1), 81–112.

Hawn, G. (2011). *10 mindful minutes: Giving our children—and ourselves—the social and emotional skills to reduce stress and anxiety for healthier, happier lives.* New York: Penguin.

Haycock, K. (1998). Good teaching matters: How well-qualified teachers can close the gap. *Thinking K–6, 3*(2), 1–14.

Headey, B., Muffels, R., & Wagner, G. G. (2010). Long-running German panel survey shows that personal and economic choices, not just genes, matter for happiness. *Proceedings of the National Academy of Sciences of the United States of America, 107*(42), 17922–17926.

Heckman, J. J. (2006). Skill formation and the economics of investing in disadvantaged children. *Science, 312*(5782), 1900–1902.

Heller, A. S., van Reekum, C. M., Schaefer, S. M., Lapate, R. C., Radler, B. T., Ryff, C. D., et al. (2013). Sustained striatal activity predicts eudaimonic well-being and cortisol output. *Psychological Science, 24*(11), 2191–2200.

Heller, S., Pollack, H. A., Ander, R., & Ludwig, J. (2013). *Preventing youth violence and dropout: A randomized field experiment* (Working Paper No. 19014). Cambridge, MA: National Bureau of Economic Research. Accessed at www.nber.org/papers/w19014 on January 14, 2016.

Henderson, W. (2012). *All the world's their stage: Connecting content to students' futures.* Accessed at http://tntp.org /assets/documents/TNTP_FishmanPrizeSeries_2012.pdf on October 22, 2015.

Himmelstein, M. S., Young, D. M., Sanchez, D. T., & Jackson, J. S. (2015). Vigilance in the discrimination-stress model for Black Americans. *Psychology and Health, 30*(3), 253–267.

Ho, Y.-C., Cheung, M.-C., & Chan, A. S. (2003). Music training improves verbal but not visual memory: Cross-sectional and longitudinal explorations in children. *Neuropsychology, 17*(3), 439–450.

Hoff, E. (2013). Interpreting the early language trajectories of children from low-SES and language minority homes: Implications for closing achievement gaps. *Developmental Psychology, 49*(1), 4–14.

Hofferth, S. L. (1996). Child care in the United States today. *The Future of Children, 6*(2), 41–61.

Hofstetter, S., Tavor, I., Moryosef, S. T., & Assaf, Y. (2013). Short-term learning induces white matter plasticity in the fornix. *Journal of Neuroscience, 33*(12), 844–850.

Holmes, J., Gathercole, S. E., Place, M., Dunning, D. L., Hilton, K. A., & Elliott, J. G. (2010). Working memory deficits can be overcome: Impacts of training and medication on working memory in children with ADHD. *Applied Cognitive Psychology, 24*(6), 827–836.

Honora, D. T. (2002). The relationship of gender and achievement to future outlook among African American adolescents. *Adolescence, 37*(146), 301–316.

Hoy, W. K., Tarter, C. J., & Hoy, A. W. (2006). Academic optimism of schools: A force for student achievement. *American Educational Research Journal, 43*(3), 425–446.

Hughes, J. N., & Kwok, O.-M. (2006). Classroom engagement mediates the effect of teacher–student support on elementary students' peer acceptance: A prospective analysis. *Journal of School Psychology, 43*(6), 465–480.

Hughes, J. N., Luo, W., Kwok, O.-M., & Loyd, L. K. (2008). Teacher–student support, effortful engagement, and achievement: A 3-year longitudinal study. *Journal of Educational Psychology, 100*(1), 1–14.

Hughes, M. G., Day, E. A., Wang, X., Schuelke, M. J., Arsenault, M. L., Harkrider, L. N., et al. (2013). Learner-controlled practice difficulty in the training of a complex task: Cognitive and motivational mechanisms. *Journal of Applied Psychology, 98*(1), 80–98.

Hurlemann, R., Hawellek, B., Matusch, A., Kolsch, H., Wollersen, H., Madea, B., et al. (2005). Noradrenergic modulation of emotion-induced forgetting and remembering. *Journal of Neuroscience, 25*(27), 6343–6349.

Huttenlocher, J., Waterfall, H., Vasilyeva, M., Vevea, J., & Hedges, L. V. (2010). Sources of variability in children's language growth. *Cognitive Psychology, 61*, 343–365.

Hyerle, D. (1996). *Visual tools for constructing knowledge.* Alexandria, VA: Association for Supervision and Curriculum Development.

Illinois Public Health Institute. (2013). *Enhancing P.E. in Illinois: Naperville Central High School.* Accessed at http://iphionline.org/pdf/P.E._Case_Study_Naperville.pdf on January 14, 2016.

Immordino-Yang, M. H., & Damasio, A. (2007). We feel, therefore we learn: The relevance of affective and social neuroscience to education. *Mind, Brain, and Education, 1*(1), 3–10.

Irish, J. (2012). *Crush Lusher: Investing students in something bigger than themselves.* Accessed at http://tntp.org /assets/documents/TNTP_FishmanPrizeSeries_2012.pdf on October 22, 2015.

Isen, A. M., Daubman, K. A., & Nowicki, G. P. (1987). Positive affect facilitates creative problem solving. *Journal of Personality and Social Psychology, 52*, 1122–1131.

Iversen, R. R., & Farber, N. B. (1996). Transmission of family values, work, and welfare among poor urban black women. *Work and Occupations, 23*(4), 437–460.

Jackson, R. R. (2011). *How to motivate reluctant learners*. Alexandria, VA: Association for Supervision and Curriculum Development.

Jackson, Y. (2011). *The pedagogy of confidence: Inspiring high intellectual performance in urban schools*. New York: Teachers College Press.

Jacoby, J. M., & Podell, L. (2013). *Mentoring for school success: Creating positive changes*. Newark, NJ: Adolescent Mentoring.

Jaeggi, S. M., Buschkuehl, M., Jonides, J., & Perrig, W. J. (2008). Improving fluid intelligence with training on working memory. *Proceedings of the National Academy of Sciences of the United States of America, 105*(19), 6829–6833.

JayMJ23. (2006, August 25). *Michael Jordan "failure" Nike commercial* [Video file]. Accessed at www.youtube.com /watch?v=45mMioJ5szc on October 28, 2015.

Jennings, P. A. (2015). *Mindfulness for teachers: Simple skills for peace and productivity in the classroom*. New York: Norton.

Jensen, E. (n.d.). *The "Bobby McFerrin effect" on your brain*. Accessed at www.jensenlearning.com/news/the-bobby -mcferrin-effect-on-your-brain/bra on April 15, 2016.

Jensen, E. (2014). *A descriptive study of differences between teachers at high and low performing Title I elementary schools* (UMI No. 3616282). Santa Barbara, CA: Fielding Graduate University.

Jensen, E. (2019). *Poor students, rich teaching: Seven high-impact mindsets for students from poverty* (Rev. ed.). Bloomington, IN: Solution Tree Press.

Jerald, C. D. (2001). *Dispelling the myth revisited: Preliminary findings from a nationwide analysis of "high-flying" schools*. Washington, DC: Education Trust.

Jimerson, S., Egeland, B., Sroufe, L. A., & Carlson, B. (2000). A prospective longitudinal study of high school dropouts: Examining multiple predictors across development. *Journal of School Psychology, 38*(6), 525–549.

Job, V., Walton, G. M., Bernecker, K., & Dweck, C. S. (2015). Implicit theories about willpower predict self-regulation and grades in everyday life. *Journal of Personality and Social Psychology, 108*, 637–647.

Johnson, J. F., Uline, C. L., & Perez, L. G. (2014). The quest for mastery. *Educational Leadership, 72*(2), 48–53.

Johnson, S. M. (2010). How best to add value? Strike a balance between the individual and the organization in school reform. *Voices in Urban Education, 27*, 7–15.

Kagan, L., Kagan, M., & Kagan, S. (1997). *Cooperative learning structures for teambuilding*. San Clement, CA: Kagan Cooperative Learning.

Kahneman, D. (2013). *Thinking, fast and slow*. New York: Farrar, Straus and Giroux.

Kaiman, J., Holpuch, A., Smith, D., Watts, J., & Topping, A. (2013, October 18). *Beyond Malala: Six teenagers changing the world*. Accessed at www.theguardian.com/world/2013/oct/18/teenagers-changing-world-malala -yousafzai on October 21, 2015.

Kelley, P., & Whatson, T. (2013). Making long-term memories in minutes: A spaced learning pattern from memory research in education. *Frontiers in Human Neuroscience, 7*(589), 1–9. Accessed at http://doi.org/10.3389 /fnhum.2013.00589 on October 9, 2018.

Kennedy, J. F. (1962, September). *Address at Rice University on the nation's space effort*. Speech presented at Rice University, Houston, TX.

Keshavan, M. S., Giedd, J., Lau, J. Y., Lewis, D. A., & Paus, T. (2014). Changes in the adolescent brain and the pathophysiology of psychotic disorders. *Lancet Psychiatry, 7*, 549–558.

Kim, P., Neuendorf, C., Bianco, H., & Evans, G. W. (2015). Exposure to childhood poverty and mental health symptomatology in adolescence: A role of coping strategies. *Stress and Health*. Accessed at http://onlinelibrary .wiley.com/doi/10.1002/smi.2646/abstract on May 18, 2016.

Kim, Y. Y., Choi, J. M., Kim, S. Y., Park, S. K., Lee, S. H., & Lee, K. H. (2002). Changes in EEG of children during brain respiration-training. *American Journal of Chinese Medicine, 30*(2–3), 405–417.

Kimble, M., Boxwala, M., Bean, W., Maletsky, K., Halper, J., Spollen, K., et al. (2014). The impact of hypervigilance: Evidence for a forward feedback loop. *Journal of Anxiety Disorders, 28*(2), 241–245.

Kirsch, I. (Ed.). (1999). *How expectancies shape experience.* Washington, DC: American Psychological Association.

Kirschner, P. A., Sweller, J., & Clark, R. E. (2006). Why minimal guidance during instruction does not work: An analysis of the failure of constructivist, discovery, problem-based, experiential, and inquiry-based teaching. *Educational Psychologist, 41*(2), 75–86.

Klanker, M., Feenstra, M., & Denys, D. (2013). Dopaminergic control of cognitive flexibility in humans and animals. *Frontiers in Neuroscience, 7*, 201.

Kluger, A. N., & DeNisi, A. S. (1996). The effects of feedback interventions on performance: A historical review, a meta-analysis, and a preliminary feedback intervention theory. *Psychological Bulletin, 119*(2), 254–284.

Knecht, S., Breitenstein, C., Bushuven, S., Wailke, S., Kamping, S., Flöel, A., et al. (2004). Levodopa: Faster and better word learning in normal humans. *Annals of Neurology, 56*(1), 20–26.

Knowles, M., Rabinowich, J., Ettinger de Cuba, S., Cutts, D. B., & Chilton, M. (2015). "Do you wanna breathe or eat?": Parent perspectives on child health consequences of food insecurity, trade-offs, and toxic stress. *Maternal and Child Health Journal*, 1–8.

Knudsen, E. I., Heckman, J. J., Cameron, J. L., & Shonkoff, J. P. (2006). Economic, neurobiological, and behavioral perspectives on building America's future workforce. *Proceedings of the National Academy of Sciences of the United States of America, 103*(27), 10155–10162.

Kohl, J. V. (2012). Human pheromones and food odors: Epigenetic influences on the socioaffective nature of evolved behaviors. *Socioaffective Neuroscience and Psychology, 2*, 17338.

Konrath, S. H., O'Brien, E. H., & Hsing, C. (2011). Changes in dispositional empathy in American college students over time: A meta-analysis. *Personality and Social Psychology Review, 15*(2), 180–198.

Krashen, S. (2002). *Poverty has a powerful impact on educational attainment, or, don't trust Ed Trust.* Chicago: Substance.

Kraus, M. W., Piff, P. K., & Keltner, D. (2009). Social class, sense of control, and social explanation. *Journal of Personality and Social Psychology, 97*(6), 992–1004.

Kulik, C.-L. C., & Kulik, J. A. (1987). Mastery testing and student learning: A meta-analysis. *Journal of Educational Technology Systems, 15*(3), 325–345.

Ladd, G. W., & Dinella, L. M. (2009). Continuity and change in early school engagement: Predictive of children's achievement trajectories from first to eighth grade? *Journal of Educational Psychology, 101*(1), 190–206.

Lally, P., van Jaarsveld, C. H. M., Potts, H. W. W., & Wardle, J. (2010). How are habits formed: Modelling habit formation in the real world. *European Journal of Social Psychology, 40*(6), 998–1009.

Lamm, C., Batson, C. D., & Decety, J. (2007). The neural substrate of human empathy: Effects of perspective-taking and cognitive appraisal. *Journal of Cognitive Neuroscience, 19*(1), 42–58.

Landis, D., Gaylord-Harden, N. K., Malinowski, S. L., Grant, K. E., Carleton, R. A., & Ford, R. E. (2007). Urban adolescent stress and hopelessness. *Journal of Adolescence, 30*(6), 1051–1070.

Latif, A., Choudhary, A. I., & Hammayun, A. A. (2015, April 15). Economic effects of student dropouts: A comparative study. *Journal of Global Economics, 3*(2). Accessed at www.omicsonline.org/open-access/economic -effects-of-student-dropouts-a-comparative-study-2375-4389-1000137.php?aid=57059 on September 13, 2018.

Layous, K., & Lyubomirsky, S. (2014). The how, why, what, when, and who of happiness: Mechanisms underlying the success of positive activity interventions. In J. Gruber & J. T. Moskowitz (Eds.), *Positive emotion: Integrating the light sides and dark sides* (pp. 473–495). New York: Oxford University Press.

Layous, K., Nelson, S. K., Oberle, E., Schonert-Reichl, K. A., & Lyubomirsky, S. (2012). Kindness counts: Prompting prosocial behavior in preadolescents boosts peer acceptance and well-being. *PLOS ONE, 7*(12).

Lee, H., Devlin, J. T., Shakeshaft, C., Stewart, L. H., Brennan, A., Glensman, J., et al. (2007). Anatomical traces of vocabulary acquisition in the adolescent brain. *Journal of Neuroscience, 27*(5), 1184–1189.

Lee, T. M., Wong, M. L., Lau, B. W., Lee, J. C., Yau, S. Y., & So, K. F. (2014). Aerobic exercise interacts with neurotrophic factors to predict cognitive functioning in adolescents. *Psychoneuroendocrinology, 39,* 214–224.

Lenhart, A. (2009). *Teens and sexting: How and why minor teens are sending sexually suggestive nude or nearly nude images via text messaging.* Washington, DC: Pew Internet and American Life Project. Accessed at www.pew internet.org/files/old-media//Files/Reports/2009/PIP_Teens_and_Sexting.pdf on April 12, 2014.

Leotti, L. A., Cho, C., & Delgado, M. R. (2015). The neural basis underlying the experience of control in the human brain. In P. Haggard & B. Eitam (Eds.), *The sense of agency.* Oxford, England: Oxford University Press.

Lewis, G. J., & Bates, T. C. (2010). Genetic evidence for multiple biological mechanisms underlying in-group favoritism. *Psychological Science, 21*(11), 1623–1628.

Lewis, G. J., Kanai, R., Rees, G., & Bates, T. C. (2014). Neural correlates of the "good life": Eudaimonic well-being is associated with insular cortex volume. *Social Cognitive and Affective Neuroscience, 9*(5), 615–618.

Lewitus, G. M., & Schwartz, M. (2009). Behavioral immunization: Immunity to self-antigens contributes to psychological stress resilience. *Molecular Psychiatry, 14,* 532–536.

Lieberman, M. D. (2014). *Social: Why our brains are wired to connect.* New York: Broadway Books.

Lieberman, M. D., Eisenberger, N. I., Crockett, M. J., Tom, S. M., Pfeifer, J. H., & Way, B. M. (2007). Putting feelings into words: Affect labeling disrupts amygdala activity in response to affective stimuli. *Psychological Science, 18*(5), 421–428.

Liew, J., Chen, Q., & Hughes, J. N. (2010). Child effortful control, teacher-student relationships, and achievement in academically at-risk children: Additive and interactive effects. *Early Childhood Research Quarterly, 25*(1), 51–64.

Liu, Y., & Wang, Z. (2014). Positive affect and cognitive control: Approach-motivation intensity influences the balance between cognitive flexibility and stability. *Psychological Science, 25*(5), 1116–1123.

London, R. A., & Castrechini, S. (2011). A longitudinal examination of the link between youth physical fitness and academic achievement. *Journal of School Health, 81*(7), 400–408.

Luby, J. L., Barch, D. M., Belden, A., Gaffrey, M. S., Tillman, R., Babb, C., et al. (2012). Maternal support in early childhood predicts larger hippocampal volumes at school age. *Proceedings of the National Academy of Sciences of the United States of America, 109*(8), 2854–2859.

Luby, J. L., Belden, A., Botteron, K., Marrus, N., Harms, M. P., Babb, C., et al. (2013). The effects of poverty on childhood brain development: The mediating effect of caregiving and stressful life events. *Journal of the American Medical Association Pediatrics, 167*(12), 1135–1142.

Lyons, K. (2012). *"You are here": Inspiring curiosity by making content personal.* Accessed at http://tntp.org/assets /documents/TNTP_FishmanPrizeSeries_2012.pdf on October 22, 2015.

Lysakowski, R. S., & Walberg, H. J. (1982). Instructional effects of cues, participation, and corrective feedback: A quantitative synthesis. *American Educational Research Journal, 19*(4), 559–578.

Lyubomirsky, S., Dickerhoof, R., Boehm, J. K, & Sheldon, K. M. (2011). Becoming happier takes both a will and a proper way: An experimental longitudinal intervention to boost well-being. *Emotion, 11*(2), 391–402.

Lyubomirsky, S., King, L., & Diener, E. (2005). The benefits of frequent positive affect: Does happiness lead to success? *Psychological Bulletin, 131*(6), 803–855.

Lyubomirsky, S., Sousa, L., & Dickerhoof, R. (2006). The costs and benefits of writing, talking, and thinking about life's triumphs and defeats. *Journal of Personality and Social Psychology, 90*(4), 692–708.

Mackey, A. P., Singley, A.T. M., Wendelken, C., & Bunge, S. A. (2015). Characterizing behavioral and brain changes associated with practicing reasoning skills. *PLOS ONE, 10*(9).

Mackey, A. P., Whitaker, K. J., & Bunge, S. A. (2012). Experience-dependent plasticity in white matter microstructure: Reasoning training alters structural connectivity. *Frontiers in Neuroanatomy, 6*(32), 1–9.

Macnamara, B. N., Hambrick, D. Z., & Oswald, F. L. (2014). Deliberate practice and performance in music, games, sports, education, and professions: A meta-analysis. *Psychological Science, 25*(8), 1608–1618.

Mahar, M. T., Murphy, S. K., Rowe, D. A., Golden, J., Shields, A. T., & Raedeke, T. D. (2006). Effects of a classroom-based program on physical activity and on-task behavior. *Medicine and Science in Sports and Exercise, 38*(12), 2086–2094.

Maier, S. F., & Watkins, L. R. (2005). Stressor controllability and learned helplessness: The roles of the dorsal raphe nucleus, serotonin, and corticotropin-releasing factor. *Neuroscience & Biobehavioral Reviews, 29*(4–5), 829–841.

Maldonado-Carreño, C., & Votruba-Drzal, E. (2011). Teacher-child relationships and the development of academic and behavioral skills during elementary school: A within- and between-child analysis. *Child Development, 82*(2), 601–616.

Mangels, J. A., Good, C., Whiteman, R. C., Maniscalco, B., & Dweck, C. S. (2012). Emotion blocks the path to learning under stereotype threat. *Social Cognitive and Affective Neuroscience, 7*(2), 230–241.

Mangen, A., & Velay, J.-L. (2010). Digitizing literacy: Reflections on the haptics of writing. In M. H. Zadeh (Ed.), *Advances in haptics*. Rijeka, Croatia: IntechOpen. Accessed at www.intechopen.com/books/advances-in-haptics /digitizing-literacy-reflections-on-the-haptics-of-writing on April 25, 2014.

Mani, A., Mullainathan, S., Shafir, E., & Zhao, J. (2013). Poverty impedes cognitive function. *Science, 341*(6149), 976–980.

Marks, H. M. (2000). Student engagement in instructional activity: Patterns in the elementary, middle, and high school years. *American Educational Research Journal, 37*(1), 153–184.

Marin-Burgin, A., & Schinder, A. F. (2012). Requirement of adult-born neurons for hippocampus-dependent learning. *Behavioural Brain Research, 227*(2), 391–399.

Marzano, R. J. (1998). *A theory-based meta-analysis of research on instruction.* Aurora, CO: Mid-continent Regional Educational Laboratory. Accessed at www.peecworks.org/peec/peec_research/I01795EFA.2/Marzano%20 Instruction%20Meta_An.pdf on March 22, 2015.

Marzano, R. J. (2001). *Classroom instruction that works: Research-based strategies for increasing student achievement.* Alexandria, VA: Association for Supervision and Curriculum Development.

Marzano, R. J. (2003). *Classroom management that works: Research-based strategies for every teacher.* Alexandria, VA: Association for Supervision and Curriculum Development.

Marzano, R. J. (2017). *The new art and science of teaching.* Bloomington, IN: Solution Tree Press.

Marzano, R. J., & Pickering, D. J. (2011). *The highly engaged classroom.* Bloomington, IN: Marzano Research.

Marzano, R. J., Pickering, D. J., & Pollock, J. E. (2001). *Classroom instruction that works: Research-based strategies for increasing student achievement.* Alexandria, VA: Association for Supervision and Curriculum Development.

Marzano, R. J., & Simms, J. A. (2014). *Questioning sequences in the classroom.* Bloomington, IN: Marzano Research.

Mason, C., Rivers Murphy, M. M., & Jackson, Y. (2019). *Mindfulness practices: Cultivating heart centered communities where students focus and flourish.* Blooming, IN: Solution Tree Press.

Maslow, A. H. (1943). A theory of human motivation. *Psychological Review, 50*(4), 370–396.

Maxwell, L. A. (2014). U.S. school enrollment hits majority-minority milestone. *Education Week.* Accessed at www.edweek.org/ew/articles/2014/08/20/01demographics.h34.html on October 23, 2015.

May, A., Hajak, G., Gänssbauer, S., Steffens, T., Langguth, B., Kleinjung, T., et al. (2007). Structural brain alterations following 5 days of intervention: Dynamic aspects of neuro-plasticity. *Cerebral Cortex: Oxford Journals, 17*(1), 205–210.

Mayer, R. E. (1989). Models for understanding. *Review of Educational Research, 59*(1), 43–64.

Mazziotta, J. C., Woods, R., Iacoboni, M., Sicotte, N., Yaden, K., Tran, M., et al. (2009). The myth of the normal, average human brain—the ICBM experience: (1) Subject screening and eligibility. *Neuroimage, 44*(3), 914–922.

McDaniel, M. A., Fadler, C. L., & Pashler, H. (2013). Effects of spaced versus massed training in function learning. *Journal of Experimental Psychology: Learning, Memory, and Cognition, 39*(5), 1417–1432.

McEwen, B. S. (2000). The neurobiology of stress: From serendipity to clinical relevance. *Brain Research Interactive, 886*(1–2), 172–189.

McEwen, B. S. (2002). *The end of stress as we know it*. New York: Dana Press.

McEwen, B. S. (2008). Central effects of stress hormones in health and disease: Understanding the protective and damaging effects of stress and stress mediators. *European Journal of Pharmacology, 583*(2–3), 174–185.

McGaugh, J. L. (2013). Making lasting memories: Remembering the significant. *Proceedings of the National Academy of Sciences of the United States of America, 110*(2), 10402–10407.

McGonigal, K. (2012). *The willpower instinct: How self-control works, why it matters, and what you can do to get more of it*. New York: Avery.

McGuigan, L., & Hoy, W. K. (2006). Principal leadership: Creating a culture of academic optimism to improve achievement for all students. *Leadership and Policy in Schools, 5*(3), 203–229.

McLanahan, S. S. (1999). Parent absence or poverty: Which matters more? In G. J. Duncan & J. Brooks-Gunn (Eds.), *Consequences of growing up poor* (pp. 35–48). New York: Russell Sage Foundation.

McLoyd, V. C. (1988). Socioeconomic disadvantage and child development. *American Psychologist, 53*(2), 185–204.

McNamara, T. P. (2005). *Semantic priming: Perspectives from memory and word recognition*. New York: Psychology Press.

McTighe, J., & Wiggins, G. (2013). *Essential questions: Opening doors to student understanding*. Alexandria, VA: Association for Supervision and Curriculum Development.

Mehrabian, A. (2000). Beyond IQ: Broad-based measurement of individual success potential or "emotional intelligence." *Genetic, Social, and General Psychology Monographs, 126*(2), 133–239.

Mehta, J., & Fine, S. (2012). Teaching differently . . . learning deeply. *Phi Delta Kappan, 94*(2), 31–35.

Melby-Lervåg, M., & Hulme, C. (2013). Is working memory training effective? A meta-analytic review. *Developmental Psychology, 49*(2), 270–291.

Meneses, A., & Liy-Salmeron, G. (2012). Serotonin and emotion, learning and memory. *Reviews in the Neurosciences, 23*(5–6), 543–553.

Milad, M. R., Wright, C. I., Orr, S. P., Pitman, R. K., Quirk, G. J., & Rauch, S. L. (2007). Recall of fear extinction in humans activates the ventromedial prefrontal cortex and hippocampus in concert. *Biological Psychiatry, 62*(5), 446–454.

Miles, S. W. (2014). Spaced vs. massed distribution instruction for L2 grammar learning. *System, 42*(1), 412–428.

Miller, C. A., & Sweatt, J. D. (2007). Covalent modification of DNA regulates memory formation. *Neuron, 53*(6), 857–869.

Miller, G. (1956). Chunks: The magical number seven, plus or minus two: Some limits on our capacity for processing information. *Psychological Review, 63*, 81–97.

Miller, J. C., & Krizan, Z. (2016). Walking facilitates positive affect (even when expecting the opposite). *Emotion, 16*(5), 775–785.

Miller, S. L., & Maner, J. K. (2010). Scent of a woman: Men's testosterone responses to olfactory ovulation cues. *Psychological Science, 21*(2), 276–283.

Miller-Lewis, L. R., Sawyer, A. C., Searle, A. K., Mittinty, M. N., Sawyer, M. G., & Lynch, J. W. (2014). Student-teacher relationship trajectories and mental health problems in young children. *BMC Psychology, 12,* 27.

Mishel, L. (2013, January 30). *Vast majority of wage earners are working harder, and for not much more.* Accessed at www.epi.org/publication/ib348-trends-us-work-hours-wages-1979-2007 on October 9, 2018.

Molenberghs, P., Cunnington, R., & Mattingley, J. B. (2009). Is the mirror neuron system involved in imitation? A short review and meta-analysis. *Neuroscience and Biobehavioral Reviews, 33*(7), 975–980.

Morel, N., Villain, N., Rauchs, G., Gaubert, M., Piolino, P., Landeau, B., et al. (2014). Brain activity and functional coupling changes associated with self-reference effect during both encoding and retrieval. *PLOS ONE, 9*(3).

Morgan, P. L., Farkas, G., Hillemeier, M. M., & Maczuga, S. (2009). Risk factors for learning-related behavior problems at 24 months of age: Population-based estimates. *Journal of Abnormal Child Psychology, 37*(3), 401–413.

Moriceau, S., & Sullivan, R. M. (2005). Neurobiology of infant attachment. *Developmental Psychobiology, 47*(3), 230–242.

Mueller, C. M., & Dweck, C. S. (1998). Praise for intelligence can undermine children's motivation and performance. *Journal of Personality and Social Psychology, 75*(1), 33–52.

Murty, V. P., DuBrow, S., & Davachi, L. (2015). The simple act of choosing influences declarative memory. *Journal of Neuroscience, 35*(16), 6255–6264.

Nagel, D. (2006). *Music in education: Study finds link with attendance and graduation rates.* Accessed at https://thejournal.com/articles/2006/11/06/music-in-education-study-finds-link-with-attendance-and-graduation-rates.aspx on July 5, 2016.

National Center for Health Statistics. (2008). Births, marriages, divorces, and deaths: Provisional data for 2007. *National Vital Statistics Reports, 56*(21). Accessed at www.cdc.gov/nchs/data/nvsr/nvsr56/nvsr56_21.pdf on May 22, 2015.

National Governors Association Center for Best Practices & Council of Chief State School Officers. (2010). *Common Core State Standards for English language arts and literacy in history/social studies, science, and technical subjects.* Washington, DC: Authors. Accessed at www.corestandards.org/assets/CCSSI_ELA%20Standards.pdf on February 25, 2016.

Nayar, D. (Producer), & Chadha, G. (Producer and Director). (2003). *Bend it like Beckham* [Motion picture]. United States: 20th Century Fox Home Entertainment.

Nelson, P. M., Demers, J. A., & Christ, T. J. (2014). The responsive environmental assessment for classroom teaching (REACT): The dimensionality of student perceptions of the instructional environment. *School Psychology Quarterly, 29,* 182–197.

The New Teacher Project. (2013). *Josalyn Tresvant.* Accessed at http://tntp.org/fishhman-prize/winners/fishman-prize-2013/josalyn-tresvant on May 31, 2016.

Nesbitt, R. E. (2009). *Intelligence and how to get it: Why schools and cultures count.* New York: Norton.

NGSS Lead States. (2013). *Next Generation Science Standards: For states, by states.* Washington, DC: National Academies Press.

Nicholls, J. G., & Miller, A. T. (1984). Reasoning about the ability of self and others: A developmental study. *Child Development, 55,* 1990–1999.

Noble, K. G., Norman, M. F., & Farah, M. J. (2005). Neurocognitive correlates of socioeconomic status in kindergarten children. *Developmental Science, 8*(1), 74–87.

Noble, K. G., Tottenham, N., & Casey, B. J. (2005). Neuroscience perspectives on disparities in school readiness and cognitive achievement. *Future of Children, 15*(1), 71–89.

Noble, K. G., Wolmetz, M. E., Ochs, L. G., Farah, M. J., & McCandliss, B. D. (2006). Brain-behavior relationships in reading acquisition are modulated by socioeconomic factors. *Developmental Science, 9*(6), 642–654.

Noggle, J. J., Steiner, N. J., Minami, T., & Khalsa, S. B. S. (2012). Benefits of yoga for psychosocial well-being in a US high school curriculum: A preliminary randomized controlled trial. *Journal of Developmental and Behavioral Pediatrics, 33*(3), 193–201.

Novak, S., & Slattery, C. (2017). *Deep discourse: A framework for cultivating student-led discussions*. Bloomington, IN: Solution Tree Press.

NPR, Robert Wood Johnson Foundation, & Harvard School of Public Health. (2013). *Education and health in schools: A survey of parents—Summary*. Accessed at www.rwjf.org/content/dam/farm/reports/surveys_and_polls/2013/rwjf407960 on June 2, 2016.

Oberle, E., Schonert-Reichl, K. A., & Thomson, K. C. (2010). Understanding the link between social and emotional well-being and peer relations in early adolescence: Gender-specific predictors of peer acceptance. *Journal of Youth and Adolescence, 39*(11), 1330–1342.

Ohira, K., Takeuchi, R., Shoji, H., & Miyakawa, T. (2013). Fluoxetine-induced cortical adult neurogenesis. *Neuropsychopharmacology, 38*(6), 909–920.

O'Keefe, P. A., & Linnenbrink-Garcia, L. (2014). The role of interest in optimizing performance and self-regulation. *Journal of Experimental Social Psychology, 53*, 70–78.

Olejnik, S., & Algina, J. (2000). Measures of effect size for comparative studies: Applications, interpretations, and limitations. *Contemporary Educational Psychology, 25*(3), 241–286.

Oppezzo, M., & Schwartz, D. L. (2014). Give your ideas some legs: The positive effect of walking on creative thinking. *Journal of Experimental Psychology: Learning, Memory, and Cognition, 40*(4), 1142–1152.

O'Rourke, N., Haimovitz, K., Ballweber, C., Dweck, C. S., & Popović, Z. (2014). *Brain points: A growth mindset incentive structure boosts persistence in an educational game*. Proceedings of the ACM Conference on Human Factors in Computing Systems (CHI 2014), Toronto, Ontario, Canada.

Otake, K., Shimai, S., Tanaka-Matsumi, J., Otsui, K., & Fredrickson, B. L. (2006). Happy people become happier through kindness: A counting kindnesses intervention. *Journal of Happiness Studies, 7*(3), 361–375.

Ouweneel, E., Le Blanc, P. M., & Schaufeli, W. B. (2014). On being grateful and kind: Results of two randomized controlled trials on study-related emotions and academic engagement. *Journal of Health Psychology, 148*(1), 37–60.

Palardy, G. J., & Rumberger, R. W. (2008). Teacher effectiveness in first grade: The importance of background qualifications, attitudes, and instructional practices for student learning. *Educational Evaluation and Policy Analysis, 30*(2), 111–140.

Palincsar, A. S., & Brown, A. L. (1984). Reciprocal teaching of comprehension-fostering and comprehension-monitoring activities. *Cognition and Instruction, 1*(2), 117–175.

Parrett, W. H., & Budge, K. M. (2012). *Turning high-poverty schools into high-performing schools*. Alexandria, VA: Association for Supervision and Curriculum Development.

Parsad, B., & Spiegelman, M. (2012). *Arts education in public elementary and secondary schools: 1999–2000 and 2009–2010*. Accessed at http://nces.ed.gov/pubs2012/2012014rev.pdf on June 2, 2016.

Passolunghi, M. C., Mammarella, I. C., & Altoe, G. (2008). Cognitive abilities as precursors of the early acquisition of mathematical skills during first through second grades. *Developmental Neuropsychology, 33*(3), 229–250.

Passolunghi, M. C., Vercelloni, B., & Schadee, H. (2007). The precursors of mathematics learning: Working memory, phonological ability and numerical competence. *Cognitive Development, 22*(2), 165–184.

Pereira, A. C., Huddleston, D. E., Brickman, A. M., Sosunov, A. A., Hen, R., McKhann, G. M., et al. (2007). An in vivo correlate of exercise-induced neurogenesis in the adult dentate gyrus. *Proceedings of the National Academy of Sciences of the United States of America, 104*(13), 5638–5643.

Peterson, C., Maier, S. F., & Seligman, M. E. (1995). *Learned helplessness*. London: Oxford University Press.

Petty, G. (2006). *Evidence-based teaching: A practical approach*. Cheltenham, England: Nelson Thornes.

Petty, G. (2009). *Evidence-based teaching*. Cheltenham, England: Nelson Thornes.

Pew Research Center. (2016). *America's shrinking middle class: A close look at changes within metropolitan areas*. Accessed at www.pewsocialtrends.org/2016/05/11/americas-shrinking-middle-class-a-close-look-at-changes -within-metropolitan-areas on May 18, 2016.

Pfeffer, F. T., & Hällsten, M. (2012). *Mobility regimes and parental wealth: The United States, Germany, and Sweden in comparison* (PSC Research Report No. 12–766). Accessed at www.psc.isr.umich.edu/pubs/pdf/rr12–766.pdf on October 14, 2015.

Phinney, J. S., Lochner, B. T., & Murphy, R. (1990). Ethnic identity development and psychological adjustment in adolescence. In A. R. Stiffman & L. E. Davis (Eds.), *Ethnic issues in adolescent mental health* (pp. 53–72). Newbury Park, CA: SAGE.

Pianta, R. C., Belsky, J., Houts, R., & Morrison, F. (2007). Opportunities to learn in America's elementary classrooms. *Science, 315*(5820), 1795–1796.

Pianta, R. C., Hamre, B. K., & Allen, J. P. (2012). Teacher-student relationships and engagement: Conceptualizing, measuring, and improving the capacity of classroom interactions. In S. L. Christenson, A. L. Reschly, & C. Wylie (Eds.), *Handbook of research on student engagement* (pp. 365–386). New York: Springer Media.

Ping, R., & Goldin-Meadow, S. (2010). Gesturing saves cognitive resources when talking about nonpresent objects. *Cognitive Science, 34*, 602–619.

Pink, D. H. (2009). *Drive: The surprising truth about what motivates us*. New York: Riverhead Books.

Plomin, R., Haworth, C. M., & Davis, O. S. (2009). Common disorders are quantitative traits. *Nature Reviews Genetics, 10*(12), 872–878.

Polikoff, M. S., McEachin, A. J., Wrabel, S. L., & Duque, M. (2013). The waive of the future? School accountability in the waiver era. *Educational Researcher, 43*(1), 45–54.

Pratt, L. A., & Brody, D. J. (2014). *NCHS data brief: Depression in the U.S. household population, 2009–2012* (No. 172). Hyattsville, MD: National Center for Health Statistics.

Priest, N., Paradies, Y., Trenerry, B., Truong, M., Karlsen, S., & Kelly, Y. (2013). A systematic review of studies examining the relationship between reported racism and health and wellbeing for children and young people. *Social Science and Medicine, 95*, 115–127.

Pungello, E. P., Kainz, K., Burchinal, M., Wasik, B. H., Sparling, J. J., Ramey, C. T., et al. (2010). Early educational intervention, early cumulative risk, and the early home environment as predictors of young adult outcomes within a high-risk sample. *Child Development, 81*(1), 410–426.

Quintana, S. M. (2007). Racial and ethnic identity: Developmental perspectives and research. *Journal of Counseling Psychology, 54*(3), 259–270.

Raichle, M. E., MacLeod, A. M., Snyder, A. Z., Powers, W. J., Gusnard, D. A., & Shulman, G. L. (2001). A default mode of brain function. *Proceedings of the National Academy of Sciences of the United States of America, 98*(2), 676–682.

Rank, M. R., & Hirschl, T. A. (2015). The likelihood of experiencing relative poverty over the life course. *PLOS ONE, 10*(7).

Ramirez, G., & Beilock, S. L. (2011). Writing about testing worries boosts exam performance in the classroom. *Science, 331*(6014), 211–213.

Rand, K. L. (2009). Hope and optimism: Latent structures and influences on grade expectancy and academic performance. *Journal of Personality, 77*(1), 231–260.

Ratey, J. J. (2008). *Spark: The revolutionary new science of exercise and the brain*. New York: Little, Brown.

Rattan, A., Good, C., & Dweck, C. S. (2012). "It's ok—Not everyone can be good at math": Instructors with an entity theory comfort (and demotivate) students. *Journal of Experimental Social Psychology*, 48(3), 731–737.

Rattan, A., Savani, K., Chugh, D., & Dweck, C. S. (2015). Leveraging mindsets to promote academic achievement: Policy recommendations. *Perspectives on Psychological Science*, 10(6), 721–726.

Rauner, R. R., Walters, R. W., Avery, M., & Wanser, T. J. (2013). Evidence that aerobic fitness is more salient than weight status in predicting standardized math and reading outcomes in fourth- through eighth-grade students. *Journal of Pediatrics*, 163(2), 344–348.

Raver, C. C., Blair, C., & Willoughby, M. (2013). Poverty as a predictor of 4-year-olds' executive function: New perspectives on models of differential susceptibility. *Developmental Psychology*, 49(2), 292–304.

Rector, R. (2012). *Marriage: America's greatest weapon against child poverty*. Washington, DC: U.S. Census Bureau. Accessed at http://factfinder2.census.gov/faces/tableservices/jsf/pages/productview.xhtml?pid=ACS_09_3YR_S1702&prodType=table on October 14, 2015.

Reeves, L. M., & Weisberg, R. W. (1994). The role of content and abstract information in analogical transfer. *Psychological Bulletin*, 115(3), 381–400.

Reis, S., Colbert, R., & Hébert, T. (2005). Understanding resilience in diverse, talented students in an urban high school. *Roeper Review*, 27(2), 110–120.

Reyes, M. R., Brackett, M. A., Rivers, S. E., White, M., & Salovey, P. (2012). Classroom emotional climate, student engagement, and academic achievement. *Journal of Educational Psychology*, 104(3), 700–712.

Riedl, K., Jensen, K., Call, J., & Tomasello, M. (2015). Restorative justice in children. *Current Biology*, 25(13), 1731–1735.

Risley, T. R., & Hart, B. (2006). Promoting early language development. In N. F. Watt, C. Ayoub, R. H. Bradley, J. E. Puma, & W. A. LeBoeuf (Eds.), *The crisis in youth mental health: Critical issues and effective programs* (Vol. 4, pp. 83–88). Westport, CT: Praeger.

Ritchart, R., Church, M., & Morrison, K. (2011). *Making thinking visible: How to promote engagement, understanding, and independence for all learners*. San Francisco: Jossey-Bass.

Ritchie, S. J., Della Sala, S., & McIntosh, R. D. (2013, November 12). Retrieval practice, with or without mind mapping, boosts fact learning in primary school children. *PLOS ONE*, 8(11). Accessed at https://doi.org/10.1371/journal.pone.0078976 on October 9, 2018.

Rivkin, S. G., Hanushek, E. A., & Kain, J. F. (2005). Teachers, schools, and academic achievement. *Econometrica*, 73(2), 417–458.

Robertson-Kraft, C., & Duckworth, A. L. (2014). True grit: Trait-level perseverance and passion for long-term goals predicts effectiveness and retention among novice teachers. *Teachers College Record*, 116(3), 1–27.

Robinson, K. (2013). *Gettin' Messi: How mistakes make mathematicians*. Accessed at http://tntp.org/assets/documents/TNTP_FishmanPrizeSeries_2013.pdf on November 10, 2015.

Rockoff, J. E. (2004). The impact of individual teachers on student achievement: Evidence from panel data. *American Economic Review*, 94(2), 247–252.

Roediger, H. L., III, Agarwal, P. K., McDaniel, M. A., & McDermott, K. B. (2011). Test-enhanced learning in the classroom: Long-term improvements from quizzing. *Journal of Experimental Psychology: Applied*, 17(4), 382–395.

Rohrer, D., Dedrick, R. F., & Stershic, S. (2015). Interleaved practice improves mathematics learning. *Journal of Educational Psychology*, 107(3), 900–908.

Roorda, D. L., Koomen, H. M. Y., Spilt, J. L., & Oort, F. J. (2011). The influence of affective teacher–student relationships on students' school engagement and achievement: A meta-analytic approach. *Review of Educational Research*, 81(4), 493–529.

Rosenfeld, L. R., Richman, J. M., & Bowen, G. L. (1998). Low social support among at-risk adolescents. *Social Work in Education*, 20(4), 245–260.

Rosenshine, B., & Meister, C. (1994). Reciprocal teaching: A review of the research. *Review of Educational Research*, *64*(4), 479–530.

Rosenthal, R., & Jacobson, L. (1966). Teachers' expectancies: Determinants of pupils' IQ gains. *Psychological Reports*, *19*(1), 115–118.

Rosenthal, R., & Jacobson, L. (1992). *Pygmalion in the classroom: Teacher expectation and pupils' intellectual development* (Expanded ed.). New York: Irvington.

Ross, L. (2012). *Here we grow again: Building a winning team in the classroom*. Accessed at http://tntp.org/assets /documents/TNTP_FishmanPrizeSeries_2012.pdf on October 22, 2015.

Rowe, G., Hirsh, J. B., & Anderson, A. K. (2007). Positive affect increases the breadth of attentional selection. *Proceedings of the National Academy of Sciences of the United States of America*, *104*(1), 383–388.

Ruhl, K. L., Hughes, C. A., & Schloss, P. J. (1987). Using the pause procedure to enhance lecture recall. *Teacher Education and Special Education*, *10*, 14–18.

Rumberger, R. (2004). Why students drop out of school. In G. Orfield (Ed.), *Dropouts in America: Confronting the graduation rate crisis* (pp. 131–155). Cambridge, MA: Harvard Education Press.

Russell, I. J., Hendricson, W. D., & Herbert, R. J. (1984). Effects of lecture information density on medical student achievement. *Journal of Medical Education*, *59*(11), 881–889.

Russo, N. M., Hornickel, H., Nicol, T., Zecker, S., & Kraus, N. (2010). Biological changes in auditory function following training in children with autism spectrum disorders. *Behavioral and Brain Functions*, *6*(60), 1–8.

Ryff, C. D. (2014). Self-realization and meaning making in the face of adversity: A eudaimonic approach to human resilience. *South African Journal of Psychology*, *24*, 1–12.

Sanders, W. L., & Horn, S. P. (1998). Research findings from the Tennessee Value-Added Assessment System (TVAAS) database: Implications for educational evaluation and research. *Journal of Personnel Evaluation in Education*, *12*(3), 247–256.

Santiago, C. D., Etter, E. M., Wadsworth, M. E., & Raviv, T. (2012). Predictors of responses to stress among families coping with poverty-related stress. *Anxiety, Stress, and Coping*, *25*(3), 239–258.

Sartori, G., Lombardi, L., & Mattiuzzi, L. (2005). Semantic relevance best predicts normal and abnormal name retrieval. *Neuropsychologia*, *43*(5), 754–770.

Schaefer, S., Lovden, M., Wieckhorst, B., & Lindenberger, U. (2010). Cognitive performance is improved while walking: Differences in cognitive-sensorimotor couplings between children and young adults. *European Journal of Developmental Psychology*, *7*, 371–389.

Scheffer, B. K., & Rubenfeld, M. G. (2001). Critical thinking: What is it and how do we teach it? In J. M. Dochterman & H. K. Grace (Eds.), *Current issues in nursing* (6th ed.; pp. 352–359). St. Louis, MO: Mosby.

Schellenberg, E. G. (2004). Music lessons enhance IQ. *Psychological Science*, *15*(8), 511–514.

Schoenthaler, S. J., Bier, I. D., Young, K., Nichols, D., & Jansenns, S. (2000). The effect of vitamin-mineral supplementation on the intelligence of American schoolchildren: A randomized, double-blind placebo-controlled trial. *Journal of Alternative and Complementary Medicine*, *6*(1), 19–29.

Schumann, K., Zaki, J., & Dweck, C. S. (2014). Addressing the empathy deficit: Beliefs about the malleability of empathy predict effortful responses when empathy is challenging. *Journal of Personality and Social Psychology*, *107*(3), 475–493.

Schwenninger, S. R., & Sherraden, S. (2011, April). *The American middle class under stress*. Washington, DC: New America Foundation. Accessed at http://garysmettler.com/wp-content/uploads/2014/09/The-American-Middle -Class-Under-Stress-2011.pdf on May 22, 2015.

Scruggs, T. E., Mastropieri, M. A., Berkeley, S., & Graetz, J. E. (2010). Do special education interventions improve learning of secondary content? A meta-analysis. *Remedial and Special Education*, *31*(6), 437–449.

Seastrom, M., Hoffman, L., Chapman, C., & Stillwell, R. (2005, October). *The averaged freshman graduation rate for public high schools from the Common Core of data: School years 2001–02 and 2002–03* (NCES 2006–601). Washington, DC: National Center for Education Statistics. Accessed at http://nces.ed.gov/pubs2006/2006601.pdf on April 1, 2012.

Segretin, M. S., Lipina, S. J., Hermida, M. J., Sheffield, T. D., Nelson, J. M., Espy, K. A., et al. (2014). Predictors of cognitive enhancement after training in preschoolers from diverse socioeconomic backgrounds. *Frontiers in Psychology, 5,* 205.

Seligman, M. E. P. (2006). *Learned optimism: How to change your mind and your life.* New York: Vintage.

Sellers, R. M., Caldwell, C. H., Schmeelk-Cone, K. H., & Zimmerman, M. A. (2003). Racial identity, racial discrimination, perceived stress, and psychological distress among African American young adults. *Journal of Health and Social Behavior, 44*(3), 302–317.

Serrano, M. A., Moya-Albiol, L., & Salvador, A. (2014). Endocrine and mood responses to two working days in female teachers. *Spanish Journal of Psychology, 17*(2), 1–11.

Sesma, H. W., Mahone, E. M., Levine, T., Eason, S. H., & Cutting, L. E. (2009). The contribution of executive skills to reading comprehension. *Child Neuropsychology, 15*(3), 232–246.

ShadowStats.com. (2016). *Alternate inflation charts.* Accessed at www.shadowstats.com/alternate_data/inflation-charts on January 6, 2016.

Shaefer, H. L., & Edin, K. (2012, February). *Extreme poverty in the United States, 1996 to 2011* [Policy brief]. Ann Arbor, MI: National Poverty Center. Accessed at www.npc.umich.edu/publications/policy_briefs/brief28/policybrief28.pdf on May 22, 2015.

Shah, A. K., Mullainathan, S., & Shafir, E. (2012). Some consequences of having too little. *Science, 338*(6107), 682–685.

Sharot, T., Shiner, T., Brown, A. C., Fan, J., & Dolan, R. J. (2009). Dopamine enhances expectation of pleasure in humans. *Current Biology, 19*(24), 2077–2080.

Shaw, G. B. (1903). *Man and Superman: A comedy and a philosophy.* New York: Brentano's.

Sheldon, K. M., & Lyubomirsky, S. (2006). How to increase and sustain positive emotion: The effects of expressing gratitude and visualizing best possible selves. *Journal of Positive Psychology, 1,* 73–82.

Shellshear, L., MacDonald, A. D., Mahoney, J., Finch, E., McMahon, K., Silburn, P., et al. (2015). Levodopa enhances explicit new-word learning in healthy adults: A preliminary study. *Human Psychopharmacology: Clinical and Experimental, 30*(5), 341–349.

Shernoff, D. J., Csikszentmihalyi, M., Schneider, B., & Shernoff, E. S. (2003). Student engagement in high school classrooms from the perspective of flow theory. *School Psychology Quarterly, 18*(2), 158–176.

Sheynikhovich, D., Otani, S., & Arleo, A. (2013). Dopaminergic control of long-term depression/long-term potentiation threshold in prefrontal cortex. *Journal of Neuroscience, 33*(34), 13914–13926.

Shinaver, C. S., III, Entwistle, P. C., & Söderqvist, S. (2014). Cogmed WM training: Reviewing the reviews. *Applied Neuropsychological Child, 3,* 163–172.

Shors, T. J., Olson, R. L., Bates, M. E., Selby, E. A., & Alderman, B. L. (2014). Mental and physical (MAP) training: A neurogenesis-inspired intervention that enhances health in humans. *Neurobiology of Learning and Memory, 115,* 3–9.

Siegler, R. S., & Alibali, M. W. (2005). *Children's thinking* (4th ed.). Upper Saddle River, NJ: Pearson.

Sinek, S. (2009). *Start with why: How great leaders inspire everyone to take action.* New York: Portfolio.

Singh, M., & Singh, G. (2005). Assessment of mental health status of middle-aged female school teachers of Varanasi City. *Internet Journal of Health, 5*(1), 1–10.

Skeels, H. M. (1966). Adult status of children with contrasting early experience: A follow-up study. *Monographs of the Society for Research in Child Development, 31,* 1–65.

Skoe, E., & Kraus, N. (2012). A little goes a long way: How the adult brain is shaped by musical training in childhood. *Journal of Neuroscience, 3*(34), 11507–11510.

Slepian, M. L., & Ambady, N. (2012). Fluid movement and creativity. *Journal of Experimental Psychology: General, 141*(4), 625–629.

Smiley, P. A., & Dweck, C. S. (1994). Individual differences in achievement goals among young children. *Child Development, 65*(6), 1723–1743.

Social Security Online. (2016). *Wage statistics for 2014*. Accessed at www.ssa.gov/cgi-bin/netcomp.cgi?year=2014 on January 6, 2016.

Söderqvist, S., & Nutley, S. B. (2015). Working memory training is associated with long term attainments in math and reading. *Frontiers in Psychology, 10*, 1711.

Soloveichik, S. (1979). Odd way to teach, but it works. *Soviet Life Magazine, 5*, 18–22.

Song, X., Wang, H., Zheng, L., Chen, D., & Wang, Z. (2010). The relationship between problem behavior and neurotransmitter deficiency in adolescents. *Journal of Huazhong University of Science and Technology (Medical Sciences), 30*(6), 714–719.

Southgate, D. E., & Roscigno, V. J. (2009). The impact of music on childhood and adolescent achievement. *Social Science Quarterly, 90*(1), 4–21.

Sperry, D. E., Sperry, L. L., & Miller, P. J. (2018, April 30). *Reexamining the verbal environments of children from different socioeconomic backgrounds*. Accessed at https://doi.org/10.1111/cdev.13072 on October 9, 2018.

Spilt, J. L., Koomen, H. M., & Harrison, L. J. (2015). Language development in the early school years: The importance of close relationships with teachers. *Developmental Psychology, 51*(2), 185–196.

Sripada, R. K., Swain, J. E., Evans, G. W., Welsh, R. C., & Liberzon, I. (2014). Childhood poverty and stress reactivity are associated with aberrant functional connectivity in default mode network. *Neuropsychopharmacology, 39*(9), 2244–2251.

Standley, J. M. (2008). Does music instruction help children learn to read? Evidence of a meta-analysis. *Update: Applications of Research in Music Education, 27*, 17–32.

Steptoe, A., Wardle, J., & Marmot, M. (2005). Positive affect and health-related neuroendocrine, cardiovascular, and inflammatory processes. *Proceedings of the National Academy of Sciences of the United States of America, 102*(18), 6508–6512.

Steiger, S., Haberer, W., & Müller, J. K. (2011). Social environment determines degree of chemical signaling. *Biology Letters, 7*(6), 822–824.

Stewart, L., Henson, R., Kampe, K., Walsh, V., Turner, R., & Frith, U. (2003). Brain changes after learning to read and play music. *Neuroimage, 20*(1), 71–83.

Stipek, D. (2002). Good instruction is motivating. In A. Wigfield & J. S. Eccles (Eds.), *Development of achievement motivation* (pp. 309–332). San Diego, CA: Academic Press.

Suitts, S. (2015). *A new majority: Low income students now a majority in the nation's public schools* (Research bulletin). Atlanta, GA: Southern Education Foundation. Accessed at www.southerneducation.org/Our-Strategies /Research-and-Publications/New-Majority-Diverse-Majority-Report-Series/A-New-Majority-2015-Update-Low -Income-Students-Now on May 22, 2015.

Sutoo, D., & Akiyama, K. (2003). Regulation of brain function by exercise. *Neurobiology of Disease, 13*(1), 1–14.

Swanson, C. B. (2009). *Cities in crisis 2009: Closing the graduation gap—Educational and economic conditions in America's largest cities*. Bethesda, MD: Editorial Projects in Education. Accessed at www.edweek.org/media /cities_in_crisis_2009.pdf on January 13, 2016.

Sweller, J., van Merrienboer, J. J. G., & Paas, F. G. W. C. (1998). Cognitive architecture and instructional design. *Educational Psychology Review, 10*(3), 251–296.

Suitts, S. (2015). *A new majority research bulletin: Low income students now a majority in the nation's public schools.* Atlanta, GA: Southern Education Foundation. Accessed at www.southerneducation.org/Our-Strategies/Research -and-Publications/New-Majority-Diverse-Majority-Report-Series/A-New-Majority-2015-Update-Low-Income -Students-Now.aspx on January 6, 2016.

Tanner, M. (2014). *War on poverty at 50: Despite trillions spent, poverty won.* Washington, DC: Cato Institute. Accessed at www.cato.org/publications/commentary/war-poverty-50-despite-trillions-spent-poverty-won on October 14, 2014.

Telzer, E. H., Fuligni, A. J., Lieberman, M. D., & Galván, A. (2014). Neural sensitivity to eudaimonic and hedonic rewards differentially predict adolescent depressive symptoms over time. *Proceedings of the National Academy of Sciences of the United States of America, 111*(18), 6600–6605.

Temple, E., Deutsch, G. K., Poldrack, R. A., Miller, S. L., Tallal, P., Merzenich, M. M., et al. (2003). Neural deficits in children with dyslexia ameliorated by behavioral remediation: Evidence from functional MRI. *Proceedings of the National Academy of Sciences of the United States of America, 100*(5), 2860–2865.

Terjestam, Y., Jouper, J., & Johansson, C. (2010). Effects of scheduled qigong exercise on pupils' well-being, self-image, distress, and stress. *Journal of Alternative and Complementary Medicine, 16*(9), 939–944.

Tine, M. (2014). Working memory differences between children living in rural and urban poverty. *Journal of Cognition and Development, 15*(4), 599–613.

Todd, R. M., & Anderson, A. K. (2009). Six degrees of separation: The amygdala regulates social behavior and perception. *Nature Neuroscience, 12*, 1217–1218.

Toga, A. (2005, October 15). *Keynote address.* Presented at the Learning Brain EXPO, Newport Beach, CA.

Tomlinson, C. A. (2014). *The differentiated classroom: Responding to the needs of all learners* (2nd ed.). Alexandria, VA: Association for Supervision and Curriculum Development.

Tomporowski, P. D., Davis, C. L., Miller, P. H., & Naglieri, J. A. (2008). Exercise and children's intelligence, cognition, and academic achievement. *Educational Psychology Review, 20*(2), 111–131.

Tough, P. (2012). *How children succeed: Grit, curiosity, and the hidden power of character.* New York: Houghton Mifflin Harcourt.

Tucker-Drob, E. M., Rhemtulla, M., Harden, K. P., Turkheimer, E., & Fask, D. (2011). Emergence of a Gene X socioeconomic status interaction on infant mental ability between 10 months and 2 years. *Psychological Science, 22*, 125–133.

Ullman, S. E., Townsend, S., Filipas, H. H., & Starzynski, L. L. (2007). Structural models of the relations of assault severity, social support, avoidance coping, self-blame, and PTSD among sexual assault survivors. *Psychology of Women Quarterly, 31*(1), 23–37.

University of Pennsylvania School of Arts and Sciences. (2011). *12-item grit scale.* Accessed at https:// angeladuckworth.com/grit-scale on May 22, 2015.

Urban Prep Academies. (2016). *Urban Prep announces 100% of seniors admitted to college and launch of "10andChange" campaign to refocus the narrative of black boys/young men on positive stories.* Accessed at www.prnewswire.com/news-releases/urban-prep-announces-100-of-seniors-admitted-to-college-and-launch-of -10andchange-campaign-to-refocus-the-narrative-of-black-boysyoung-men-on-positive-stories-300237717.html on June 2, 2016.

U.S. Census Bureau. (n.d.a). *American FactFinder: Community facts.* Accessed at http:// factfinder2.census.gov/faces /nav/jsf/pages/community_facts.xhtml on May 22, 2015.

U.S. Census Bureau. (n.d.b). *Historical poverty tables—people: Table 2. Poverty status, by family relationship, race, and Hispanic origin.* Accessed at www.census.gov/hhes/www/poverty/data/historical/people.html on May 22, 2015.

U.S. Census Bureau. (n.d.c). *Survey of income and program participation.* Accessed at www.census.gov/programs -surveys/sipp.html on January 6, 2016.

U.S. Census Bureau. (2010). *American FactFinder: Poverty status in the past 12 months of families (2010 American Community Survey 1-year estimates)*. Accessed at http://factfi der2.census.gov/faces/tableservices/jsf/pages /productview.xhtml?pid=ACS_10_1YR_S1702&prodType=table on April 10, 2012.

U.S. Census Bureau. (2011). *More young adults are living in their parents' home, Census Bureau reports* [Press release]. Accessed at www.census.gov/newsroom/releases/archives/families_households/cb11–183.html on January 6, 2016.

U.S. Department of Agriculture, Food and Nutrition Service. (2013). *National School Lunch Program*. Accessed at www.fns.usda.gov/sites/default/files/NSLPFactSheet.pdf on October 14, 2015.

U.S. Department of Agriculture, Food and Nutrition Service. (2016). *Supplemental Nutrition Assistance Program participation and costs*. Accessed at www.fns.usda.gov/sites/default/files/pd/SNAPsummary.pdf on January 6, 2016.

U.S. Department of Agriculture, Office of Inspector General. (2013). *Overlap and duplication in Food and Nutrition Service's nutrition programs* (Audit Report No. 27001–0001–10). Washington, DC: Author. Accessed at www.usda.gov/oig/webdocs/27001–0001–10.pdf on May 22, 2015.

U.S. Department of Education Office for Civil Rights. (2014). *Civil rights data collection: Data snapshot—School discipline*. Accessed at http://ocrdata.ed.gov/Downloads/CRDC-School-Discipline-Snapshot.pdf on October 14, 2015.

U.S. Department of Labor, Bureau of Labor Statistics. (2015). *The employment situation—December 2015* [Press release]. Accessed at www.bls.gov/news.release/pdf/empsit.pdf on January 14, 2016.

U.S. Department of the Treasury. (2007). *Income mobility in the U.S. from 1996 to 2005*. Washington, DC: Author. Accessed at www.treasury.gov/resource-center/tax-policy/Documents/incomemobilitystudy03–08revise.pdf on May 22, 2015.

U.S. News & World Report. (2016). *High schools: Preuss School UCSD*. Accessed at www.usnews.com/education/best -high-schools/california/districts/san-diego-unified-school-district/preuss-school-ucsd-3216 on June 1, 2016.

Vacha-Haase, T., & Thompson, B. (2004). How to estimate and interpret various effect sizes. *Journal of Counseling Psychology, 51*(4), 473–481.

Valentine, J. (2005). *Statistical differences for the percentages of student engagement as measured by IPI categories between very successful and very unsuccessful middle schools*. Columbia, MO: Middle Level Leadership Center.

Valentine, J., & Collins, J. (2011, April 11). *Student engagement and achievement on high-stakes tests: A HLM analysis across 68 middle schools*. Presented at the annual conference of the American Educational Research Association, New Orleans, LA.

van Gelder, T. (2004). *Using argument mapping to improve critical thinking skills*. Accessed at www.reasoninglab.com /wp-content/uploads/2013/10/TvG-Using-argument-mapping-to-improve-critical-thinking-skills-2015.pdf on May 18, 2016.

van Gelder, T. (2015). *Using argument mapping to improve critical thinking skills*. Accessed at www.reasoninglab.com /wp-content/uploads/2013/10/TvG-Using-argument-mapping-to-improve-critical-thinking-skills-2015.pdf on May 18, 2016.

van Gelder, T., Bissett, M., & Cumming, G. (2004). Cultivating expertise in informal reasoning. *Canadian Journal of Experimental Psychology, 58*(2), 142–152.

van Holstein, M., Aarts, E., van der Schaaf, M. E., Geurts, D. E., Verkes, R. J., Franke, B., et al. (2011). Human cognitive flexibility depends on dopamine D2 receptor signaling. *Psychopharmacology, 218*(3), 567–578.

van Praag, H., Fleshner, M., Schwartz, M. W., & Mattson, M. P. (2014). Exercise, energy intake, glucose homeostasis, and the brain. *Journal of Neuroscience, 34*(46), 15139–15149.

Vargas Lascano, D. I., Galambos, N. L., Krahn, H. J., & Lachman, M. E. (2015). Growth in perceived control across 25 years from the late teens to midlife: The role of personal and parents' education. *Developmental Psychology, 51*(1), 124–135.

Volkow, N. D., Wang, G. J., Fowler, J. S., Telang, F., Maynard, L., Logan, J., et al. (2004). Evidence that methylphenidate enhances the saliency of a mathematical task by increasing dopamine in the human brain. *American Journal of Psychiatry, 161*(7), 1173–1180.

Voss, J. L., Gonsalves, B. D., Federmeier, K. D., Tranel, D., & Cohen, N. J. (2011). Hippocampal brain-network coordination during volitional exploratory behavior enhances learning. *Nature Neuroscience, 14*(1), 115–120.

Wanless, S. B., McClelland, M. M., Acock, A. C., Chen, F.-M., & Chen, J.-L. (2011). Behavioral regulation and early academic achievement in Taiwan. *Early Education and Development, 22*(1), 1–28.

Wanless, S. B., McClelland, M. M., Tominey, S. L., & Acock, A. C. (2011). The influence of demographic risk factors on children's behavioral regulation in prekindergarten and kindergarten. *Early Education and Development, 22*(3), 461–488.

Watanabe-Crockett, L. (2019). *Future-focused learning: Ten essential shifts of everyday practice.* Bloomington, IN: Solution Tree Press.

Wegner, M., Schüler, J., & Budde, H. (2014). The implicit affiliation motive moderates cortisol responses to acute psychosocial stress in high school students. *Psychoneuroendocrinology, 48*, 162–168.

Wenglinsky, H. (2000). *How teaching matters: Bringing the classroom back into discussions of teacher quality.* Princeton, NJ: Educational Testing Service.

Wenglinsky, H. (2002). How schools matter: The link between teacher classroom practices and student academic performance. *Education Policy Analysis Archives, 10*(12). Accessed at http://epaa.asu.edu/ojs/article/download/291/417 on May 22, 2015.

Wentzel, K. R. (1997). Student motivation in middle school: The role of perceived pedagogical caring. *Journal of Educational Psychology, 89*(3), 411–419.

Wiliam, D. (2018). *Embedded formative assessment* (2nd ed.). Bloomington, IN: Solution Tree Press.

Wiliam, D., & Thompson, M. (2007). Integrating assessment with instruction: What will it take to make it work? In C. A. Dwyer (Ed.), *The future of assessment: Shaping teaching and learning* (pp. 53–82). Mahwah, NJ: Erlbaum.

Williams, J. H. G., Perrett, D. I., Waiter, G. D., & Pechey, S. (2007). Differential effects of tryptophan depletion on emotion processing according to face direction. *Social Cognitive and Affective Neuroscience, 2*(4), 264–273.

Willett, J. B., Yamashita, J. J. M., & Anderson, R. D. (1983). A meta-analysis of instructional systems applied in science teaching. *Journal of Research in Science Teaching, 20*(5), 405–417.

Willingham, D. T. (2008). Critical thinking: Why is it so hard to teach? *Arts Education Policy Review, 109*(4), 21–32.

Wilson, T. D. (2011). *Redirect: The surprising new science of psychological change.* New York: Little, Brown.

Wilson, W. J. (1997). *When work disappears: The world of the new urban poor.* New York: Knopf.

Winerman, L. (2013). What sets high achievers apart? *Monitor on Psychology, 44*(11), 28–31.

Winn, W. (2003). Research methods and types of evidence for research in educational technology. *Educational Psychology Review, 15*(4), 367–373.

Winter, B., Breitenstein, C., Mooren, F. C., Voelker, K., Fobker, M., Lechtermann, A., et al. (2007). High impact running improves learning. *Neurobiology of Learning and Memory, 87*(4), 597–609.

Wu, M., Morgan, K., Hur, J., Schifrin, K., Gordon, L., Russell, G., et al. (2012). *The irreplaceables: Understanding the real retention crisis in America's urban schools.* Brooklyn, NY: New Teacher Project. Accessed at www.tntp.org/assets/documents/TNTP_Irreplaceables_2012.pdf on March 5, 2013.

World Memory Sports Council. (2015). *World Memory Championships 2015: Names and faces result.* Accessed at www.worldmemorychampionships.com/wp-content/uploads/2015/12/WMC-2015-Full-Scores.pdf on May 14, 2016.

Yamashita, A. (2015). *Mindfulness for beginners: A practical guide to awakening and finding inner peace in your life!* Seattle, WA: CreateSpace.

Yau, S. Y., Li, A., Xu, A., & So, K.-F. (2015). Fat cell-secreted adiponectin mediates physical exercise-induced hippocampal neurogenesis: An alternative anti-depressive treatment? *Neural Regeneration Research, 10*(1), 7–9.

Yazzie-Mintz, E. (2007a). *National high school student engagement survey by IU reveals unengaged students* [Press release]. Accessed at www. indiana.edu/~soenews/news/news1172622996.html on April 12, 2012.

Yazzie-Mintz, E. (2007b). *Voices of students on engagement: A report of the 2006 High School Survey of Student Engagement.* Bloomington, IN: Center for Evaluation and Education Policy. Accessed at http://ceep.indiana.edu/hssse/images /HSSSE%20Overview%20 Report%20-%202006.pdf on May 22, 2015.

Yeager, D. S., Henderson, M. D., Paunesku, D., Walton, G. M., D'Mello, S., Spitzer, B. J., et al. (2014). Boring but important: A self-transcendent purpose for learning fosters academic self-regulation. *Journal of Personality and Social Psychology, 107*(4), 559–580.

Yehuda, R., Flory, J. D., Southwick, S., & Charney, D. S. (2006). Developing an agenda for translational studies of resilience and vulnerability following trauma exposure. *Annals of the New York Academy of Sciences, 1071*, 379–396.

Yerkes, R. M., & Dodson, J. D. (1908). The relation of strength of stimulus to rapidity of habit-formation. *Journal of Comparative Neurology & Psychology, 18*(5), 459–482.

Zak, P. J. (2015, February). *Why inspiring stories make us react: The neuroscience of narrative.* Accessed at www.dana .org/Cerebrum/2015/Why_Inspiring_ Stories_Make_Us_React The_Neuroscience_of_Narrative/ on January 13, 2016.

Zepeda, C. D., Richey, J. E., Ronevich, P., & Nokes-Malach, T. J. (2015). Direct instruction of metacognition benefits adolescent science learning, transfer, and motivation: An in vivo study. *Journal of Educational Psychology, 107*(4), 954–970.

Zink, C. F., Tong, Y., Chen, Q., Bassett, D. S., Stein, J. L., & Meyer-Lindenberg, A. (2008). Know your place: Neural processing of social hierarchy in humans. *Neuron, 58*(2), 273–283.

Index

Solution Tree

Solution Tree's mission is to advance the work of our authors. By working with the best researchers and educators worldwide, we strive to be the premier provider of innovative publishing, in-demand events, and inspired professional development designed to transform education to ensure that all students learn.

LEARN. TEACH. LEAD.

ASCD is a global nonprofit association dedicated to the whole child approach that supports educators, families, community members, and policy makers. We provide expert and innovative solutions to facilitate professional development through print and digital publishing, on-site learning services, and conferences and events that empower educators to support the success of each child.